Crossing New Europe

POSTMODERN TRAVEL AND THE EUROPEAN ROAD MOVIE

Ewa Mazierska and Laura Rascaroli

WALLFLOWER PRESS
LONDON & NEW YORK

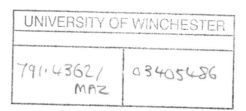
First published in Great Britain in 2006 by
Wallflower Press
6a Middleton Place, Langham Street, London W1W 7TE
www.wallflowerpress.co.uk

A catalogue for this book is available from the British Library

ISBN 1-904764-67-3 (pbk)
ISBN 1-904764-68-1 (hbk)

Book design by Elsa Mathern

Printed in Great Britain by Antony Rowe Ltd, Chippenham, Wiltshire

Cr

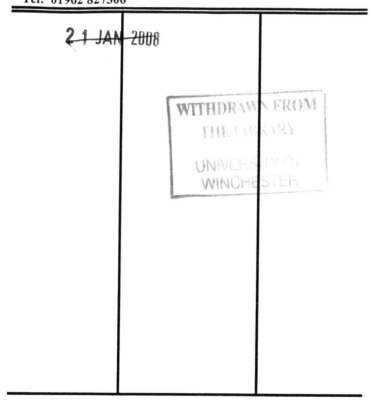

CONTENTS

ACKNOWLEDGEMENTS

Our thanks go, first and foremost, to Tom Carroll and Gifford Kerr for their constant and loving support. We also wish to express our gratitude to Yoram Allon at Wallflower Press for his assistance and enthusiasm, and to the following individuals, who have helped us in various ways in our work: John Walton at the University of Central Lancashire; Adam Wyżyński at Warsaw's National Film Archive; Caitríona Leahy at Trinity College Dublin; Stefano Baschiera, Mary Noonan and the incomparable Aisling O'Leary at the National University of Ireland, Cork; Matteo Zambetti and Giulia Russo at Associazione Alasca; Robert Hughes; Patrick Keiller; and Nanni Moretti.

The stills in this book are courtesy of the following organisations and individuals: the National Film Archive, Warsaw; Associazione Alasca, Torre Boldone; Sacher Film; Patrick Keiller; and Werner Herzog Film. All efforts have been made to clear the copyright for all pictures. We thank those who have granted us the right to reproduce stills and are grateful for the financial support of the Research Publication Fund of the College of Arts, Celtic Studies and Social Sciences, University College Cork.

This book, as with each of our joint works, is the fruit of genuine and intensive collaboration on all chapters and aspects of the volume. Each of us was principally responsible for writing almost exactly half of the book, as follows: Ewa Mazierska wrote Chapters One, Two, Three, Eight, and the section 'Nowhere to run: women in Eastern European road films' of Chapter Seven; Laura Rascaroli wrote the Introduction, Chapters Four, Five, Six, and all remaining sections of Chapter Seven. All translations of texts in languages other than English are by the authors.

The early versions of some of the chapters were previously published as articles, and we wish to thank the editors of the respective journals for allowing us to reproduce our work here: Ewa Mazierska (2001) 'Travelling to the margins of Europe', *Kinema*, 16, 5–22; and (2002) 'Road to authenticity and stability: Representation of holidays, relocation and movement in the films of Eric Rohmer', *Tourist Studies*, 2, 3, 223–46; Laura Rascaroli (2003) 'New voyages to Italy: Postmodern travellers and the Italian road movie', *Screen*, 44, 1, 71–91.

For this research project, Laura Rascaroli was granted a Government of Ireland Research Fellowship by the Irish Research Council for the Humanities and Social Sciences.

dedicated to my friends (EM)
to Alba, Cristiana, and Vera – travel partners (LR)

INTRODUCTION

'The use of travelling is to regulate imagination by reality, and, instead of thinking how things may be, to see them as they are.'
— Samuel Johnson

Travel, space and identity in postmodern Europe

Movement and lack of permanency have today become a lifestyle for a significant
number of Europeans. Accordingly, Zygmunt Bauman (1996) has proposed three
figures of mobility as the embodiment of postmodernity: the stroller, the tourist and the vagabond. The purpose of this book is to examine the ways in which
recent European travel films have mirrored and explored the complex question
of movement in and through Europe in the last thirty years. Our intention is to
determine to what extent travel films have engaged with the notion of a changing
European socio-geographical space, which has in turn produced new forms of
national and transnational identity. Experiences of displacement, diaspora, exile,
migration, nomadism, homelessness, border-crossing and tourism are all relevant
to contemporary Europe, as indeed they have been in earlier epochs. Nevertheless, in the last two to three decades, mobility – understood as changing country,
nationality, culture, as well as one's identity – is a phenomenon that no longer
concerns a minority of Europeans but has become the condition of large groups of
citizens. Mobility has ceased to be the exception to the rule, and has itself become
the rule: 'If the *modern* "problem of identity" was how to construct an identity and
keep it solid and stable, the *postmodern* "problem of identity" is primarily how to
avoid fixation and keep the options open' (Bauman 1996: 18).

This situation is the result of a set of social, economic and political transformations that have taken place in the last twenty to thirty years, a period to which we
will apply the term 'postmodernity'. These events include: the fall of Communism,
the disintegration of the Soviet Union and the Eastern European bloc, and the decay of totalising ideologies; the advent of post-Fordism, the growth of disorganised

capitalism and of globalisation; the strengthening of the European Union, which has promoted in a contradictory fashion both the shedding of national identities and the encouragement of transnational identification, and, at the same time, the strengthening of feelings of regional and local belonging; the disappearance of (some) customs and borders, the diffusion of a common currency, and the formation of a single market; the intensification of an ethnic component in politics; conflicts such as those in the Balkans, which have made refugees of many and have reconfigured whole geographical areas; and the continuing poverty and unrest of the so-called Third World, which has produced ever-increasing immigration into Europe. These factors have reduced barriers and raised the stakes on movement, putting in motion people from outside and inside Europe, impacting on the socio-geographical fixity of a continent of nation-states, and putting in flux the idea of Europe itself.

Our choice to examine these questions through the travel film is justified by the fact that, given its history and its characteristics, this cinematic form has the ability to mirror and interpret phenomena such as shifting European borders; the formation of new personal, regional, national and transnational identities; the transformation of communities; and, more generally, the character of movement in postmodernity. Travel films, which often involve the crossing of borders and typically require the productive and creative efforts of more than one nation, also provide an important lens through which to study the evolution of the European cinematographic industry and the effects of the spreading practices of multi-national co-production and of European-funded production.

Filmmaking on the road

Road movies are widely considered to be a peculiarly American film genre, albeit one which has been subsequently borrowed and adapted by filmmakers of other nationalities, chiefly Australian and European: 'The road movie is … a Hollywood genre that catches peculiarly American dreams, tensions and anxieties, even when imported by the motion picture industries of other nations' (Cohan & Hark 1997: 2); 'Road movies emerged from America, where notions of the open road and travel form part of a potent cultural myth far more powerful than in Europe where all possible routes were mapped long before their nation-states consolidated' (Sargeant & Watson 1999: 18). For the most part the existing critical literature concentrates on Hollywood production, and there is work still to be done on the relationship between American and non-American road movies and on the phenomenon of cross-fertilisation between road movies of different countries and continents. The road movie is not only considered to be an American genre, but it is also usually identified with a specific format that emerged during the late 1960s, is epitomised by Dennis Hopper's *Easy Rider* (1969), and is derived from 'a well-known American daydream: hitting the road' (Eyerman & Löfgren 1995: 53). Most critics see the American highway as the emblem of the genre, and maintain that only America offers the geographic and symbolic conditions required to realise a road movie proper, even when they recognise the genre's debt to European forms:

> The journey as a metaphor for life itself is not an especially American invention, the *homo viator* motif has a long European history, but the Americanisation of this type of narrative in the road movie format is a consequence of the way specific conceptions concerning the freedom and the function of the road were constructed in the United States. (Eyerman & Löfgren 1995: 55)

Accordingly, very few European directors are widely recognised as authors of road movies – and those who are, like Wim Wenders and Aki Kaurismäki, have borrowed from (but also changed and subverted) the 'American format'. However, in the 1950s directors such as Roberto Rossellini, Federico Fellini, Ingmar Bergman and Michelangelo Antonioni showed, with films such as *Viaggio in Italia* (*Voyage to Italy*, 1954), *La strada* (*The Road*, 1954), *Smultronstället* (*Wild Strawberries*, 1957) and *L'avventura* (*The Adventure*, 1959), that it is also possible to be 'on the road' in Europe, and to make at the same time a peculiarly European cinema, with little connection to American forms of the genre.

From the 1960s onward, European road movies began to engage more overtly with the rules and trappings of the Hollywood genre, although maintaining a strong European imprint. Examples of this tendency are Jean-Luc Godard's *Pierrot le fou* (1965) and *Weekend* (1967); Wim Wenders' *Alice in den Städten* (*Alice in the Cities*, 1974) and *Im Lauf der Zeit* (*Kings of the Road*, 1976); and Antonioni's *Professione: reporter* (*The Passenger*, 1975). Other road films continued to be more resolutely European – for instance Pier Paolo Pasolini's *Uccellacci e uccellini* (*Hawks and Sparrows*, 1966), Theo Angelopoulos' *O thiassos* (*The Travelling Players*, 1975), Chantal Akerman's *Les Rendez-vous d'Anna* (1978), Andrei Tarkovsky's *Andrej Rublyov* (1969) and *Stalker* (1979). In reverse, North American directors started to absorb the influence of the European road cinema, usually mediated by the 'American' films by Wim Wenders and by Werner Herzog (*Stroszek*, 1977). The most influential representative of this trend in recent times is Jim Jarmusch, starting with his *Stranger Than Paradise* from 1984.

Given that European road movies and travel cinema have not been studied extensively as a genre or at least as a body of work, the definition of our object of enquiry is itself problematic. Should the European-style road movie be seen as a completely different and (relatively) independent type of cinema, or, as many critics suggest, as a sub-genre of the Hollywood format (the road movie as seen by the directors of the old continent)? Evidently, if we straightforwardly identify the road movie genre with the American format of the 1960s and after, none of the pre-1960 European films mentioned above belong to the genre. On the other hand, all academic works on American road movies include films made in the United States since the 1930s, beginning with Mark Sandrich's *The Gay Divorcee* (1934) and Frank Capra's *It Happened One Night* (1934), thus recognising that the genre existed long before it crystallised into the prevailing format, three decades later. Films that adopted the road and travelling as fundamental narrative functions were made in Europe as early as (or even earlier than) in Hollywood. Bertram M. Gordon argues that 'films made in the first decade, roughly 1894 to 1904, were almost all travel films' (2003: 7) – Gordon mentions, amongst others, *L'Arrivée d'un train à la Ciotat* (1895) by Louis and Auguste Lumière and Georges Méliès' *Voyage dans la lune* (*A Trip to the Moon*, 1902) (2003: 8–9). Think also of the Italian *Rotaie* (1930) by Mario Camerini and *Treno popolare* (1933) by Raffaello Matarazzo – which, with titles meaning, respectively, 'railway tracks' and 'working-class train', had railway travel at the centre of their narratives; or of the Polish *Włóczęgi* (*Vagabonds*, 1939) by Michał Waszyński, whose title speaks for itself. The European 'road film' thus developed alongside the Hollywood road movie, being influenced by and influencing it at the same time.

A widespread impression is that, whereas it is possible to study the American road movie as a compact category obeying a relatively consistent set of rules, European films 'on the road' cannot be contained within a coherent genre, and are instead characterised by their extreme richness and diversity. This belief is consonant with broader distinctions frequently argued or assumed between 'industrial' Hollywood cinema and 'artisanal' European filmmaking, and between the critical discourses with which they are associated: genre criticism on the one hand, and a particular articulation of *auteurism* on the other. Such an approach, though, is an oversimplification, and a recent book by David Laderman (2002) aptly shows how the American road movie also has cut across a wide variety of film styles and contexts, while maintaining a constant generic core: the journey as cultural critique, as exploration both of society and of self.[1] This broad definition of the genre applies equally well to European road movies and travel films. In fact, we argue that the main similarity between European and American travel films is that the directors on both continents use the motif of the journey as a vehicle for investigating metaphysical questions on the meaning and purpose of life. Travel, thus, commonly becomes an opportunity for exploration, discovery and transformation (of landscapes, of situation and of identity).

Nevertheless, there are significant differences between American and European road movies. The type and characteristics of the actual roads along which the films are set produce perhaps the most important distinction – the open spaces of North America, with their straight, boundless highways and the sense of freedom and opportunity to reinvent one's life, are in clear contrast with the European reality of a mosaic of nations, cultures, languages and roads, which are separated by geographical, political and economic boundaries and customs.[2] In European films the emphasis is either placed on crossing national borders or, in the case of national travel, on the landscapes that the voyagers traverse, moving, for instance, from deprived to wealthy areas, from the country to the city, or simply through regions presenting different cultures and characteristics. Furthermore, whereas the main vehicles for traversing the North American expanse are the private car (preferably a convertible) and the motorbike (Harley Davidson), European films often opt for public transport (trains, buses), if not hitchhiking or travelling on foot.[3] Another general distinction is that, whereas in American films the travellers tend to be outcasts and rebels looking for freedom or escape, in Europe it is rather the 'ordinary citizen' who is on the move, often for practical reasons (for work, immigration, commuting or holiday-making).

For the purposes of our study, which aims to explore movement in Europe in the last thirty years as reflected in European cinema, we will consider various types of films: those that may be seen as European versions of the American road movie genre established in the 1960s, and those that belong more directly to the long tradition of European travel cinema. Our object of study will therefore coincide with films made by a European director and produced or co-produced by European countries, whose narrative is centred on a trip through or to Europe, and in which emphasis is placed on the trip and on the road covered. We will nevertheless include in our study films such as the international co-productions *Felicia's Journey* (1999), one of the most distinctive road films set recently in Britain and Ireland, and *Calendar* (1993), both directed by Armenian-Canadian filmmaker Atom Egoyan. These two films engage with discourses on travel and Europe, respectively at the centre of the continent and at its margins, yet Egoyan is interesting here also as the representative of a diasporic cinema, in contrast to the other filmmakers who will be analysed in this book, most of whom travel instead for choice. We will also discuss, on account of their strong European character, and as a means to compare and contrast European and American road cinema, films by European directors (such as Werner Herzog and Aki Kaurismäki) that are not set in Europe. Our interpretation of Europe will be broad and will include nations, such as Poland, which are often neglected by academic work on 'European cinema' or countries, such as Armenia, whose belonging to Europe is problematic.

Fig. 1 Atom Egoyan's *Felicia's Journey* (US/Canada, 1999) © Icon Productions

With some exceptions (Herzog's television work, for instance), most of our examples belong to what we could define as 'non-mainstream' cinema; with this expression we refer to a wide range of films, including those which are marketed as art-house cinema; those that are more difficult to label as such (for example, Patrick Keiller's experimental films); those that are perceived as 'authorial' (as is often the case with directors such as Atom Egoyan, Eric Rohmer and Nanni Moretti); as well as non-fiction. The book's extensive geographical and cinematographic scope is justified by our desire to travel broadly and to reach the boundaries both of the European continent and of its road cinema.

It is necessary in this Introduction to point to some distinctions, which risk being obliterated by the subsequent analysis: between the 'urban journey' film, in which the travelling space is the city itself, and the travel film, where the road covered is national or transnational; between multi-location films, in which the emphasis is on the crossing of different socio-economic and physical landscapes, and films in which the road (or railway) itself is the transformative element; and, as mentioned above, between films that refer self-consciously to the American genre, even when subverting it and making it 'very European' (as in the case of the early Wim Wenders and of Aki Kaurismäki), and films which use the road to express a national (or European) imaginary and space. Finally, we are aware that the election of a 'European travel film' as our object of study implies the risk of homogenising different experiences and products; in the course of our work we will strive not to lose sight of the specificity of national, regional and local contexts.

Routes

This book engages with a variety of discourses and has the ambition to contribute to several areas of research. Some of these are specific to Film Studies, such as the theory and history of film genres. We feel that the under-representation of a European perspective in the existing literature seriously distorts the current perception of the history and characteristics of road movies and of travel cinema; we hope that this book will be an important contribution to our understanding of these cinematic forms. Our book is also a continuation and extension of a previous co-authored work on the European postmodern city (Mazierska & Rascaroli 2003), and as such contributes to the growing area of work dedicated to the representation of space in film: both the roads travelled and the urban and rural landscapes bordering them will be the objects of our study. *Crossing New Europe* furthermore proposes to offer a significant contribution to discussions on the existence and essence of a 'European cinema', and in particular of European postmodern cinema, through comparisons between European and Hollywood film, between art-house and mainstream filmmaking, and between the centre and the periphery of cinematic production.

Crossing New Europe is also one of the first major works to discuss comprehensively postmodern versus modern or pre-modern experiences of travel in film, thus contributing from a cinematic perspective to the exciting strands of research on the theory and history of movement in modernity and postmodernity currently undertaken in social and cultural history, social geography, cultural studies, sociology and tourist studies. Among the foremost contributions from these areas with which we will engage in the course of our work are those by Edward Said, Stuart Hall, Homi K. Bhabha, Zygmunt Bauman, Rob Shields, John Urry, Gilles Deleuze and Félix Guattari, Iain Chambers and Caren Kaplan. We propose to examine many different forms of travel, all of which have deep theoretical as well as historical, cultural and social repercussions: displacement, diaspora, exile, migration, nomadism, homelessness, border-crossing, tourism, relocation, commuting, exploration, adventuring, pilgrimage, tourism, conquest, escape and *flâneurism*. These will be discussed and put in their socio-historical as well as theoretical and cultural contexts. Finally, we hope that this work will contribute to our understanding of the last thirty years of the socio-political history of Europe, and will be a lens through which to view the transformations that Europe has undergone since the fall of the Berlin Wall.

Being at the intersection of all these discourses, our study will naturally draw on a range of theoretical and analytical tools, including author theory, genre and gender criticism, *mise-en-scène* criticism, social and cultural history, social geography, cultural studies, sociology, tourist studies, modernism and postmodernism theory. Although, when useful for our discussion, we will refer to the films' productive contexts, it must be stated that this is not a book on production or on reception. Our main interest here lies in representation; we have decided to produce a discussion of our topic through an engagement with theory and a practice of close textual analysis. Every monograph is, unavoidably, the fruit of a series of subjective choices, the product of a selection. Although we strived for both breadth and depth, the reader will certainly find omissions. A work of this type is also always the product of discourse, and not simply a description of an existing phenomenon; hence, this monograph will, somehow, produce its object – 'European travel film' – rather than merely describe it.

We feel that our objectives are best served by dividing the book into two sections, one devoted to authors and one to themes. The first section, entitled 'Authors on the road', looks at the cinema of four directors: Aki Kaurismäki, Eric Rohmer, Patrick Keiller and Werner Herzog, who devoted their work wholly or in large part to the representation of travel and created a very distinctive style of road cinema. The ability to create such a style, rather than the sheer number of road films that they made, was the principal criterion for the choice of these directors. The inclusion of some of them may seem unusual: apart from Kaurismäki, who is a widely recognised author of road movies, Rohmer, Keiller and Herzog have rarely been seen in this light. Rohmer has been chosen because we claim that the questions of holidaymaking and tourism are at the centre of the filmmaker's *oeuvre*; Keiller is the author of atypical but revolutionary contributions to the genre of travel cinema; and, despite many critics having looked at the question of travel in specific films by Herzog, rarely if ever has his body of work been analysed thoroughly from this perspective. The most evident absence from this section is Wim Wenders, probably the most famous European author of road movies; so much critical literature on Wenders concentrates precisely on this topic that we felt there was little interest in returning on this author. Nevertheless, one film by Wenders, *Lisbon Story*, is analysed in depth in chapter eight, 'Travelling to the Margins of Europe'.

The second section of the book, 'Geographies', provides a choice of case studies of films and themes. This section allows us to explore and study the routes and places crossed by cinematic travellers, the most typical reasons for travelling, and the connections between the aims of the trips and their geographical destination. Hence, the mapping of cinematic journeys in geographical terms will be connected with the drawing of a 'social map' of the cinematic travellers. Here we discuss

Fig. 2 Wim Wenders' *Lisbon Story* (Germany/Portugal, 1994) © Road Movies Filmproduktion

the meaning of home and of various types of movement, and the implications of crossing borders: national, natural (such as the sea), cultural and social. The emphasis is put not only on the places visited by the travellers, but also on the changes experienced by them, including of their identity; for instance, in chapter seven, 'When women hit the road', as well as elsewhere, we examine how the gender and sexuality of the travellers influence their attitude to travelling, the type of problems they encounter on the road, and the satisfaction resulting from their being on the move. In 'Geographies' we also look in depth at some important theoretical categories related to travel, including nomadism and diaspora.

On the whole, our book will argue that much European cinema has been from very early on and continues to this day to be deeply interested in the representation of travel. The journey has been used in different stages of national European production to reflect on various cultural and historical experiences. In the last twenty to thirty years, European travel films and road movies have mirrored the ever-increasing mobility of the population and have served as a reflection on the many and elusive shifts of borders, identities and cultures that we have been experiencing. Even if they cannot be considered as a genre in the traditional Hollywood sense of the word, European travel films constitute a multiform and dense body of work that offers an extraordinary lens through which to look at the changing realities of the continent and of its cinema.

SECTION ONE **Authors on the Road**

chapter one
BETWEEN HELSINKI, MEMPHIS AND 'NO DIRECTOR'S LAND': AKI KAURISMÄKI'S ROAD CINEMA

Aki Kaurismäki is, alongside Wim Wenders, the European filmmaker most widely identified with road cinema. This is not surprising, as over half of the films he has directed contain the motif of travel. Even *Dogs Have No Hell*, his ten-minute contribution to the co-authored *Ten Minutes Older: The Trumpet* (2002), is a travel film. Moreover, with the exception of Wim Wenders' films, his work is closer to the American model of road cinema than that of most European directors interested in travel. At the same time, Kaurismäki succeeded in creating a unique style of road cinema, producing the perception that he is an atypical, marginal representative of the genre. Even in the few publications that discuss the European input into this genre, such as David Laderman's *Driving Visions* (2002), Kaurismäki's films are omitted from the analysis. This chapter will examine the relationship of Kaurismäki's films to American road cinema and his use of magical realism, which appears to us as the most original aspect of his work.

American experience?

Although Kaurismäki alludes to American road films, he does not imitate them. He often parodies the road experience as represented by American directors or blends American motifs with specifically Finnish/Scandinavian and Eastern European perspectives on the road. We find similarities between Kaurismäki's representation of America and that offered by other European directors who worked in this country, especially Werner Herzog, as well as that of American filmmakers who specialise in road cinema, while being regarded as untypical representatives of this genre, such as Jim Jarmusch and David Lynch. Kaurismäki's films are rarely clear-cut generic productions; instead, he mixes elements of different genres. For example, a press kit describes *Ariel* (1988) in the following terms: 'A film that begins as an unemployment story, turns into a hanging-out movie, has a touch of love story about ordinary people, becomes a crime and prison film before ending up as an over-romantic melodrama. Contains truth about life in a typical Western "everything for sale" society. Some drama included' (quoted in Soila *et al*. 1998: 93).

Rather than distilling elements of the American road movie from Kaurismäki's films, in this chapter we will examine his cinema as being influenced by but also resistant to American traditions of representing the road, considering such issues as setting and iconography, camerawork, choice of protagonists and character of their journey. For this purpose, it is useful to reconstruct some paradigmatic features of the American road movie and examine whether they are present in the films of the Finnish author.

In terms of iconography, the American road movie is defined by highways and open landscape bordered by the horizon. As David Laderman observes, 'These expansive spaces obviously recall the western's compelling articulation of the frontier, and more generally the shifting nature/culture divide. However, the road movie reinvents the western's preindustrial iconography of slow-paced horse treks as motorised motion and speed' (2002: 14). The landscape, crossed by road movie travellers, as in many westerns, is typically romanticised, becoming a sign of the infinite opportunities awaiting travellers. According to Jack Sargeant and Stephanie Watson:

> The vision of the open road eternally vanishing into the horizon always prom-ises greater possibilities and journeys to come. Road movies offer audiences a glimpse at an ecstatic freedom. Following the classic westerns the *mise-en-scène* emphasises the vastness of the terrain, not only locating the individual protagonist's journey within the greater zone of the wilderness, but also allow-ing the audience the visual pleasure of the spectacle of the landscape, itself a mythical and poetic aspect of the construction of the American identity ... On the road anything appears possible because nothing seems fixed, the journey itself represents a degree of seduction as the protagonists leave the confines of their world and see the geographical expanse of their future before them. (1999: 13–15)

Three of Kaurismäki's films, *Leningrad Cowboys Go America* (1989), *Leningrad Cowboys Meet Moses* (1994) and the short *Thru the Wire* (1987), are entirely or partly set in the USA. They also allude to some narrative structures common to American road movies, especially escape. The films about the Leningrad Cow-boys present a group of immigrants from Eastern Europe (the rock musicians in the band that gives its name to the films) attempting to find success in America, whereas *Thru the Wire* shows an escape from prison. Yet, unlike in the descrip-

Fig. 3 Aki Kaurismäki's *Leningrad Cowboys Go America* (Finland/Sweden, 1989) © Sputnik Oy

tion provided by Laderman and Sargeant and Watson, Kaurismäki's America does not come across as being at the top of or at the centre of the world. Neither is it a land of infinite possibilities. On the contrary, it lacks any features that can attract tourists or immigrants and looks provincial, with dingy and scarcely frequented bars and clubs, ugly houses and old-fashioned workshops, streets which are almost empty in towns devoid of historical centres and cultural monuments. If there are people on the streets at all, they are usually poorly-clad black children or old people hanging out, with nothing else to do. This description applies even to places whose names are associated with vibrant culture and first-class entertainment, such as New York and Memphis. Unlike in the bulk of American road movies, which recognise and celebrate the variety and beauty of American landscapes, especially when one moves from the North to the South of the country, the landscape in *Leningrad Cowboys Go America* changes little. It is mainly industrial and postindustrial: gigantic factory plants, electrical installations, heaps of scrap metals and disused cars. There are few images of the countryside, one of them being the apparently famous resort in *Leningrad Cowboys Go America*, boasting a beach and other tourist attractions. However, when the Cowboys visit the beach, it is cold and empty. Their manager Vladimir even has to force them to sunbathe (claiming that their lack of suntan prejudices audiences against their music) and they do it in full clothing, which makes them look ridiculous and undermines the apparent attractiveness of the place they visit.

Kaurismäki's representation of America bears considerable similarity with his portrayal of Finland and other European countries. For example, the landscape passed by Valto and Reino, the main characters in *Pidä huivista kiinni, Tatjana* (*Take Care of Your Scarf, Tatjana*, 1994), set in Finland, is very monotonous and grey, mainly forests covered in snow, small provincial towns and villages, and cheap motels and drive-in bars. There are very few people in the places the travellers visit and all have a parochial atmosphere. Take, for example, the enormous and almost empty restaurant in which Valto, Reino and their female companions find themselves at the end of their journey. Such restaurants, where there was usually very little to eat, were commonplace in the Eastern block, and their ambience is also not uncommon in Finland, where there is more habitable land than people to inhabit it. Similarly, people whom Valto and Reino meet on their trek usually look parochial, wearing outmoded clothes and dancing in an old-fashioned way to kitsch Finnish music for a middle-aged audience. Dingy nightclubs and milk bars are frequented by Taisto in *Ariel*, another of Kaurismäki's films set in Finland. In common with the Leningrad Cowboys, at some stage Taisto makes an effort to be a tourist by taking a woman named Irmeli, whom he meets on the road, and her son to a beach. Yet, in spite of the good will and effort of all the travellers, the outcome of their trip is far from successful, as it was in the case of the Cowboys. The wind makes the passengers shiver in the car, as Taisto does not know how to close the car's sunroof; when they reach the beach, it is again too cold and windy to stay there for long. The best indication that the beach is not really an attractive place for visitors is the fact that there are no other people there. The beach episodes in *Leningrad Cowboys Go America* and *Ariel* also bear a resemblance to Jim Jarmusch's *Stranger Than Paradise*, in which the main characters travel first to the Great Lakes and then to Florida, only to experience boredom, sleepiness and silence. Everywhere is the same; landscape resembles townscape, looking ugly or dull – such a conclusion can equally be drawn from Jarmusch's and from Kaurismäki's films. For both directors an important means of conveying this experience is the use of colour – the majority of their films, including the three by Kaurismäki set in America, are shot in black and white. Jarmusch's films, at least for their setting, are regarded as close to European cinema. The director of *Stranger Than Paradise* even admitted in an interview that he wanted his films to look as if they were set in Eastern Europe. Hence, the comparison with Jarmusch does not really establish the similarity of Kaurismäki's films to their American equivalents, but rather the fact that the Finnish director discovered or revisited his European cinematic heritage through an American intermediary – not an unusual case in postmodern cinema.

The link between Kaurismäki and Jarmusch can also be explained by the cultural homogenisation of different parts of the world, which has taken place through the levelling of different cultures down to the lowest common denominator. This phenomenon is encapsulated by the fast food consumed by the characters, and by the 'basic English' used in the films of both directors by Americans and immigrants in their minimalist communication. The impression that 'everywhere is the same' also derives from choosing marginal characters as their protagonists: immigrants, the unemployed and petty criminals who have no intellectual and material resources to engage in social and cultural life. Yet, in comparison with travellers in Kaurismäki's films, Jarmusch's protagonists are more active and inquiring about life. They make their own choices rather than being pressurised into particular decisions. Also, they feel more at home in America than their counterparts in Kaurismäki's films do. This difference is particularly striking when we compare foreigners in the films of the respective directors. In Jarmusch's movies, they typically outwit the locals. Take, for example, the Italian prisoner played by Roberto Benigni in *Down by Law* (1986), who shows his cellmates how to escape, or Hungarian Eva in *Stranger Than Paradise*, who manages to acquire a large sum of money. Moreover, these foreigners generally have no problems with communication; it is the Americans who are unable to express themselves. In comparison with them, Kaurismäki's immigrants give the impression of being inarticulate, clumsy and lost when left to their own devices.

National borders matter little for Kaurismäki; his characters cross them with little difficulty and, as previously mentioned, distant places look as if they were parts of the same country. By contrast, the border between sea and mainland is of great significance for them. Not only do the characters often travel across the sea, but the sea promises them new opportunities, which cannot be fulfilled on land, such as the chance to find love, regain freedom and start life afresh. One such example is *Take Care of Your Scarf, Tatjana* in which Reino and Valto decide to follow Tatjana and her girlfriend only after the women boarded a ferry to Tallin. In *Ariel* the sea offers Taisto hope on more than one occasion: first when he finds work in docklands, later when he and Irmeli board a ship named Ariel leaving for Mexico. Crossing the boundary between sea and land is always much more dramatic than simply hitting the road or crossing other types of border. The impression is conveyed that there is no way back once one has left the solid land. We argue that the importance of the sea connects Kaurismäki's films with the European rendering of travel; it suffices to think of the first travel narrative of world recognition: Homer's *Odyssey*. By contrast, in American road movies the sea features only in the background, as an element of landscape, or as the limit of the movement for the characters. Due to the importance of the sea, Kaurismäki's stories also appear more open, avoiding both the happy ending that is the norm in most Hollywood narratives and the tragic one that dominates American road movies – which were largely born out of rebellion against the dominant, optimistic ideologies.

Another important connection between Kaurismäki's films and the American road movie is that his characters travel mainly by car. Unlike in European films, where, as John Orr suggests, cars are disposable, transient, temporary and impersonal (1993: 132), the cars in Kaurismäki's films are always owned by the travellers, who are very attached to them and dislike to leave them even for a short time. Outside them they feel out of place, thus the rule 'I own [a car]/drive, therefore I am' (ibid.), which determines the behaviour of the protagonists of American movies, also applies to them. They are even less willing to abandon them for good, and they suffer greatly when their vehicles are stolen or when they are forced to sell them. On such occasions they do not quarrel about the price, and quickly accept what they are offered, even if it is only a fraction of the car's true value – examples are Taisto in *Ariel* and Lauri in *Kauas pilvet karkaavat* (*Drifting Clouds*, 1996), who sell their stylish vehicles to unscrupulous dealers. Such behaviour on the one hand suggests their desperation, on the other it shows that they do not treat their cars as an ordinary commodity. This renders them similar to travellers in American films, who treat their cars as their best and priceless friends. Moreover, the car favoured by Kaurismäki's characters is the Cadillac, irrespective of the country in which the film is set. Cadillacs feature in the films with Leningrad Cowboys, and in *Thru the Wire*, *Ariel*, *Drifting Clouds* and *Take Care of Your Scarf, Tatjana*.

Although cars are 'transported', so to speak, by Kaurismäki from the visual vocabulary of the American road movie, he gives them a different function in his films. Unlike in Arthur Penn's *Bonnie and Clyde* (1967), Terrence Malick's *Badlands* (1973) or David Lynch's *Wild at Heart* (1990), they are not instruments of romantic journeys, but largely of comical trips. This results from the way they are used by their owners and from the context in which they appear. For example, Taisto in *Ariel*, who drives a convertible Cadillac, does not know how to close the sunroof, an essential device in a cold northern climate. To protect himself from the wind he puts a scarf on his head, which makes him look like a Russian 'babushka', not an archetypal male driver whose virility is augmented by his car. Taisto's expensive car also looks ridiculous when parked in the docklands, where he waits with other unemployed men for some casual work. It appears even funnier when parked amongst the caravans, where penniless Taisto decides to spend the night, after being thrown out of a cheap hotel. However, conforming to the American ideology by which the car is used by men to lure women, thanks to his Cadillac Taisto meets Irmeli, who becomes the love of his life. Irmeli, a traffic warden, suggests to Taisto that they have lunch together as an alternative to his paying a parking ticket, and later invites him home, where they make love. Yet the incredible ease of their acquaintance and the speed of their romance cast doubts on the seriousness of Kaurismäki's attitude to the value of a car as a means of seducing women. The most idiosyncratic feature of the Cadillac driven by Valto in *Take Care of Your Scarf, Tatjana* is a coffee machine attached to the steering wheel, which he uses almost continuously, being addicted to coffee. This device transforms his car into a portable home, but also signifies his inability to break with his old habits and enjoy the pleasures of the road, making the most of the opportunity to start his life afresh.

The cars in which the Leningrad Cowboys travel are also used differently to American cinema. Firstly, they are extremely overcrowded due to the number of Cowboys – some members of the group are even forced to travel in the boot. The result is extreme constraint, rather than the freedom enjoyed by characters of American road movies. It is even difficult to imagine their car reaching high speed. Moreover, for most of their journey they carry a coffin on the rooftop, in which Vladimir, the manager of the group, keeps a corpse as well as cans of beer, which looks ridiculous, even absurd, making them resemble a travelling circus. On the whole the car, although nominally American, does not help the Cowboys fit into American culture but, on the contrary, marks them as alien – similarly to Stroszek in Herzog's film, who also tried in vain to assimilate into the American milieu by means of a car – a house on wheels. However, being enormous and not a proper car, somehow 'more American than American cars', this vehicle ultimately set Stroszek apart from his adopted compatriots.

Cars are always driven by men, which until the enormous success of Ridley Scott's *Thelma & Louise* (1991) was also the norm for American movies. Travelling women in Kaurismäki's films literally take a back seat. The only exception is the woman who helps the fugitive in *Thru the Wire*. Yet women have great influence on male travellers by providing them with company, telling them where to go and stop, and sometimes how to behave in a car. In addition, female company makes male journeys more adventurous. Take the characters in *Take Care of Your Scarf, Tatjana* who, after driving a long distance with two women from Estonia, decide to visit them in their native country. Women do not need to exert much pressure to make Kaurismäki's men behave like their unpaid chauffeurs – they regard it as a price worth paying for their company. It could be argued that meeting women is an important, albeit unspoken, reason for his characters to go on the road.

The importance of women to male travellers, particularly their ability to change an unstructured drift into a purposeful journey, can be regarded as a sign of their crisis of masculinity. Kaurismäki draws attention to many other symptoms of Finnish/Eastern European men losing in social prestige and self-confidence, such as their unenviable job situation, resulting from the disappearance of traditionally masculine industries and, conversely, of female labour gaining in importance. For example, after being made redundant Taisto in *Ariel* has great difficulties in finding even a casual job and a place to stay, while his lover Irmeli works in several different places and is able to support herself, her son, and pay for their nice apartment. Both wife and husband in *Drifting Clouds* are made redundant, but whereas her husband is rejected everywhere he goes for work and eventually turns to alcohol, Ilona does not give up hope of finding a job and eventually opens her own restaurant. Kaurismäki suggests that her husband, who has no better prospects, will also work there. Valto in *Take Care of Your Scarf, Tatjana* lives with his mother and works from home, on a sewing machine. Again, we can assume that he is employed by his own mother. For many of these men travelling is a way of dealing with the difficulty of finding a new role, when it is impossible to continue to play the old one. This feature renders Kaurismäki's films close to a certain tradition in American cinema, where the road was used as a means to depict men's experiences during the depression of the 1930s, as in Mervyn LeRoy's *I Am a Fugitive from a Chain Gang* (1932), Fritz Lang's *You Only Live Once* (1937) and John Ford's *The Grapes of Wrath* (1940).

For those men who once had a car, to lose it implies a loss of independence and dignity: the ultimate downfall and metaphoric castration. Take Lauri in *Drifting Clouds* and Taisto in *Ariel*, who without their cars become completely helpless and sedentary. Kaurismäki's women, because they always had to rely on public transport or the kindness of strangers, do not suffer a comparable problem. In the city they even prove more mobile than men, like Ilona, who moves from one job or employment agency to the next by bus or taxis or walking, or Irmeli, who constantly changes jobs and still finds time to visit Taisto in jail. Hence, a car in Kaurismäki's cinema does not guarantee mobility and freedom, and mobility and freedom are not excluded by not having a car.

The importance of cars in American road movies lies not only in the role they play in the narrative and depiction of the characters, but also in structuring the gaze of the protagonists and the audience. Laderman, whose previously cited book is significantly entitled *Driving Visions*, quotes Michael Atkinson:

> Few cultural developments outside the first atomic bomb test at Los Alamos have had such a decisive impact on movies. The structure of the car, designed both to conform to our bodies' shortcomings and powerfully extend them, has become how we regard the world (through the screen-like, Panavision-shaped lens of the windscreen and, like a miniature movie within a movie, the rear view mirror). (Quoted in 2002: 3)

In the American paradigmatic examples of the genre we experience the world as viewed by the driver of a car (or motorcycle). His vision constitutes the perspective adopted by the film, both in a literal and moral sense. Even if his perception of something, be it landscape, society or himself, is very different from the representation that dominates in his culture, we are meant to identify with his gaze, believing that it is correct. The very point of many road movies is to convince us about the superiority of the drivers' sight over other comparable visions.

In Kaurismäki's films, by contrast, the vision of the driver is not privileged. More often than looking at the world through his eyes, we are looking at him from outside. The point of view usually adopted by Kaurismäki is that of the objective, impersonal camera, or of a critical passenger. The first situation takes place in the films about Leningrad Cowboys and in *Ariel*, the second in *Take Care of Your Scarf, Tatjana*. In the latter film, the director juxtaposes the gaze of Reino and Valto with that of the women from the ex-Soviet Union. This leads to a paradox: the foreign women appear to be more in tune with their surroundings and 'normal' than the Finnish men who act as total outsiders. The fair share of comedy in Kaurismäki's films results from the fact that his drivers are the object of somebody else's gaze. This is also one of the reasons why his films feel rather static.

Kaurismäki's characters hit the road or board a train or a ferry, as in classical American movies, in order to escape. Taisto in *Ariel* leaves the coalmine estate after the mine is closed down and he is made redundant together with all the other workers. Valto in *Take Care of Your Scarf, Tatjana* flees his home after his mother upsets him by not buying him the coffee to which he is addicted. The Leningrad Cowboys head for New York after failing to achieve success in their own country. The main protagonist in *Thru the Wire* first escapes from prison, then from various places where he is chased by the police. An additional factor in the departure of many of these people seems to be an ordinary boredom and, if not poverty as such, at least lack of prospects. Their home towns and villages are always inconspicuous, sparsely populated and devoid of entertainment, not mentioning high culture, and suffering harsh climate. Another factor in their desire to leave is a lack of desirable women. In the Siberian village from which the Leningrad Cowboys begin their journey, there are virtually no women. Even a baby in a cradle is looked after by a man.

Leaving the place of departure is easy for Kaurismäki's characters, because they have little attachment to what they abandon: their homes, families, friends and their country. These things either do not exist in their lives at all, or bear only negative connotations for them. Although this lack of attachment primarily reflects their personal situation, it also encapsulates the history of Finland, marked by periods of deep poverty and the suppression of indigenous culture (see Häikio

1992). Furthermore, 'Finland has been a country of outward migration for most of its modern history. The land is too poor to attract large numbers of new settlers and from the nineteenth century onwards there have been times when many young Finns faced the stark reality of "emigrate or starve"' (Singleton 1998: 158). Finland was part of Sweden until 1809, when she became an autonomous part of Russia. Only in 1917 did Finland achieve political independence. Even nowadays many Finns admit that they have a postcolonial culture and mentality. The vast majority of the products for cultural consumption is imported either from Sweden or from the USA, and Finns suffer an inferiority complex towards their larger and more powerful neighbours. In the films about the Leningrad Cowboys the lack of connection with one's home and country might signify cultural and economic deprivation, resulting from long decades of communist rule. The Leningrad Cowboys' homeland, Siberia, used to be the part of Soviet Union most exposed to and affected by communist 'enculturation'. In this region more new, artificial cities were created than in any other part of the Soviet Union (see Lewis & Rowland 1976). Here also natural demographic processes were disturbed by enforced migration of hundreds of thousands of people from other parts of the Stalinist empire and its satellites, such as Poland. Not having connections with their home and country results in a lack of nostalgia in Kaurismäki's characters. Alternatively, as in *Leningrad Cowboys Go America*, the homesickness of travellers is represented in a way which undermines its seriousness – through the picture of a rather unappealing woman carried by one of the Leningrad Cowboys, and their happiness at the view of some tractors ploughing a field in rural America.

On the other hand, Kaurismäki demonstrates that a lack of roots is an obstacle in finding a reason and direction of travel and, ultimately, a new home. His characters do not seek any new experiences that travelling may offer them, and are uninterested in the geographical and cultural landscapes which they traverse. They do not leave their cars, unless they are forced to, and hardly look through the windows. In *Take Care of Your Scarf, Tatjana* Reino tells his friend Valto how, during a coach holiday in Czechoslovakia, his group was invited to view some ruins; '...as if Finland was lacking in ruins', he adds with a sneer. The same lack of interest applies to Reino and Valto's trip through Finland: they do not talk to people whom they meet on the road, nor explore their surroundings; they do not even have a map. Their low-key attitude to travelling is sometimes funny, as when they clumsily adapt certain elements of the American 'road ethos': clothes, gestures and expressions. As Jonathan Romney writes: 'Reino may dress up in leathers and snakeskin shirt, and he and Valto may live the tough life, camping by night (Valto, morosely toasting a sausage by firelight, remarks that a rocker's must surely be a hard life); but they seem to miss out entirely on the traditional pleasures of the road' (1995: 51). Their lacking a spirit of adventure and 'travelling culture' is revealed not only by what they fail to notice on the road, but also by what manages to attract their attention: a shop selling mechanical tools. On the other hand, it is difficult to imagine what remarkable views and cultural landmarks Reino and Valto are missing – the landscape which they pass in their cars is monotonous and similar to that left at home.

Another important reason why Kaurismäki's characters remain attached to their cars, instead of exploring the places which they are visiting, is financial difficulties. Being unemployed, economic migrants or provincials with a limited budget for tourist pleasures, they cannot afford expensive hotels and restaurants, let alone museums or galleries. The Leningrad Cowboys' poverty in America is so extreme that it becomes comical. On their arrival in New York each receives 25 cents from their manager, Vladimir, with the advice not to spend all this money at once. When they complain of hunger they receive some onions which Vladimir bought for them in a supermarket. They are forced to play and beg on the streets, and even pretend to be crippled to get more money from the passers-by. At the same time Vladimir drinks hundreds of cans of beer on their way from New York to Memphis and has lavish meals in restaurants, while the Cowboys go hungry outside. In spite of the grotesque exaggeration, Kaurismäki conveys some important aspects of the experience of many new immigrants to the West: poverty, helplessness, fear and isolation, as well as dependence on various types of 'guardians' who organise work for them in exchange for a high proportion of their wages.

Discussing American road movies, Ron Eyerman and Orvar Löfgren argue that 'the freedom to move upward and outward, is one of the most central and persistent images America has of itself ... "If you don't like it here, go somewhere else", was a cry heard very early on in American history; the phrase always contained the sense of possibility, the positive, within its negative instruction' (1995: 55). By contrast, Kaurismäki shows that there is little chance for his characters who travel in America to move upward. The Leningrad Cowboys can be regarded as a seminal case. Although initially they are welcomed in the US and their prospects are impressive (playing on large stages and stadiums for audiences of thousands of people), they fail to make a big career or even find a modest but secure existence. In addition, they are constantly humiliated, persecuted and bullied and even go to jail for some days after trying to organise a funeral for their colleague without having permission from the local authority. Wherever they go, after a short time they hear from their hosts the same, unwelcoming words: 'Leave and never come back', in spite of the Cowboys' genuine attempts to fit into American society by speaking English, learning how to play country and rock 'n' roll and even, in the case of one Cowboy, spending a small fortune on a typical cowboy outfit (or more precisely, as such an outfit is represented in the media). This experience of America as a deceptive lure, as a fake promised land, is reminiscent of the image created by some other European directors who worked in the US, most notably by Werner Herzog in *Stroszek*. The main idea informing both films is that if you do not have money or good prospects of becoming rich, in America you are nobody and the country will get rid of you as waste.

The aspiration to fit into American society and the immense difficulty to fulfil this desire is inscribed in the very name of the group. The oxymoron 'Leningrad Cowboys' puts together the city in Russia with a symbol of rural America. However, the musicians are not even from Leningrad, but from an obscure village in the tundra. Metaphorically speaking, the name 'Leningrad Cowboys' signifies the distance of the musicians from their own inherited traditions and their craving for a new identity by appropriating elements of different cultures. The idea of freeing oneself from a previous identity and appropriating a new spiritual homeland and generally changing identity 'on demand' is a postmodern concept. It is only in the last decades when it became possible (or assumed to be possible) to have an unstable identity and to influence cultural identity in a major way. Writers such as Fredric Jameson, Anthony Giddens, Zygmunt Bauman and Stuart Hall draw attention to various causes and consequences of a 'liquid' identity. In this context particularly worthy of attention are the views of Zygmunt Bauman, who uses extensively metaphors from the discourse on travelling and tourism to depict the times in which we live. Bauman maintains that the desire to have one's identity unfixed, to keep one's options open, leads to the risk of having no identity, of becoming a vagabond (1996: 29). Such an opinion captures the position in which the Leningrad Cowboys find themselves. In terms of belonging to any culture, they are neither real cowboys nor real Americans, neither 'here nor there', they are model vagabonds. Still, Kaurismäki shows that the position of even the humblest travellers in America is better than their counterparts in Finland and Russia. They might not be able to move upward, achieving higher social status and becoming true Americans, but can relatively easily move outward: to new cities, new states, even new countries. When Kaurismäki's men start their journey in Finland, which is the case of the characters in *Ariel* and in *Take Care of Your Scarf, Tatjana*, their opportunities are even more restricted. In spite of the relatively large size of the country, Finland appears claustrophobic. The impression of confinement is excellently conveyed by a man who shares a cell with Taisto in *Ariel*. When asked by Taisto about the chances of escaping from prison, he says that there is no point to flee, because even if the escape was successful, nothing would change: those who escaped would be soon found in Finland or Sweden, and put back in prison.

The trips depicted by Kaurismäki do not have any definite outcome. *Ariel* finishes when Taisto, Irmeli and her son, equipped with false passports, board a ship which is meant to take them to Mexico. A group of men in *Calamari Union* (1985) head for a trip across Helsinki to find a better place in the picturesque Eira district by the sea. Nobody in the group, however, reaches the original goal. One after the other the men meet their fate: some are killed, some just disappear. One of the men in *Take Care of Your Scarf, Tatjana* follows Tatjana to her village in Estonia. The other, Valto, after passing through a large part of Finland and crossing the sea, returns to his home in Finland, which looks exactly the same as at the beginning of his journey. Valto even starts his work on the sewing machine at the place he abandoned some days or weeks before. Nothing suggests that the journey changed his attitude to life or his manners: he is as taciturn and introverted as before he accepted Reino's offer to hit the road. Similarly to Valto's trip, the journeys in *Leningrad Cowboys Go America* and *Leningrad Cowboys Meet Moses* are circular. The Cowboys first go to America, then to Mexico, then to Europe, passing through countries such as Czechoslovakia and Poland, and are eventually back in Siberia. Ultimately, nothing changes in their lives, either in economic, social or psychological terms. With the exception of meeting a cousin who migrated to the US many years before, no friendships are forged during their journey. Even the internal dynamics of the group remains as when they left their home village. The Cowboys get rid of Vladimir on their way to Mexico, but he reappears as Moses in *Leningrad Cowboys Meet Moses*, and continues to overpower and bully the hapless musicians. The 'ordinary' Cowboys get on with each other fine en route, as they did when they lived in Siberia. Yet their relationships with each other are lacking any real attachment; they remain emotionally inarticulate or suppressed. On the whole, the road in Kaurismäki's films does not fulfil its traditional road movie functions of a way to reach a better place or rite of passage, of an instrument to gain wisdom and maturity. However, in its emphasis on the process of travelling, his cinema is true road cinema, as opposed to a cinema of 'leaving and arriving'.

Magical realism

In many ways Kaurismäki's characters and the journeys they undertake feel painfully authentic; in other respects they feel unreal, even magical. For this reason the term 'magical realism', or similar ones such as 'fantastical anti-realism', have been used by critics to describe the style of Kaurismäki's films (see Pulleine 1990: 71; Romney 1997: 11). The term 'magical realism' was introduced into the artistic discourse in the mid-1920s through the German expression *Magischer Realismus*, used by Franz Roh to depict the 'counter-movement in art through which the charm of the object was rediscovered' (Simpkins 1995: 146). In due course it was applied to Latin American literature, represented by authors such as Alejo Carpentier, Carlos Fuentes, Julio Cortázar, José Donoso and, most of all, Gabriel García Márquez. Their books were about miracles in the real world, they dealt with such phenomena as 'the fusion of the realms which we know to be separated, the abolition of the laws of statics, the loss of identity, the distortion of natural size and shape, the suspension of the category of objects, the destruction of personality, and the fragmentation of historical order' (Nigro 1975: 220). Typical inhabitants of the world of magical realism are people who live for centuries and newborn babies or foetuses that have the appearances and knowledge of adult people. Some critics argue that magical realism is essentially realism, because it does not use dream motifs or create imagined worlds. It is an epistemological rather than an ontological concept, articulating a particular way of perceiving things (for instance, through strange juxtapositions), as opposed to seeing a supernatural world. The fact that magical realism (although being present also in the work of some European and American writers, such as Günter Grass and Vladimir Nabokov) flourished in Latin America is often explained by the fact that 'the postcolonial experience involved sharp discrepancies between the cultures of technology and superstition' (Ousby 1993–95). For the characters in the literature belonging to this paradigm, magic is often the only way to understand the world and survive in hostile circumstances; it is a secret weapon of the disadvantaged and marginalised.

In the 1990s Fredric Jameson used the notion of 'magical realism' in reference to the Soviet science fiction cinema of the 1970s and 1980s, created by Andrei Tarkovsky and Aleksandr Sokurov. Films such as Tarkovsky's *Stalker* and Sokurov's *Dni zatmeniya* (*Days of Eclipse*, 1988) depicted strange, inexplicable events in a world which in many respects bore close affinity to the Soviet reality of late Communism. They were set at the margins of the civilised world ('magical gulags in real physical space') and often represented characters who were crippled, emaciated, eccentric and almost always unhappy. In common with Latin American magical realism, albeit to a larger extent, the Soviet one conveyed an ambiguous attitude towards science and technology, showing that more often than alleviating poverty and illness, they exacerbate them. Similarly, it drew attention to the utter mystery and inexplicability of human existence and social life (see Jameson 1992).

A different type of magical realism can be found in the films of Ingmar Bergman. Bergman creates a sense of the unreal by introducing characters who use magic as a way of earning their living – magicians, actors, circus artists, as in *Det Sjunde Inseglet* (*The Seventh Seal*, 1956), *Ansiktet* (*The Magician*, 1958) and *Fanny och Alexander* (*Fanny and Alexander*, 1982), or people who decline into insanity as a means of coping with the outside world which they find hostile, as in *Såsom i en spegel* (*Through a Glass Darkly*, 1961). It could be argued that Bergman's use of magical realism is also a means to articulate his emotional distance from the cold Scandinavian climate, and his disillusionment with rational Lutheran religion, by juxtaposing it with pagan and 'cheap' sorcery. We suggest that Bergman's magical realism is largely epistemological.

The seminal example of European magical realism in cinema is the work of Werner Herzog. He traces what is inexplicable in human history, as in *Jeder für sich und Gott gegen alle* (*The Enigma of Kaspar Hauser*, 1974), concentrates on 'holy madmen' and 'idiot saints', explores ways of seeing which are far from the ordinary. His version of magical realism is both epistemological and ontological. According to Herzog, the real world is full of miracles, but people can also see miracles whose existence is problematic. This usually happens when they are isolated from their native culture and put in extreme circumstances. We find a similar type of magic as that of Herzog in the films by Emir Kusturica, namely magic resulting from seeing the world in an idiosyncratic way and magic inherent in reality, especially the cultural reality of certain marginalised nations or groups, such as Gypsies (see Gocić 2001).

Many authors discussing magical realism notice its affinity with postmodernism. Theo L. D'haen maintains that 'they now seem almost the only shorthands available to categorise contemporary developments in Western fiction. Increasingly, though, it has proved difficult to distinguish the categories covered by these terms clearly' (1995: 193). This is not surprising as postmodernism is marked by such characteristics as self-reflexivity, discontinuity, generic eclecticism, parody, the dissolution of character and narrative stance, the destabilisation of the reader, as well as interest in marginal characters and cultures (ex-centricity) and rejection of or distrust towards any kind of hegemony, many of which undermine or exclude realistic treatment of the subject matter. D'haen argues that magical realism is the cutting edge of postmodernism. He also notices the reluctance to apply the term 'magical realism' to American literature (ibid.). This is also true, in our opinion, of American cinema; for example, the work of David Lynch is hardly classified in this way and instead he is regarded as the epitome of postmodernism in American film.

Kaurismäki's films largely conform to the aforementioned description, sharing many features with magical realism and postmodernism at large, and their particular incarnations in cinema. Firstly, they represent characters who are outsiders. Take the Leningrad Cowboys, who are marginal in many ways, first by living, as the subtitle announces, 'in tundra, in no man's land' and apparently having no contact with anybody beyond their own idiosyncratic village, populated exclusively by people and animals with strange hairstyles and shoes, and devoid of women.

Fig. 4 Aki Kaurismäki's *Leningrad Cowboys Go America* (Finland/Sweden, 1989) © Sputnik Oy

Although the Cowboys' village does not look as depressing as those in the films by Tarkovsky and Sokurov, it is hardly represented as a place which one wants to visit as a tourist, not least to stay permanently. The 'beaks' decorating the heads and feet of the villagers might be regarded as a sign of some catastrophe affecting their health and physical appearance – which was also a typical motif of the cinema of Russian magical realists. In America and other countries where they travel, the Cowboys are even more marginal due to being foreign, not knowing the local people or understanding the indigenous culture, as demonstrated in an episode in which they admit that they do not know what rock 'n' roll is. They are also marginal because, as was previously mentioned, they are rarely in charge of their fate; usually they are at the mercy of their manager and hostile circumstances. Other examples of peripheral characters in Kaurismäki's films are Valto and Reino in *Take Care of Your Scarf, Tatjana*, who live in the solipsistic world of drinking coffee and alcohol, and Taisto in *Ariel* who is first marginalised by his unemployment, then by his homelessness and eventually his incarceration. In common with the Leningrad Cowboys, these characters live at the margin of a margin, as the countries and regions where they come from, Finland and Lapland, are very sparsely populated and provincial.

We can assume that such people, more than the members of more civilised and prosperous societies, need magic to survive and Kaurismäki generously grants miracles to them to correct the injustices resulting from the differences between cultural centre and periphery. For example, magic is the only tool to allow the Leningrad Cowboys to breach the border between Siberia and New York, two regions which are extremely distant from each other in geographical, cultural, political and technological terms. Kaurismäki makes the tundra seem more civilised in certain respects than we might expect, and New York more backward. For example, the Leningrad Cowboys' manager phones New York from a public telephone attached to an old-fashioned barn and is able to convince his American caller that the musicians are in reality American, only their name is Russian. The international airport, from which the Siberian group begins their journey, is so close to their village that they reach it on foot, without any difficulty in crossing the vast Siberian forest, the 'taiga'. The airport in New York where they arrive, on the other hand, looks more like a dingy bus station in a provincial town than one of the largest airports in the world.

During the Cowboys' journey various physical and human laws are suspended or violated, to allow them to continue their movement. First, the cost of their trip is covered by a relative in a hamlet, who simply takes a bag full of money (or gold) from a cradle where a 'baby cowboy' is sleeping and gives it to Vladimir, without asking him to repay his loan. Such an extravagant attitude to money is at odds with the common knowledge (conveyed elsewhere in the narrative) that Siberia is a poor place, where ordinary people must save all their lives in order to have enough money for a Transatlantic journey. The Cowboys go to America seemingly without passports or American visas, which Soviet citizens normally only obtain with great difficulty. Moreover, they carry with them a coffin with the corpse of one of the musicians, who died of frost bite when practicing late at night. Needless to say, such a piece of luggage requires plenty of extra documents and additional expenses. In America the Leningrad Cowboys are always reaching their destination without possessing exact addresses. They go to New York or Mexico as if these were small villages where everybody knows everybody else. Moreover, on their way they meet at a petrol station their cousin who immigrated to the country a long time before. He reached his destination in an even more bizarre way than the Cowboys – he was left in a little boat in Siberia and some weeks later found himself in America.

Even more mysterious and improbable is the journey of Igor, the village idiot, who is also dumb. He goes to America in spite of Vladimir forbidding him to do so. Unnoticed by anybody, he boards the plane and flies to New York hidden in the luggage compartment. There he leaves the plane in the same inconspicuous manner as he boarded it and starts to follow the Leningrad Cowboys. Although they travel by car and he on foot, he reaches every destination at the same time as they, or even arrives earlier. Moreover, in spite of his apparent stupidity, he proves to be more resourceful than his more intelligent compatriots. For example, while the Cowboys are starving and passively waiting for some food or money being given to them by Vladimir, Igor manages to catch an enormous fish, big enough to feed the whole group.

The character of the village idiot is a common figure in Russian fairytales (where he has a name, 'iurodivy') and in Scandinavian folklore, as well as in the traditions of other European nations and magical realist narratives. One example is Tarjei Vesaas' novel *The Birds* which was adapted for the screen by the Polish director Witold Leszczyński, resulting in the film *Żywot Mateusza* (*The Life of Matthew*, 1967), one of the most successful examples of magical realism in Polish cinema. He is typically represented as somebody who has low intelligence and is physically impaired (dumb, blind, crippled), but possesses some abilities beyond the reach of most people, such as the power of clairvoyance and of understanding animals and plants. Due to his otherness he is rejected by the community, but it is suggested that the society makes a mistake in overlooking his talents. Similarly, in the films about the Leningrad Cowboys Kaurismäki conveys the idea that Igor would be very useful to the Cowboys. The European part of the Leningrad Cowboys' trek, as well as the journeys of Kaurismäki's other characters, is also full of unlikely or inexplicable events, such as Taisto's escape from prison. Again, one gets the impression that by the use of magic or unlikely coincidences the director wanted to correct the harsh social reality in which his characters found themselves. In these examples magic operates also as a means to produce comical situations. To be precise, it is not magic itself, but the clash of magical events on the one hand and, on the other, strange relationships with the realistic surroundings.

Realism is further undermined by the episodic structure of Kaurismäki's narratives, a structure which is sometimes explained by the low budget at his disposal, and which is often emphasised by intertitles that are largely irrelevant or redundant, such as 'Later' or 'Highway'. Some of his films, including those with the Leningrad Cowboys, feel almost like a series of gags, joined together by the participation of the same characters. Little explanation is given as to why certain decisions are made and how the characters reach a particular destination. They simply do, as if helped by a fairy's wand. In common with the narrative, time is treated by Kaurismäki in a nonchalant manner. Firstly, we are given little information as to how much time passes in the characters' lives. A long period can be depicted as if it was a short while and (albeit less often) tiny episodes last very long. Secondly, the laws of time are violated. Take, for example, the dead corpse of one of the Cowboys, which does not undergo decomposition but, on the contrary, is brought back to life after several weeks. Neither the friends of the resurrected Cowboy nor the man himself find this particularly strange. Another, although more plausible, example of resurrection is Vladimir, who keeps returning in the story in different disguises and keeps finding the Cowboys when they supposedly need him. Kaurismäki's characters also seem to live according to different clocks than those of normal people. In *Take Care of Your Scarf, Tatjana* two friends manage to cross the whole of Finland and find themselves in Tallin, while the mother of one of them is locked in the cupboard all the time. When eventually released from her imprisonment, she carries on as if no time has passed. Moreover, the change of seasons hardly affects the characters; they wear the same clothes and behave in the same way irrespective of whether it is summer or winter. One gets the impression that, as in fairytales, time in Kaurismäki's films is not linear, but circular. People do not die, but appropriate new identities, or perhaps only new names. Hence, there is a parallel between life and road, as represented by Kaurismäki's: both are circular, there is no progress either in individual or in social life.

The aura of magic and improbability, as well as the grotesque, is also introduced by Kaurismäki's reference to cultural archetypes, particularly those involving travelling. The very word 'cowboy' in the name of the group of musicians and the films in which they are cast as protagonists refers to the American predecessor of the road movie: the western. *Leningrad Cowboys Meet Moses*, as the title indicates, alludes to the characters and narrative of the Bible, which can be regarded as one of the first 'road narratives' ever written. Yet the Leningrad Cowboys are not from America but from Russia, hence they cannot be true successors of cowboys. Similarly, Kaurismäki's Moses is in reality Vladimir and his appropriation of Moses' persona invites ridicule. We would suggest that by quoting these archetypes Kaurismäki draws attention to the possibility of time and history not being linear, but circular. In this respect he is not alone amongst creators of road cinema – the Coen brothers in *O Brother, Where Art Thou?* (2000) used archetypes of travel in a similar way.

The Finnish director uses magical realism as a strategy assuring his characters' survival in a difficult or hostile environment. In this respect, it is a testimony of his solidarity with the economically, socially and culturally disadvantaged. We also argue that Kaurismäki employs magical realism as a style of counter-culture and a means to defy genre conventions. It allows him to look at well-known objects afresh; to defamiliarise and denaturalise American landscapes and journeys, and the road cinema that depicts them. Consequently, it is a way to correct or even subvert road cinema as a genre which has its roots in the western understood as a narrative of conquest of the strongest and fittest over the weak. However, magic in Kaurismäki's films, as in many other examples of cinematic or literary magical realism, operates dialectically. On the one hand, it reverses (at least partially) the social order who favours the fittest and most ruthless; on the other, it draws attention to the fact that in 'real life' people similar to his characters would not survive. Similarly, at the same time as opposing generic conventions and mainstream culture, it testifies to their strength as a template towards which any cinematic rebel must define his position.

chapter two
THE ROAD TO AUTHENTICITY AND STABILITY: HOLIDAYS, RELOCATION AND MOVEMENT IN THE FILMS OF ERIC ROHMER

'François Truffaut once said that if he had not discovered the cinema, he might have ended up in prison. As for his former *nouvelle vague* colleague Eric Rohmer, he might have ended up a travel agent.'
– John Wrathal

In the same article from which the above quote is taken, John Wrathal claims that 'no other director [than Rohmer] has chronicled in such minute detail what people do – or, more to the point, don't do – on holiday' (1996: 53), an opinion which we share. We also argue that Rohmer has few rivals in another area – discovering holiday pleasures and hazards in people's everyday, working lives. The aim of this chapter is to examine the holiday aspect of the lives of Rohmer's characters, and the wider problem of the significance of geographical change in their lives. Ultimately, we wish to illuminate key issues in the representation and evaluation of tourism through an analysis of the work of this director. What interests us in particular is that which for the director constitutes an enjoyable and morally valuable tourist experience and, more broadly, a satisfactory transition from one place to another.

Rather than adopting a rigid definition of tourism and holiday-making, we will reconstruct Rohmer's own discourse on tourism. However, we will refer to the work of several authors, including Zygmunt Bauman and John Urry, who discuss tourism both as an actual experience and as a metaphor of the modern/postmodern condition. We will also refer to the literature that acknowledges and explores gender differences in the travel experience, as well as the relationship between tourism and social class.

As is well known, Eric Rohmer (b. 1920), real name Jean-Marie Maurice Schérer, is one of the initiators of the French New Wave. The young directors who rallied around André Bazin, their mentor and friend, and editor of the famous journal *Cahiers du cinéma*, were in favour of naturalness, achieved through location shooting, use of hand-held camera, improvisation and narrative fragmentation, which was meant to reflect the unpredictability of real life. Geographical authenticity, especially the emphasis on representing various aspects of Paris, and the relationship between character and physical environment were among their major concerns. In Rohmer's case, it meant setting the narratives of many of his films during holidays, when the physical environment is of special importance for the characters. However, we argue that, in the subsequent decades, only Rohmer remained faithful to his original interest in the relationship between film characters and their geographical surroundings and continued to study in minute detail various French locations, hence his uniqueness within the original 'Bazin circle'. As a result of his interests in 'social geography', Rohmer is also a rarity against the wider backdrop of contemporary French and European cinema. It is all the more surprising that his work has hardly ever been analysed from the perspective here outlined.

In order to emphasise the continuity of Rohmer's preoccupation with holidays, relocation and movement, as well as his changing attitude towards place and transition, we will refer to films made at different stages of his cinematic career, which spans over forty years – although it is impossible here to discuss his considerable *oeuvre* in its entirety.

Looking for love and permanence on vacation

According to James Monaco, Rohmer attached great importance to holiday as a subject of his art even before he became a filmmaker. Testimony to that is his writing during the Nazi Occupation a novel 'variously called *Elizabeth* and *Les Vacances*' (1976: 286). Holidays also feature in the majority of his films, including *La Collectionneuse* (*The Collector*, 1966), *Le Genou de Claire* (*Claire's Knee*, 1970), *Pauline à la plage* (*Pauline at the Beach*, 1982), *Le Rayon vert* (*The Green Ray*, 1986), *Conte d'hiver* (*A Winter's Tale*, 1992) and *Conte d'été* (*A Summer's Tale*, 1996). In each case, the holiday's purpose is to go to an attractive place, such as a village by the sea or on the edge of a lake. Rohmer often shows Parisians who visit a picturesque province, which is the case in all the films listed above. We also find foreigners coming to Paris and other parts of France, such as the Swedish female students in *The Green Ray* and *Mère et enfant, 1907*, one of the three sections of *Les Rendez-vous de Paris* (*Rendezvous in Paris*, 1995), but they hardly feature as the main characters, instead their behaviour serves as a backdrop for the activities of Parisians.

We can detect in Rohmer's holidaymakers a certain hostility towards tourists or, more precisely, towards those whom they regard as typical or common tourists. Léna in *A Summer's Tale* reproaches her boyfriend, Gaspard, by telling him: 'You behave like an ordinary tourist.' Henri in *Pauline at the Beach* simply states: 'I hate tourists.' Their dislike of tourism is shared by Jérome and Laura in *Claire's Knee*, and to a certain extent by Delphine in *The Green Ray* and Adrien in *The Collector*. In their aversion to tourism Rohmer's characters are by no means original. James Buzard maintains that denigration of tourism has existed almost as long as tourism itself (1993: 1–5). It is worth mentioning here Henry James' opinion that 'tourists are vulgar, vulgar, vulgar' (quoted in Pearce & Moscardo 1986: 121), and Reverend Francis Kilvert's claim that 'If there is one thing more hateful than another it is being told what to admire and having objects pointed out to one with a stick. Of all noxious animals too the most noxious is a tourist' (1971: 79).

The perceived low status of 'tourism' in a hierarchy of human pleasures results, as Buzard argues, from it being undertaken on the 'beaten track', which 'succinctly designates the space of the "touristic" as a region in which all experience is predictable and repetitive, all cultures and objects mere "touristy" self-parodies' (1993: 4). Buzard observes that the detractors of tourists claim that these do not go where they want to, but where the industry directs them (1993: 3). In common with Buzard, John Urry observes that tourism became regarded as commodified, inauthentic, clichéd, and as a way of experiencing 'pseudo-events': 'All over the world the unsung armies of semioticians, the tourists, are fanning out in search of the signs of Frenchness, typical Italian behaviour, exemplary Oriental scenes, typical American thruways, traditional English pubs' (1990: 3). The popular tourist guides, published in millions of copies, not only inform the tourist about the cultural treasures of a given area, but also often simplify its complex cultural character, increasing the danger of tourism being clichéd. Tourists, especially those who take part in its mass form of which the 'package holiday' is a model, are also criticised because their behaviour is frequently marked by a certain excess, resulting from an ostentatious breaking with the established routines of everyday life, and this is potentially disruptive for the local community (see Urry 1990; Shields 1991). In its perceived inauthenticity, commodification and kitsch, 'tourism' is typically contrasted with 'travelling', regarded as a more authentic and noble pastime. Unlike tourists, travellers are individuals: they go where they want and stay in a chosen place for as long as they please. Moreover, they are guided by some personal quest, not by a published guide. Buzard, however, argues that tourists and travellers have more in common than the latter are willing to admit: 'Rather than being a description of objective differences, the tourist/traveller dichotomy has functioned primarily, as [Jonathan] Culler says, "to convince oneself that one is not a tourist ... the desire to distinguish between tourists and real travellers [being] part of tourism – integral to it rather than outside it or beyond it"' (1993: 4–5).

Chris Ryan, applying the perspective of a more sophisticated, self-reflexive tourist (who might even call himself 'a traveller') observes that

> the irony of tourism is that for many tourists they achieve the highest levels of satisfaction when they feel that they have ceased to be a 'tourist' … The touristic critique of tourism is based on a desire to go beyond the other 'mere' tourists to a more profound appreciation of society and culture, and it is by no means limited to intellectual statements. All tourists desire this deeper involvement with society and culture to some degree; it is a basic component of their motivation to travel. (1991: 35)

Hence (ordinary) tourists are reproached for two principal vices: following in the footsteps of other tourists, and not achieving the status of a guest in the visited community. As a result, a touristic experience is regarded as both repetitive and superficial.

Rohmer's characters join in the choir of those who criticise tourism for the same or similar reasons. Laura in *Claire's Knee* complains that the campers who visit the beautiful village of Talloires on Lake Annecy are primitive, unpleasant, noisy and produce a lot of rubbish. Laura is a permanent resident of this idyllic village, but her ill disposition towards the campers can also be attributed to the majority of Rohmer's holidaymakers. However, unlike the majority of the critics of tourism, that which Rohmer's characters dislike about it is not that it is undertaken on the 'beaten track', but on a track that is not beaten enough, in the sense of not being sufficiently internalised by those who use it. Rohmer's protagonists do not aspire to discover any new locations, new objects or new communities. They are content to return and gaze at the same objects and people. Accordingly, 'tourism' in Rohmer's films is not contrasted with 'travelling', but with 'holiday', or more precisely, with a certain type of holiday, which is represented in his films.

Rohmer's characters come to their chosen location unassisted, without the help of a travel agent, not because as model travellers they seek adventure and want to get lost in a new place, but, on the contrary, because they know the place so well that they do not need any guides. Often they perceive themselves as 'semi-natives', returning to the same place year after year, sometimes ever since their childhood, even owning houses in the resorts, and knowing the people who live there. If they do not seem to belong to the place they visit, they swiftly leave it. Needless to say, hotels and guesthouses hardly feature in Rohmer's holiday films and they appear only as places where 'the others', the ordinary tourists, stay. Moreover, the places where his characters lodge always have a stamp of their individuality – such as a poster of the pop group Oasis in the flat rented for the summer

Fig. 5 Eric Rohmer's *Conte d'hiver* (*A Winter Tale*, France, 1992) © Les Films du Losange

by Gaspard in *A Summer's Tale* – which helps them to feel at home. Their sense of belonging to the holiday location is strengthened by the fact that some lack roots in their everyday lives. Take, for example, Jérome in *Claire's Knee* and Henri in *Pauline at the Beach*, who travel extensively or live abroad because of their professional duties. Henri, who works as an ethnologist, does not even have a permanent home, so that his summer house, although it is very sparsely furnished, serves as his proper home. It is the only place where he can stay with his daughter, who spends the rest of the year with his ex-wife.

Moreover, Rohmer's characters seek on vacation a genuine and lasting human contact. This opinion is clearly expressed by the titular teenage heroine of *Pauline at the Beach*, who comments on a recent trip to Spain with her parents, where every day she was in a different place: 'It was interesting, but it was not fun.' Apart from not allowing her to rest, this trip prevented her from making any friends of her own age. The conviction of the superiority of the social pleasures of the vacation over its other aspects is also held by Pauline's cousin, Marion, who barely conceals the fact that on holiday she looks for 'love which will burn her', or Delphine in *The Green Ray*, who leaves every holiday resort which she visits – Brittany, La Plagne, Biarritz – after failing to meet anyone with whom she can communicate in a meaningful way, or whose lifestyle would suit her own (she is a vegetarian who loves walking). Delphine also refuses to spend a night with a sailor without giving any reason, but we suspect that she simply does not want to engage romantically with somebody who will leave her the next day. It could be said that Rohmer's characters do seek adventure on holiday, but adventure 'with a purpose' and 'to be continued', not a temporary break from the everyday routine without further consequences.

The vacation often marks an important change in the lives of Rohmer's characters, and is taken following some crucial decision. Jérome in *Claire's Knee* goes on holiday before getting married and moving to Sweden, Delphine in *The Green Ray* after breaking up with her boyfriend, Marion in *Pauline at the Beach* after getting divorced. In Marion one can detect the desire to find, while on holiday in a place that she used to visit before she got married, her old self and her lost innocence. Jérome, who is uneasy about his impending emigration, by returning to a place of his childhood, seems to seek some kind of unity in his existence, which he thinks is in danger of being fragmented. Delphine searches on holiday for a love that will give meaning to her life. All these desires go against the ethos of both modern tourism (see Urry 1995) and travelling (see Buzard 1993) which, by favouring new, unknown places and activities, ignore the danger of being fragmented and displaced, of being an exile.

It might seem excessive to compare the discourse on tourism and travel with that on exile but, as Caren Kaplan (1998) argues, the border between the respective types of travel are blurred, largely because they can be accompanied by similar states of mind. Hence the exiles who accept and welcome their predicament of being far away from home can be regarded as tourists, while tourists and travellers, particularly when venturing in unknown and dangerous places, can easily become exiles.[1] In comparing 'tourism' to 'exile' it is also worth referring to Zygmunt Bauman, who argues that the figure of the tourist as somebody who avoids 'being fixed' and always 'keeps his options open' has become the epitome of the condition of postmodernity, which is marked by fragmentation of communities and individual selves (1997: 88–94). Bauman also claims that although initially the condition of a tourist looks attractive, signifying freedom and choice, with time it can become painful. Postmodern tourists often change into vagabonds, 'who travel because they have no other choice'[2] (1997: 94).

Marion, Jérome and the vast majority of Rohmer's holidaymakers do not wish to be tourists or travellers, even less so vagabonds, largely because they identify tourism with exile and they fear being displaced in the same way as exiles are. They want to be at home, or at least near home, wherever they go, both in the geographical and in the cultural sense. They are true holidaymakers, not travellers and tourists in the metaphorical sense, as defined by Bauman, as holiday implies having a home and regular work somewhere, while travelling and 'tourism', as Bauman argues, only indicate moving from one place to another, and even from one identity to another, without feeling obliged to return home and to become one's old self.

Rohmer suggests that a necessary condition for feeling at home on vacation is to know the local language and indigenous traditions. Therefore, foreigners have less chance of experiencing such a vacation than those who holiday in their own country. Rohmer also shows us some discord between foreign and French tourists and residents. In *The Green Ray* Delphine, who is French, meets a Swedish young woman called Lena. They spend some time together, walking, sunbathing and visiting cafés, but it is obvious that Delphine does not feel comfortable in Lena's presence. For the Swedish tourist everything is temporary, and she does not mind outraging anyone with her appearance (she swims and sunbathes topless) or behaviour (she uses men for her own gratification and discards them when she finds them boring). Delphine, by contrast, looks for love, not for one-night stands or a mere summer romance. Even less successful is the meeting in *The Collector* between Adrien and an American, Sam, who is utterly materialistic, hedonistic, shallow, lecherous and obscenely rich. He reminds us of Prokosch in Godard's *Le Mépris* (*Contempt*, 1963). One gets the impression that people like that almost pollute the beautiful French Riviera. In the same way that foreigners cannot enjoy France as much as the French, one can find in Rohmer's films the opinion that there is little reason for French people to go abroad, especially to countries with a very different climate and culture. For example, Delphine refuses to go with her family to Ireland, claiming that 'it will not be her type of holiday'. Needless to add, package holidays to distant countries are not considered at all by Rohmer's characters.

Another pleasure enjoyed by Rohmer's holidaymakers is passivity and routine. Adrien in *The Collector* rejects all efforts and goes to any length to justify the moral superiority of his own idle holiday, as well as of his idle existence (as he equates life with holidaymaking), over other types of vacation and life arguing that, contrary to popular opinion, idleness is very difficult, while work is easy. The apparent heroism and artistry inscribed in idleness result from the intellectual challenge it poses: it forces one to empty one's mind and think afresh, to find out what is important in life. Moreover, it purifies people from prejudices and makes them open to events and encounters. Work, on the other hand, prevents people from controlling their physical and mental activities, and consequently enforces and justifies social conformity and intellectual passivity; makes them follow the crowd, rather than be individual. Adrien also perceives his idle holiday in terms of the future of Western society, forced into leisure by technological advancement. He suggests that in such a society those who, like him, learn how to be idle win, while workaholics lose.[3] As C. G. Crisp suggests, for Adrien a passive holiday by the sea is 'a retreat from the hurly-burly of materialist commercial considerations which have been preoccupying him too much; paradoxically, it indicates a desire to rid himself of past excesses, to introduce a certain rigor and discipline in his lax life' (1988: 46). The search for passivity explains why peaceful beaches and villages are preferred over large cities, busy resorts with multi-storeyed hotels and swimming pools, theme parks and places with dramatic features, such as high mountains, forests or water-falls. If Rohmer's characters visit the surroundings of their holiday destination, they rarely get to places situated further than a few miles from their resort. Even in these circumstances 'tourism' is rarely the main reason why they go there. Jérome in *Claire's Knee* goes to the mountains because he is attracted to Laura, who encourages him to make the excursion. In *Pauline at the Beach* Marion and Pauline visit a nearby historical town because Pauline's parents expect their daughter to learn something during her vacation.

The importance of peace and stability on vacation is indicated by what Rohmer includes in his narratives and what he leaves out. Journeys are almost never shown, we only occasionally see the characters arriving or leaving the resort. This suggests that the director does not regard these activities as an essential part of the holiday experience of his protagonists. Similarly, the emphasis is on static, restful, sociable and largely uncommodified pastimes: lying on a beach, sunbathing on a terrace, lying in the water (rather than swimming or sailing), having meals and conversations in a garden.

Ordinary, mass tourism which is commodified and undertaken by large numbers of people in a 'regimented' way, is a modern phenomenon, characteristic of industrialised societies (see Veal 1987; Urry 1990 and 1995). Prior to the nineteenth century, few people could afford to travel, particularly for non-work related reasons (see Urry 1990 and 1995). Mass tourism, as tourism experienced *en masse*, is nowadays also largely regarded as a habit of the working classes. The upper classes prefer more individualised vacations, associated with what Urry describes as the 'romantic gaze', meaning gazing in solitude at 'undisturbed natural beauty' (1995: 137). Accordingly, the contempt directed to the ordinary mass tourists can be regarded as an attitude connected with class – a sentiment arising from being placed higher on the social ladder. Rohmer's holidaymakers, who are also hostile to ordinary tourists, are mainly middle class. However, we should be careful in associating holidaymaking with middle class and tourism with working class in Rohmer's films, as the search for 'authenticity', which constitutes the core of a successful holiday in his films is also a plight of Rohmer's working-class characters. In particular, the hairdresser Félicie, the heroine of *A Winter's Tale*, once had such a holiday, which transformed her entire life.

The question arises whether Rohmer shares the same disapproval of a commodified tourism, eulogy of passive and social holiday, and fear of becoming an exile through excessive travelling that characterises his protagonists. His affinity for irony, identified by many critics (for example Crisp 1988; King 1990), and his own warning not to identify the discourse of his characters with his own (Rohmer 1989: 80) discourage us from unconditionally identifying the views of his characters with his. In some cases it is indeed clear that Rohmer ridicules his protagonists' ideas. For example in *The Collectioner* Rohmer suggests that Adrien largely deludes himself by proclaiming the merits of his lifestyle. However, the very fact that he represents passive, peaceful, social and individualised holidaymaking as pleasurable, attractive, even magical, and that he practically excludes mass tourists from his films (they are mainly talked of in derogatory terms and rarely shown), suggests that he privileges the former type of vacation. Moreover, on most occasions he seems to side with those of his characters, such as Pauline or Delphine, who distrust noisy, commodified and excessive mass tourism, by making them the objects of the viewer's identification.

We always see Rohmer's characters holidaying in their own country. As Crisp observes, Rohmer almost programmatically documents various regions of France: Annecy, Clermont-Ferrand, Le Mans, Brittany, Normandy (1988: 98). His characters move in a small yet precisely reconstructed field of action, covering a few villages, beaches and islands. In *Pauline at the Beach*, which is set on the Normandy coast, the boundaries of their field of action are Rennes, Granville and Mont St. Michel. Crisp argues that the geographical authentication of the characters' existence is an important element in Rohmer's realism. We also suggest that representing landscape in minute precision serves to demonstrate the beauty, richness and versatility of French nature and culture. Rohmer refers, for example, to the meteorological phenomenon of green rays (in the film of the same name), which can be observed in Biarritz; to the blue hour, a moment of absolute silence at dawn in *4 aventures de Reinette & Mirabelle* (*Four Adventures of Reinette and Mirabelle*, 1986); to the production of glass in Nevers in *A Winter's Tale*; and wine-making in the Rhone valley in *Conte d'automne* (*An Autumn Tale*, 1998). He also conveys the impression that the sea is nowhere as blue and warm, and the beaches as sandy, as in France. According to Rohmer, even in the better known parts of France there is still plenty to explore: plants, architecture, customs, people – if only one has the time and desire to do so. On several occasions the significance of regional nature and culture is revealed by showing that it inspires outsiders. For example, Margot, one of the characters in *A Summer's Tale*, who is an ethnology student, accompanied by her musician friend, Gaspard, interviews an old sailor as part of her university project. Enchanted and inspired by the old man's stories and songs,

Gaspard writes his own song. Again, it must be stressed that the ability to be interested in history, ethnology and landscape in Rohmer's films is not limited to the middle and upper classes. Hairdressers and secretaries in his films are just as able to explore the place they visit, as artists and intellectuals do, if not more so.

Rohmer increasingly reveals in his work a preoccupation with the fragility of nature and culture, due to the threat of industrialisation and globalisation, and his desire to immortalise them before it is too late. In *Four Adventures of Reinette and Mirabelle* Reinette takes Mirabelle on a tour of the countryside, where they meet a man who uses old methods of farming, unlike the majority of French farmers. In *An Autumn Tale* the traditional ways of making wine used by the film's protagonist, Magali, are contrasted with large-scale, industrialised production. Those who, like the farmer or Magali, preserve the old traditions are depicted as artisans or even artists. These people advocate the idea of 'listening', adjusting to and conserving nature and the landscape, as opposed to conquering it, which is the modernist concept. Magali claims that she wants to honour the soil, not exploit it, which is the norm these days amongst wine growers. Guided by the same principles, she condemns the factories that spoil the beauty of the Rhône valley.[4] Delphine in *The Green Ray* is another of Rohmer's characters who listens and honours nature. She keeps finding green playing cards everywhere and tries to read them as prophecies. Eventually, she listens to the story of the green ray, which according to the novel of Jules Verne gives those who see it insight into the human soul, and begins to believe that she will soon fall in love. Indeed, on her way back to Paris, she meets a man with whom she decides to spend the rest of her holiday, in this way confirming the wisdom of nature. For Reinette and Mirabelle sharing the blue hour (although the experience was not completely successful, due to the noise of a tractor which destroyed the silence at dawn) means that they should become friends. Amongst people who listen to nature we shall also include Laura in *Claire's Knee*, who comments that living at the foot of the mountain is like being in a cradle: the mountain gives her protection against loneliness. On the whole, one gets the impression that in Rohmer's films, as in the famous book by James Lovelock (1979), the Earth is regarded as a living, thinking creature which must be respected, cared for, even obeyed.

The conviction that pleasure, idleness and contact with other people and nature are the essence of vacation is also revealed in the metaphorical blurring of the distinction between work time and the places of work on the one hand, and holiday time and holiday locations on the other. The retired taxi driver in *The Green Ray*, who never went on a holiday because he could not afford to go, insists that Paris is like a holiday resort – it has plenty of parks, good weather and a river which is like a sea; broad and inviting people to rest on its banks. Moreover, Paris suits him more than many tourist places in the mountains or by the seaside, because he prefers to drive on a flat surface.

It is easy to dismiss the taxi driver's praise of Paris as his way to come to terms with his unfortunate position of being imprisoned in one city. However, Rohmer constructs the driver as a jolly and happy man. Moreover, he uses *mise-en-scène* in a way which suggests that the old man is indeed on holiday: he sits with Delphine and her girlfriends at a large table in the garden, eating a meal, surrounded by flowers and trees; similar images are included in many of Rohmer's films set during vacations, such as *Claire's Knee, A Summer's Tale, Pauline at the Beach* and *The Green Ray*. Magali in *An Autumn Tale* is a similar character to the driver in her attitude to work and resting: she is also largely confined to the place where she works; however, as she enjoys her job and her surroundings, she does not complain about her situation.

The impression that in Rohmer's films the difference between holiday and work is relatively small also results from the fact that his characters squeeze many activities associated with holidays into their working week. They visit their summer houses at weekends and sometimes even during the week, as in *Conte de printemps* (*A Tale of Springtime*, 1989), and visit museums and galleries, as in *The Green Ray* and *Rendezvous in Paris*. Furthermore, they often engage in the type of romance that is particularly associated with vacation, which the director himself described as *l'amour par désoeuvrement* – love from idleness. In the case of Fréderic in *L'Amour l'après-midi* (*Love in the Afternoon*, 1972), the crucial factor in his romance is his afternoon boredom. The rhythm of their lives is balanced; nobody seems to be overworked, frustrated or stressed by the amount of things to be done. In various films it is also suggested that work for the characters is like a hobby – many of them are masters of their own time, being artists, writers, journalists, students, academics or self-employed.

Ordinary life in Rohmer's films also seems like a holiday because the director tends to set his stories on days free of work, such as public holidays, weekends and Christmas. His favourite season of the year is summer; the vast majority of his films are 'summer tales'. Even in the films of the 'Tales of the Four Seasons' series which are set in other seasons, summer remains important. Either, as in *A Winter's Tale*, what happened during a summer plays a crucial role in the life of the heroine, or the director depicts a chosen season of the year in relation to summer, as in *An Autumn Tale*, in which autumn is depicted as an Indian Summer, a time when the weather is still warm, nature produces bountiful fruit and people have hopes for love and romance. Consequently, there are many opportunities for lavish, restful meals in the garden, which the director often shoots in a style reminiscent of Impressionist painting.

It is worth noting that the positive connotations of holiday and idleness in general are largely the consequence of Rohmer's characters belonging to the (broadly-defined) middle class. In this social group lack of money is rarely a problem and, even when it is, as in *Le Signe du lion* (*The Sign of Leo*, 1959) or *Four Adventures of Reinette and Mirabelle*, it is relatively short-lived. Rohmer does not simply document the relaxing lifestyle of the French middle classes; by ignoring such issues as striving for professional success and affluence, he praises and promotes 'middle-class slackery'.

Various authors have noted that the dominant tradition in travel and tourism discourse is masculine. In the majority of travel literature, as well as road cinema, women are viewed either as passive objects of male travel (see Craik 1997; Laderman 2002: 20–1), or as 'pathological' travellers, for example prostitutes, often described as 'women of the streets' (see Jokinen & Veijola 1997). By contrast, in Rohmer's films about holidaying, women have the same rights to travel and associated activities, such as gazing at other people, as men have; examples are the heroines of *The Green Ray*, *Pauline at the Beach* and *A Summer's Tale*. Typically, they are even more active and self-reflexive than their male counterparts. In particular, they try to make the most of their travelling experience and if they are dissatisfied, they move on, while men stay even if they do not like the place, largely out of laziness.

Touristic Paris

The *mise-en-scène* and narratives of some of Rohmer's films confirm the impression that the division of people's time and space into holiday and work is a false dichotomy. Rohmer represents Paris in particular as a site of almost infinite pleasures, not only for tourists and holidaymakers, but also for Parisians, for example in *La Femme de l'aviateur* (*The Pilot's Wife*, 1980), which is largely set in a park with a great surface of greenery and water. Here the main characters, Christian and Lucie, enjoy the holiday atmosphere and, largely out of idleness, invent an elaborate plot about a man and a woman whom they saw in the park. The park is represented as a place where the division between nature and culture is obliterated. There are no unpleasant signs of modern civilisation there. On the other hand, the presence of a large number of people, including Japanese tourists taking photographs, suggests that Paris is an object of what Urry describes as the 'collective tourist gaze' – a place which is interesting largely because it is full of tourists (1995: 137–8). *A Winter's Tale* conveys the opinion that Paris is closer to nature than the provincial town of Nevers. Elise, Felicie's small daughter, complains that in Nevers she does not have a garden, which she enjoyed when living with her grandmother in Paris.

The aspects of Paris that make its inhabitants feel like careless holidaymakers, tourists or vagabonds (yet in some of Rohmer's films these distinctions hardly matter) are foregrounded in *The Sign of Leo, Four Adventures of Reinette and Mirabelle* and *Rendezvous in Paris*. The main character of the first film, a Dutch violinist named Pierre, has a good time with his French friends while he awaits his inheritance. Eventually, all of them go off on holiday. By the beginning of August, the 'month of the Leo', he is in Paris by himself. Moreover, he runs short of money and loses his flat. At this stage he befriends a tramp on the banks of the Seine and they start to perform for tourists in the cafés. His situation changes again in September when his friends return from their vacation and he receives his inheritance. The film is remarkable both for catching the mood of Paris in August, as a place which most Parisians have left to go on holiday (such a Paris will re-appear in *The Green Ray*), and for showing how easily one can change from a 'normal', static inhabitant of a city into a mobile tourist or vagabond. Rohmer depicts Paris in this film as very welcoming; a city where one can linger in the streets for hours without being tired or bored.

The situation of Reinette and Mirabelle, two students sharing a flat in Paris, is not very different from that of Pierre. They also run out of cash to pay the rent for their flat and have to 'perform' to stay afloat in the city. Like Pierre, Reinette is not a native; she came to Paris from the country (previously she lived in a derelict barn) and at the beginning does not understand the 'Parisian ways', as shown in the episode when she pays for a coffee with a 200 Franc note, which makes the waiter furious. More importantly the girlfriends, like proper tourists, are idle, careless and open to new experiences – the term 'adventures' in the title underlines their attitude to life. Moreover, through their interactions, their attitude to Paris changes: the worldly Parisian Mirabelle becomes more like a tourist and the dogmatic, provincial Reinette more like a native.

Rendezvous in Paris concentrates even more on the holiday pleasures of native Parisians. In its second part, entitled 'Les Bancs de Paris' ('The Benches of Paris'), the characters, meaningfully named Elle and Lui ('Everywoman' and 'Everyman'), first visit various Parisian benches, some placed in well-known locations, others in the suburbs; eventually, pretending to be tourists, they go to a hotel in Montmartre. The film reveals the difficulties of being a tourist in one's own city; Elle, in particular, feels uncomfortable in some of the places they visit together, as she associates them with her long-term boyfriend. Her visit to the hotel with Lui is spoilt when she notices that her boyfriend arrives at the same hotel with another woman. In the end the couple do not go into the hotel and part forever. 'The Benches of Paris', in common with Rohmer's films about true holidays, demonstrates that a necessary condition for a successful holiday is to be in tune and have positive associations with the place visited. This is much more important than the beauty of the place. Consequently, there are no intrinsically good or bad places for taking a holiday; it depends on the individual concerned.

Much has been written about the significance of Paris in the work of the New Wave directors (see, for example, Wilson 1999). It was even argued that representing Paris was one of the New Wave's main peculiarities, as well as a unifying feature of the work of Godard, Truffaut, Rivette and Rohmer, and that the locations they used correspond to a tourist's view of Paris – the café, the airport, Parisian streets at night, and so on (see Kuhn 1985: 42). We agree with this statement, but believe that Rohmer's vision of Paris differs from that of his fellow directors. Firstly, in the work of Godard and Truffaut Paris is primarily a locus of action; the protagonists of their films, such as Antoine Doinel in *Les quatre cents coups* (*The 400 Blows*, 1959) or Michel Poiccard in *À bout de souffle* (*Breathless*, 1960), run down the streets, often hurrying, bumping into their fellow passers-by. Rivette, on the other hand, tends to represent the city as a stage, where plays are rehearsed, performed and recorded. For Rohmer, by contrast, Paris is a place of peaceful, relaxing *flânerie*, in which the main purpose of strolling is strolling. Secondly, Rohmer extended the boundaries of the cinematic Paris. His city not only contains the famous landmarks (the Eiffel Tower, the Champs Elysées), the small cafés and cinemas, but also quarters, streets and suburbs that tourists normally do not visit. In his later films the landmarks are even overshadowed by less well-known locations and places: ordinary shops, hairdressing salons and cosmopolitan restaurants. Thirdly, for Rohmer, unlike Godard and Truffaut, Paris is never a dystopia; throughout his career he treats this city with admiration and tenderness. Even the modern quarters, which Godard portrayed as monstrous, soulless 'machines for living', for Rohmer constitute a functional, healthy, human environment. Such a representation results from his assumption that places are not good or bad in themselves, but are only so in human perception.

In search of a spiritual centre

In Rohmer's films there are more scenes set on means of transport, such as train, car or metro, and which depict his characters during their working lives, than those which are set on holiday. One can think of Fréderic in *Love in the Afternoon* and Louise in *Les Nuits de la pleine lune* (*Full Moon in Paris*, 1984), who commute every day from the suburbs of Paris to the centre and back; of Sabine in *Le beau mariage* (*A Good Marriage*, 1981), who every week travels from the historic town of Le Mans to Paris; and Félicie in *A Winter's Tale*, who lives first in Paris, then in Nevers, then in Paris again. Modern life forces these people to divide their time into many separate activities: work, study, bringing up children, socialising and rest – activities that must be undertaken in different locations. Or, to put it differently, it allows them to take part in many different businesses and events at the price of continuously changing location. The characters' second reason for travelling, albeit intrinsically connected with the first, is their search for a place where they could settle down, not only physically, but also mentally – a place which they would not like to leave, unless for a short time. This place we will call their 'spiritual centre'.

The premise of the four films mentioned above is that the characters have at least two centres around which their lives revolve – in order to discern them from spiritual centres we will describe them as 'centres of activity'. Louise in *Full Moon in Paris* has two centres of activity. She lives with her architect boyfriend, Rémi, in a new town near Paris and keeps her pied-à-terre apartment in the capital. She lived there as a student and recently had it redecorated, in order to use it when she wants to stay in Paris overnight. She assumes that such an arrangement will be the perfect solution to her problem: how to retain her freedom, contacts with old friends and opportunities to meet new people, and be close to the centre of culture and entertainment, and at the same time to remain in a permanent personal relationship (in the suburbs). However, life proves her wrong: her boyfriend is unhappy to see her only from time to time and have his pattern of life disrupted by her irregular comings and goings. Louise, on the other hand, discovers that having two homes means being displaced in both: in Paris she misses Rémi's suburban home; when in the suburbs, she yearns for Paris. Moreover, after a brief romance with a young saxophonist, she realises that she truly loves Rémi. By this time, however, he has found a new girlfriend, exercising the same right to freedom that Louise used at will.

Louise's continuous decentredness is emphasised by the scenery in which Rohmer places her and the choice of actress for this role. As Berenice Reynaud observes, 'while Rohmer's superbly mastered style eliminates all "unimportant" moments, he has carefully kept those when Louise is "in transit"' (1990: 274): running up and down the stairs, on a train, in various people's cars, on the bike of her saxophonist lover. By contrast, Rémi is typically shown at home, static. When at a party, he avoids dancing or walking about and awaits the time when he can return home without offending his hosts. Moreover, Louise, played by Pascale Ogier, looks ethereal and light; Tchéky Karyo's Rémi, on the other hand, is stout and lumpish. Louise's literal and spiritual homelessness is best rendered in one of the last scenes, in which she leaves her Paris flat at night to go to a café alone. The café, being a place which people normally attend only briefly, inbetween their errands, and which almost encapsulates the transitoriness and hurry of modern life, becomes in this episode the most stable place Louise can find, further accentuating her decentredness and lack of a real home.

Rohmer indicates that Rémi's attachment to his home and his town, and eventually his falling in love with a woman who lives nearby, is not only a question of personal taste or lack of imagination, connected with age, although these factors might play a part in his attitude, but also a moral decision. We learn that Rémi lives in the new town because he was involved in its planning. When Louise's friend, Octave, asks her jokingly whether Rémi would live in a prison if he had designed it, she answers seriously that he probably would. The premise of Octave's ironical attitude to Rémi is his taking for granted the 'disembedding of the social system', as Anthony Giddens calls it – the 'lifting out' of social relations from local contexts of interaction (1990: 21). Rémi, by contrast, disapproves of such 'disembedding' and by the choices he makes testifies to the possibility of resisting it, if not on a large social scale then at least in individual life. Interestingly, although Octave mocks Rémi's immobility and himself is very decentred in his emotional life (he claims that he loves his wife, but also tries to seduce Louise), at the same time he confides to Louise that he cannot live outside Paris, which he regards as the centre of his world.

A comparable effect of decentredness is reached in *Love in the Afternoon*. In the first scene, which bears similarities with Baudelaire's strolling through Paris, Fréderic confesses in an inner monologue that he loves Paris and compares it to the sea. The crowds of people surrounding him when he leaves the metro are like waves for him. He says that being in a crowd is invigorating, while staying in the static suburbs is depressing. Subsequently, we see him dividing his life between the city, where he works and in the afternoons meets his old friend Chloé with whom he soon becomes romantically involved, and the suburbs where he spends his evenings with his wife and two children. For a considerable time Fréderic finds this life exciting; he enjoys visiting restaurants with Chloé, helping her out when she changes flats and misses her when he has to spend his afternoons by himself. He also likes the comfort of his large family home in the suburbs and loves his wife and children. Eventually, however, he feels guilty about his 'double life' and in the last scene, while Chloé waits for him in bed, he runs away and returns contrite to his wife.

Chloé's life is even more decentred and fragmented than Fréderic's. She keeps changing jobs, men, flats and even countries continuously; before coming to Paris she lived in the US for some years and during the time of her romance with Fréderic she travelled to Spain for some weeks, where she had an affair with another man. She also keeps changing her image – initially she looks almost like a hippie, with baggy trousers, strange coats and scruffy hair; later her elegant appearance conveys power and self-confidence; in the period when she tries hardest to seduce Fréderic, her hair and clothes become very light and feminine. At the beginning of her relationship with Fréderic, Chloé seems to be happy to be constantly on the move, her stories are always packed with attractive people and interesting events, and she is very excited about every new opportunity that life brings her. Gradually, however, we learn that in reality she is not content at all. She admits that the lack of stability makes her depressed and in the past she even tried to commit suicide. Her disappointment with her unstable life is also revealed in her attachment to Fréderic and her desire to have a child fathered by him. Unfortunately for her, he cannot offer her the stability for which she yearns.

A Good Marriage is another story of the dangers of living in two different places, and of the desire to overcome them. At the beginning of the film Sabine shares her time between Paris, where she works on her thesis in Art History, and where she spends time with Simon, her married lover who is a painter, and Le Mans, where she lives with her mother and younger sister and works as a part-time assistant in an antiques shop. After being disturbed by an evening call from Simon's wife, she breaks up with him, deciding to find a husband. Soon she discovers that she is unhappy with almost all aspects of her life and gives up her job in order to invest all her energy in the pursuit of her ideal man. She chooses an affluent lawyer, Edmond, the cousin of her best friend Clarisse. Her plan, however, in spite of her commitment and Clarisse's support, fails when Edmond declares in unambiguous terms to Sabine that he has no wish to marry.

Sabine, more consciously than the characters in *Full Moon in Paris* and *Love in the Afternoon*, seeks a spiritual centre. She wants a husband precisely in order to have such a centre; she dreams about a house that she can look after and wants, as she puts it, to 'integrate herself with her husband's milieu'. However, Rohmer puts a question mark over Sabine's ability to find a husband and a suitable social environment. Firstly, we see that when she had the chance to achieve her objective, she did not take advantage of it. Her lover Simon told her to treat his studio as her own place, but she refused on the grounds that she could not stand a place full of his paintings. Neither can she accept that he has children. Later on, she is very critical of the appearance of a modest apartment of her ex-boyfriend, teacher Claude, and of everything that he has achieved in his life. It is also clear that Sabine has little understanding of Edmond's environment. Rohmer thus suggests that Sabine is unable to integrate with anybody's milieu; she wants other people to adjust to her tastes and values and provide her with the habitat she is looking for, and which she defines largely in material terms. By contrast, her friend Clarisse is happy in her environment: she likes Le Mans, loves her husband and her artisan job of painting lamps.

Rohmer hints at possible reasons why Sabine and Clarisse are so different in their attitude to their environment. Clarisse's family lived in Le Mans much longer than Sabine's, who moved there shortly after the death of her father. Secondly, Clarisse comes from a more affluent background than her friend, whose family lost a lot of money and had to adjust to a relatively modest lifestyle. Consequently, for Sabine Le Mans is only a centre of activity, as opposed to being a spiritual centre. Clarisse was also lucky in her personal life, finding a husband who had the same job as her own doctor father. Yet the main reasons why they have different attitudes to their milieu lies in their personalities: Clarisse is modest, easygoing, tolerant and unselfish; Sabine is ambitious, impatient, dogmatic and egotistic. Paradoxically, with her insisting on having a 'good marriage' rather than a good relationship, Sabine is also more old-fashioned than her provincial friend, or even than her own mother, who listens to her desire to be worshipped by her husband with utmost scepticism.

Clarisse reminds us of Rémi in *Full Moon in Paris*, while Sabine has many features of Louise in the same film. Clarisse, in common with Rémi, comes across as static; she works near home and has no desire to look for entertainment beyond her hometown and a small circle of family and friends. We never see her in a car or on the train. Sabine, on the other hand, like Louise is constantly travelling. She is rather detached from her family and looks forward to meeting new people (she looks at all men on trains as potential husbands). Furthermore, both Louise and Sabine end up being metaphorically more displaced, confused and homeless than at the beginning, although for opposite reasons: Louise because she wanted to preserve her freedom at all costs, Sabine because she wanted to settle down too much.

A Winter's Tale is another film about searching for love and home, as typically the two things are connected in Rohmer's films. The film's heroine, hairdresser Félicie, travels from Paris where she initially works and lives with her daughter in her mother's house, to Nevers where her boyfriend Maxence recently moved to take over a new hairdressing salon. She decides to move permanently to Nevers but life with Maxence does not suit her, as she has difficulty combining work with looking after her child. Félicie also feels suffocated, being dependent on a man who is rather old-fashioned in his attitude to male/female relationships and who is only a substitute for the love of her life. Her true love is Charles, the father of her daughter Elise, with whom she lost contact after a holiday in Normandy. Hoping to find him in Paris is as important a reason to return to the capital as Félicie's disappointment in living in Nevers. In the end Félicie's dream comes true – she comes across Charles in a metro and they decide to stay together.

Superficially, Félicie's life is even more fragmented and in transit than that of Louise and Sabine. Apart from having an affair with Maxence, she often stays with her other boyfriend, librarian Loic. Similarly, we see her travelling a lot: between the cities, between the suburbs and the centre of Paris, and in the city centre. Yet her movements are always purposeful; unlike Louise, she never moves for the sake of being in transit, or wishes to have two or more homes and two or more men. On the contrary, each change (of city, of house, of man, of job) is accompanied by her hope that it will be the last. She yearns for stability, but unlike Sabine, understands that this cannot be achieved on command or by the power of will, simply by adapting or 'invading' someone else's space. In her case being in transit results largely from bad luck – giving Charles a wrong address. It could also be argued that Félicie's chances of finding a spiritual centre are greater because in a sense she is a more spiritual person than the other women, who not only are not religious, but also have faith in nothing. She follows her intuition, especially her maternal instinct, and she looks for 'signs' in her life (in common with Delphine in *The Green Ray*). An example is her emotional reaction in the theatre during the staging of Shakespeare's *The Winter's Tale*. She regards this tale, in which the wife of Leontes is miraculously brought to life after sixteen years asleep, as prophetic of her own future.

These four films and, to a lesser extent, some others directed by Rohmer such as *L'Ami de mon amie* (*My Girlfriend's Boyfriend*, 1987), *A Summer's Tale* and *An Autumn Tale*, show us the flaws and dangers of physically decentred, as well as socially fragmented, lives. However, Rohmer does not advocate a return to any real or mythical home. Those of his characters who already have – or eventually find – their spiritual centre, do not necessarily find it in the place where they came from; Clarisse in this respect is an exception to the rule. Rohmer also shows that the more connections one has with a certain place, such as friends, family, work, landscape and so on, the greater the chances that it will become or remain one's spiritual centre. His films are devoid of nostalgia for traditional institutions, such as marriage (many of his most charming characters are cohabiting or single), religion (Rohmer's most religious characters, such as Félicie in *A Winter's Tale*, rarely go to church and real Catholics, such as Loic in the same film or Jean-Louis in *My Night with Maud*, prove to be lacking any spirituality) or closely-knit community, where everybody knows everybody else. Nevertheless, Rohmer insists on the relevance to modern life of some of the values that these institutions promote, such as loyalty, honesty, modesty, seriousness and altruism. Of his characters, those who possess a spiritual centre are also characterised by moral integrity: they have a coherent system of values and expectations. By contrast, those who desire things that cannot be reconciled, such as love and total freedom, stability and change, lead a physically as well as spiritually decentred life. Many critics of Rohmer's cinema draw attention to his connection with the rationalist, Enlightenment, or at least

Fig. 6 Eric Rohmer's *Conte d'été* (*A Summer Tale*, France 1996) © Les Films du Losange

pre-twentieth century moralism, mentioning such names as Pascal, Descartes or Marivaux (see Dawson 1970; Monaco 1976; Crisp 1988). Raymond Durgnat when analysing *My Girlfriend's Boyfriend* comments: 'Rohmer's evident delight in its [Cergy-Pontoise, the town where the film is set] radiance, its human order, parallels his discovery, or hypothesis that rationalist moralising is alive and well in a world often dismissed as alienated and materialistic' (1988: 198). Indeed, order and rationality are key factors in Rohmer's recipe for happiness and inner peace.

Many problems of Rohmer's characters result from having too much choice in regard to their place of living, partners and job opportunities. This abundant choice is partly the consequence of the increased affluence of French society (or Western society in general), especially of the middle classes, which are Rohmer's favourite subject, and of some cultural changes that occurred in recent decades, such as the end of old-style ideologies, the 'death of citizenship' (with the citizen being replaced by the individual) and the diffusion of consumerism. Zygmunt Bauman describes the period when these changes happened as 'liquid modernity'; other terms widely used include 'late modernity', 'postmodernity', and 'the post-industrial age'. Some thinkers even argue that, as far as Western society is concerned, 'whatever freedom was conceivable and likely to be achieved has already arrived … Men and women are fully and truly free, and so the agenda of emancipation has been all but exhausted' (Bauman 2000: 22). Rohmer does not condemn the new circumstances of life, which are so conducive to freedom; neither does he state that freedom *per se* is a bad thing, but makes us realise that we should use it with greater care and restraint, because the more choice and freedom one has, the greater one's responsibility. He seems to exclude or at least is not interested in any large-scale, structural solutions to the problems resulting from living in the late modern, post-industrial age. The hazards connected with extensive choice, which lead to the fragmentation of almost all types of communities and societies, in his films must be overcome by the individuals themselves.

Female characters in Rohmer's films are typically more displaced and decentred than men, and their situation causes them more emotional turmoil and practical problems. Their state can have two opposite explanations and Rohmer hints at both of them. Firstly, it can be suggested that freedom and its negative 'by-products', such as lack of spiritual centre, especially affect women, who in the past were more homebound as a result of having fewer job opportunities and more domestic duties than men. Women such as Chloé or Louise have not yet learnt how to use their freedom in a sensible way – they are intoxicated by it. On the other hand, it could be argued that Rohmer's women lack a stable centre not because they have too much choice, but because they have too little, especially due to their social position being much lower than men's. Women in his films, as opposed to men, typically have low-paid, junior or part-time work (waitresses, secretaries, hairdressers, shop assistants, junior designers), which gives them little job satisfaction, or even independence. Moreover, they live in houses that belong to their partners or parents, which are rarely well adapted to their needs. As a result, they have less attachment to the places that potentially could be their spiritual centres: their places of work, their houses and their neighbourhoods. Paradoxically, their difficult situation makes them even more unwilling to try to find or create a spiritual centre completely by themselves, making them dependent on males.[5] Conversely, financial independence, which is enjoyed by Rohmer's heroines such as Blanche in *My Girlfriend's Boyfriend*, Magali in *An Autumn Tale* and probably Clarisse in *A Good Marriage*, help the female characters to be in tune with their environment.

From the centre to the margins

We argued that for Rohmer there are no intrinsically good or bad locations for a holiday. The same rule of relative values applies to the places of residence and to all potential spiritual centres – since a 'spiritual centre' is one where one's emotional and intellectual requirements are fulfilled, where one's spirit feels at home. It can be indifferently in the centre of a large city, in a province or in a suburb. C. G. Crisp argues that in *Full Moon in Paris* Rohmer suggests that 'essential truths and permanent relationships can only be discovered at the fringe of things, whereas the city becomes a deceptive lure, an anonymous and uncaring world' (1988: 102). Indeed, such a conclusion can be drawn from the narrative of the film, in which Louise 'loses her soul' in the city. However, in terms of *mise-en-scène* suburbs in this film look rather unwelcoming, even alienating. When Louise walks to her train to go to work in Paris or returns to Rémi's home, she typically does not meet anybody on the way. The streets and playgrounds are deserted and the spaces that she must cross to reach her destination seem very large. Their appearance can hardly be associated with 'community'. We suggest that in this film the idea of the superiority of the margins over the centre is more postulated than demonstrated. By contrast, in *My Girlfriend's Boyfriend*, made three years after *Full Moon in Paris*, the suburbs prove attractive not only 'conceptually', but also visually. In this film the new town of Cergy-Pontoise near Paris boasts modern apartment blocks, which are not standard, grey and anonymous 'machines for living', but versatile, colourful, stylish and multi-functional homes. It also contains offices, schools and a university, shopping centres, restaurants and cafés, abundant greenery, even a lake and a wood. Blanche's material, cultural and even romantic requirements are fulfilled in and by these places. She works only minutes away from her apartment block and after finishing work visits local shops and restaurants; during her lunch breaks she swims in the local swimming pool, and at weekends windsurfs on the lake. She even falls in love with a local man, Fabien, when they visit a local wood together. Cergy-Pontoise is so pleasing for Blanche's soul and body that she hardly desires to go to Paris. When, persuaded by her girlfriend, she visits an exhibition in the centre of the capital, the city looks anonymous and uninteresting. Needless to add, having everything she wants within walking distance makes a car unnecessary for her. Raymond Durgnat goes as far as to suggest that the architecture of Cergy-Pontoise signifies moral order: 'The Enlightenment sense of psycho-moral geometry is underlined by this new town's architecture, with its "unity in diversity" of mall and precinct, of warm brick buildings and public parkland, of bright windsurfing sails (geometry sensitive to nature…) and formless water' (1988: 198). We can say even that Cergy-Pontoise is portrayed here as 'authentic', in the sense of being beneficial to people seeking genuine and lasting relationships.

Rohmer's films evolved in the way in which they represent the capital and the rest of the country: provinces, suburbs or new satellite towns of Paris. When discussing *My Night with Maud*, which is set in Clermont-Ferrand, C. S. Crisp observes:

France is perhaps the most centralised country in the world, both physically and psychologically. Everything of significance happens or is felt to happen in Paris. Provincials, more so in France than elsewhere, can seem to be living on the fringe of things, excluded from meaningful participation, grubby faces peering in the window at an elegant festivity. It is logical, then, in an age when the centre doesn't hold, that the generalised sense of loss of belonging should be translated in book and film into images of provincials who know themselves to be such – outcasts, travellers who like our narrator are as much at home in Vancouver, Canada, or in Valparaiso, Chile; and this principally because they are truly at home nowhere. As Maud says, 'Wherever you go, these days, you're condemned to the provinces.' Though, as she hastens to add, she prefers it that way: she, at least, has learnt to live in a relative world. The narrator has not, and will not. He is forced towards a religious commitment in order to regain a focus, a centre to his existence, in order to transcend his provincialism. (1988: 56–7)

We argue that over time Rohmer's films have 'decentred' and that since the 1980s the director tends to represent the margins as more attractive. *My Girlfriend's Boyfriend*, *A Good Marriage*, *Full Moon in Paris* and *An Autumn Tale* are good examples of this trend. Consequently, Paris in these films loses some of its lure. Moreover, in these films we do not find many characters like Maud who prefer to 'live in a relative way'. If they do, they are punished by the narrative, something which demonstrates the superiority of the contrasting philosophy of life.

It is worth emphasising here that authenticity, which determines the success of the travels and transitions of Rohmer's protagonists, is a widely discussed and contested concept in tourist studies. In particular, in the earlier representations of tourism, which we can roughly identify with modernity (examples of which include the previously quoted accounts of Francis Kilvert and Henry James) authenticity, understood as reaching places and engaging in activities unattainable by other travellers, was regarded as the Holy Grail of travelling. By contrast, in recent discussions of tourism, undertaken from a postmodern perspective, and especially in the works of John Urry, it is suggested that for many contemporary tourists the simulacrum, for example in the form of theme parks, is a far more precious object of the gaze than 'authentic' locations, such as mountains and seas (Urry 1995: 148–51). Moreover, the border between authentic and inauthentic objects of the tourist experience is now blurred as a result of our way of looking at objects, even those which are 'authentic', which is largely conditioned by previous touristic experience (Lash & Urry 1994: 255).

It is our opinion that, in his discourse on tourism and relocation, Rohmer reconciles the two tendencies. On the one hand, as with Kilvert and James, he edifies 'authenticity' in the experience of both travellers and non-travellers; on the other hand he regards 'authenticity' as a relative, not absolute value, depending on the individual concerned.

Road to stability and moderation

In spite of devoting the majority of his films to people who are actually and metaphorically in transition – on vacation, returning from abroad, changing homes, cities and jobs – Rohmer is not a great fan of travelling and change. His films suggest that transition is bad, unless it fulfils the function of a 'rite of passage' to permanence and stability. Moreover, Rohmer advocates a physically, morally and spiritually centred life and shows that such a life is a practical possibility.[6] The best testimony to that is the fact that this spiritually-centred life is an attribute of many of his young characters (Clarisse, Blanche and, in future, possibly also Delphine and Félicie), and not only the preserve of old people. In this conviction, he differs substantially from theorists like Anthony Giddens (1990), Stuart Hall (1992b) or Zygmunt Bauman (2000) who argue that in postmodernity it is impossible to find anything solid, that we are all condemned to liquidity, decentredness and fragmentation. However, Rohmer also shows that in a late-modern reality having a centre is, probably much more so than in earlier periods, the result of a conscious moral decision, rather than simply of circumstances. If we want to have a centre, we must look for it and do so wisely. According to Rohmer, the struggle is worth undertaking, as the alternative is hardly attractive: restlessness, confusion, emptiness and, if not literal, then metaphorical homelessness.

The emphasis, characterising Rohmer's discourse on travel and tourism, on the centrality of place in travelling and on the dialectic home/holiday destination, rather than on the sheer act of changing locations and being on the move, goes against the dominant strand in tourist studies, which concentrates on and largely celebrates tourist mobility (see Bauman 1997 and 2000). Hence, his films offer a valuable and unusual contribution to current debates in tourist studies. In advocating travelling for the sake of finding a place which is like home Eric Rohmer also sets himself apart from the majority of directors of road cinema, who convey the idea that the road (as opposed to the destination) is all that matters to travellers.

chapter three
PATRICK KEILLER'S JOURNEYS TO THE REAL AND IMAGINARY ENGLAND

In common with Eric Rohmer, Patrick Keiller, director of the shorts *Norwood* (1983) and *Stonebridge Park* (1984) and of the full-length *London* (1994) and *Robinson in Space* (1997), cannot be regarded as a typical author of road cinema. His work, even to a larger extent than Rohmer's, challenges the common understanding of the genre and widens its boundaries. The originality lies in the style of his films, marked as they are by the following features: the absence of visible actors and characters (the elusive Robinson and the Narrator, his friend and ex-lover who accompanies him on his journeys, are unseen); the extensive use of voice-over; a static camera and long frames, conveying the impression of a series of photographs rather than a film; and an essay-like content. Many of these features stand in direct contrast with the paradigmatic examples of road movies, which are characterised by the importance of actors/characters, embodying the rebellious ideology of the film; the use of travelling shots and other cinematic means suggesting mobility, such as images of landscape in motion filmed from cars, motorcycles or trains; and an omniscient or, at least, objective narration.

Nonetheless, some meaningful connections between Keiller's films and road and travel cinema, especially of the European kind, may be identified. Not only is Keiller interested in travel as an experience and in its objects, such as landscapes and townscapes, but he also uses a 'marginal intellectual' as the main protagonist of the films, and employs the journey as a way to investigate his country's past and possible future. These features bear strong associations with the films of Wim Wenders and of some postmodern filmmakers interested in this genre, especially Nanni Moretti, who in the first episode of *Caro diario* (*Dear Diary*, 1994) travels through Rome and simultaneously muses how his city has changed in the last forty years.[1] Perhaps the films that are closest to the work of Keiller are those by French filmmaker Chris Marker, especially *Sans soleil* (*Sunless*, 1983), a highly subjective but extremely persuasive portrayal of Tokyo. Both Keiller and Marker use travel in space as a means to investigate histories of cities and countries. They can both be described as essayists, as they show distrust of traditional, Hollywood-style cinematic narratives, build their films out of loosely-connected episodes, make use of various media (including still photographs) and construct mosaics or collages by juxtaposing contrasting images and ideas and by taking objects out of their normal contexts to put them into new, unexpected perspectives. For these reasons, they can be considered as model postmodernists. Paradoxically, both Marker and Keiller use postmodern techniques to denounce postmodernity as a 'condition': as a political, social and cultural system under which a large proportion of the world population lives.

In his native England, Keiller's main filmic antecedents are the creators of classical documentaries from the 1930s and 1940s, particularly of the so-called poetic documentaries, of which the work of Humphrey Jennings is the model example (see Higson 1986). Furthermore, Keiller's blending of truth and fiction, his use of invisible narrators and characters behind which to conceal himself,[2] and his preoccupation with landscape encouraged critics to compare him to his idiosyncratic fellow Englishman, Peter Greenaway and to classify Keiller's films as 'false documentaries' (see Combs 1995: 59). While acknowledging the links between Keiller on the one hand and Jennings and Greenaway on the other, we suggest that the differences between them are more important than any similarities. In particular, in Jennings' films human characters have a much more important role than in Keiller's. Moreover, although Jennings recognises the momentous changes experienced by England in the twentieth century he appears to believe in the unity and inclusiveness of the English nation; for Keiller, conversely, such unity is highly problematic. On the other hand, the documentary form, used by Greenaway in films such as *A Walk Through H* (1978), *Vertical Features Remake* (1978) or *The Falls* (1980), emphasised the silly or absurd content of his films: catalogues, lists and encyclopaedias whose usefulness he called into question. In the case of Keiller, the use of fictional characters is meant to add ironic lightness to a content which is so serious, dense and close to historical and political discourse that it could even be regarded as unsuitable to the medium of film.

The journeys undertaken by the Narrator and his male companion can be placed in two main categories: travelling in time, from the past to the (possible) future; and geographical movements. Although the first type of travel is only metaphorical, we include it to illuminate one of the main theses of this book: that the specificity of European travel cinema lies largely in its attempt to interrogate the relation between space and time, especially the history of nations and cities. We will analyse Robinson's and the Narrator's journeys by referring to several discourses which Keiller employs in his films, such as modernism and its discontents, English heritage, *flânerie* and tourism.

From pre-modernity to post-modernity and beyond – the case of London and England

'Blackpool stands between us and the revolution.'
> – The Narrator, *Robinson in Space*

In spite of the vast and ever-growing academic literature devoted to the study of modernism and postmodernism, there is little consensus on how to define and clearly distinguish the dyads 'modern/postmodern', 'modernity/postmodernity', and 'modernism/postmodernism'. Peter Brooker aptly sums up the confusion in this field:

> What you get is what you see from where you stand. What is more, these different perspectives and informing criteria do not add up. They do not together form a complete picture so much as cancel, subsume or contend with each other. A chronology of modernism would identify a range of artistic movements, decisive meetings, individual works and events, and would, for all its inevitable superficialities, underline these disparities … A fuller picture would only confirm the plurality of modernisms, across their several divergent and contrary formations. (1992: 5)

It is certainly not our purpose here to propose any 'ultimate' definition of the above terms, but to reconstruct Keiller's understanding of them, and to investigate how his understanding influences his cinematic travels. The Narrator of *London* and *Robinson in Space* does not provide us with any precise definition of modernism and modernity, but from the remarks saturating the films we understand that, for Keiller, modernity is intimately connected with what Jürgen Habermas describes as 'the project of Enlightenment':

> The project of modernity formulated in the eighteenth century by the philosophers of Enlightenment consisted in their efforts to develop objective science, universal morality and law, and autonomous art according to their inner logic. At the same time, this project intended to release the cognitive potentials of each domain from their esoteric forms. The Enlightenment philosophers wanted to utilise this accumulation of specialised culture for the enrichment of everyday life – that is, for the rational organisation of everyday social life. (1992: 132)

Using the Narrator as his mouthpiece, Keiller maintains that in continental Europe the Enlightenment project was implemented with a degree of success, largely thanks to one momentous event – the 1789 French Revolution, with its ideals of justice, equality and solidarity. By contrast, the English Revolution, which was precipitated by the execution of King Charles I in 1649, spectacularly failed. Its failure, in Keiller's view, is responsible for much of the malaise which poisons English politics and social life to this day: a bad constitution, which serves only a small section of the population, marginalising large chunks of the British people, and preventing radical political change; the troubles in Ireland; and English hostility towards Europe. The respective victory and failure of the French and English revolutions also had a major impact on the structure and social character of European cities. Cities in continental Europe, as is argued in *London*, welcome both inhabitants and tourists and encourage strolling by offering distinctive, well-maintained pedestrianised centres, boasting an abundance of public space, affordable housing and public transport. In short, they are the locus of democracy and egalitarianism. By contrast, the fiasco of English revolution assured the political and cultural dominance of narrow elites in the capital city, belonging to aristocracy and the monarchy, and people with access to considerable wealth, such as the industrial bourgeoisie, bankers and brokers. These groups, as Keiller suggests, echoing the views of Iain Chambers (1990), are not mutually exclusive; on the contrary, they live in perfect harmony, following a lengthy osmosis between agrarian capital and industrial development. The city centre, which in the bulk of European cities is enjoyed by ordinary people, in London is to a large extent inaccessible to them; it belongs to the monarch and the City, occupied by bankers and brokers. To support this opinion, the Narrator quotes official statistics, according to which the resident population of the City is only 6,000, while 300,000 people commute there every day, often from far away. This proportion bears similarities with many British and European holiday resorts, which pay for their popularity amongst affluent new arrivals with the decline of the indigenous population, whose needs are neglected.

As Keiller alleges, both the monarchy and the City anxiously protect their distance from the crowd, using private armies and, in the case of the City, an independent police force, as highlighted by the recurrent motif of fences, gates and other obstacles which prevent intruders from reaching many parts of London. They separate and segregate people and obscure the view of the city. Keiller criticises the continuous presence of the monarchy in London's cultural life for undermining or even preventing true democracy, as well as for being utterly anachronistic. He contrasts the frequency and pomp of royal occasions, such as the gilded coaches and the horses and soldiers greeting the Queen and other members of the royal family, with the poverty and squalor in which large sections of London's population live, and mentions that the Queen does not pay any taxes. Contrary to popular opinion, for Keiller the activities of the royal family are neither politically neutral nor innocuous, as they promote a certain historical discourse and embody a distinctive militaristic and reactionary political ethos. This is illustrated by the episode of the Queen Mother unveiling a monument to Sir Arthur Travers Harris, the British air marshal responsible for bombing German civilians during the Second World War.

While Keiller claims that the substance of the social and cultural structuring of London was established centuries ago by the elites, who were anxious to preserve their dominant position and were afraid of 'the mob', he also points out that since the victory of Margaret Thatcher the city declined even further. At this time London's public transport became deregulated, run-down and the most expensive in the world, whereas public spaces, such as parks and libraries, were privatised or destroyed. Moreover, putting economic prosperity above other values resulted in widespread pollution. In Keiller's film the Thames looks more like a sewer than a river. These problems are worsened by the increasing size of London, which renders human contact difficult and makes the city unmanageable and depersonalised. Keiller's overall opinion of London's present is negative, and is conveyed not only through criticism of its individual features, but also through paradoxical statements, such as the Narrator's words that open *London*: 'We came to the end of the world', as well as the claim uttered near the end of the film that 'London is the first metropolis in the world which disappeared', or the quotation from Alexander Herzen, the exiled Russian socialist who arrived in the city in 1852: 'There is no town in the world which is more adapted for training one away from people and training one into solitude.'

We suggest that many features of London that Keiller regards as anachronistic, because they encapsulate a pre-modern, pre-Enlightenment ideology, may simultaneously be regarded as post-modern. We refer to the repositioning of social and cultural activities in the suburbs and places where social interactions can be easily surveyed and policed, such as shopping malls, and the privatisation of public transport and public spaces, such as parks and libraries but also hospitals and streets, resulting in the displacement of poorer people to less desirable areas. These phenomena are recently observed in the towns of many post-communist countries, including Poland and Russia, as well as in the former East Germany, especially in Berlin (see Mazierska & Rascaroli 2003). In the same cities we also witness the proliferation of various types of barriers, which divide the population and reduce public space, and the repositioning of the rich to the suburbs, largely due to fear of crime, pollution and the mob. In other words, that which in Keiller's opinion is a sign of London's utter anachronism and abnormality is regarded as a sign of progress and normality in countries that recently joined the community of democratic and capitalist countries.

Figs. 7 and 8 Patrick Keiller's *London* (UK, 1994) © Patrick Keiller and British Film Institute

Paradoxically, Keiller's observation on London's decay and his opinion that the English, unlike the people of continental Europe, are afraid of large cities is also the source of his optimism for London's future. He hopes that the centre's unattractiveness for people of political and economic power will eventually lead to its reclamation by those who are by nature the most creative force in cities: artists, poets and all sorts of bohemian people. However, at least at the time of *London*'s production, this repossession had not happened; on the contrary, the dominance of the centre by business and power even increased, as testified by the cleaning of rough sleepers to more distant quarters, to prevent them from spoiling the ambience for the affluent Londoners. The only sign of bohemian life in the centre of London is the Notting Hill carnival, the largest festival in Europe. Robinson observes sarcastically that London is a perfect place for this type of activity, because its streets are usually empty of pedestrians. This explanation, referring to Londoners' suburban lifestyle, their fear of crowds and everything that poses a threat to their values, is reminiscent of the phenomenon of the social inversions and reversals, as discussed by David Sibley. These take place when the marginalised and the socially excluded 'occupy the centre and the dominant majority are cast in the role of spectators' (1995: 43). Sibley draws attention to the fact that 'inversions can have a role in political protest in the sense that they expose power relations by reversing them and, in the process, raise the consciousness of the oppression. They energise boundaries by parodying established power relations' (1995: 43–4). Although this is true in many cases, we suggest that inversions also serve as a 'vent' to allow the oppressed to rebel against their situation in a spatially and temporarily limited and strictly controlled environment. Accordingly, the Notting Hill carnival is accepted by those in power precisely because it is only a brief event, which does not pose a serious threat to the status quo.

Keiller's suggestion that London's positioning on the map of the world and the axis of history can be seen in two contrasting ways – as the top of the world or as its bottom, as a place which is stuck in the past or ultra-modern – renders this city particularly conducive to a discourse on postmodernism, which emphasises relativism and circularity. London supports the postmodern claim that there is no social progress, or that progress is always relative: advancement in one area of social life can be accompanied by regression in another. The motif of the relative nature of progress is further elaborated in *Robinson in Space*, in which the characters travel to the South, North, East and West of England, reaching, amongst other locations, Dover, Oxford, Cambridge, Bristol, Birmingham, Liverpool, Manchester, Halifax, Hull, Blackpool and Sellafield. As in the previous film, on his way Robinson discusses England's past and present, concentrating on the shortcomings of his native country: the lack of true democracy, the dominance of the upper classes in politics and economy, the resistance of those in power to change in politics and social life, the despicable situation of the English intelligentsia. We are shown historical and modern buildings, the countryside and urban areas, factories and supermarkets, roads and bridges, demonstrating the comprehensive character of Robinson's project: to show the whole of England, including areas which are typically hidden from the camera. Paradoxically – as we will argue below – such an approach also exposes what is normally concealed and cannot be seen by a tourist.

Robinson engages with two competing paradigms or narratives of England, and tries to destroy two myths that are embedded in them. According to one, which can be described as sentimental, England at its best is a pre-modern, 'heritage country': rural, tranquil, refined, picturesque, full of lavish, aristocratic houses and well-mannered people, living in small, closely-knit communities. This is the image conveyed by numerous 'heritage films' produced in Britain in the 1980s and 1990s, examples being the Merchant-Ivory adaptations of E. M. Forster's novels, as well as by many earlier filmic representations, such as war propaganda films and Ealing comedies. The heritage films were described by critics as 'postmodern', because they forged simulacra of English history, rather than accurate recreations. The Narrator of *Robinson in Space* refers to this phenomenon by mentioning six adaptations of Jane Austen's novels shot during the year of his journey. He also visually engages in the discourse proposed by heritage cinema. As Andrew Higson (1993: 110) argues, while the narratives of these films are often concerned with subjecting aristocratic values to a moral critique, the images reground these values with alluring heritage spectacle. The visual style of heritage films is marked by 'studied compositions', long shots and long takes with elegant, stately camera movements showing off heritage spectacle. Higson and John Hill maintain that 'such shots exceed the narrative requirements of the depiction of character point of view and … establish a public gaze which has heritage spectacle as its object. The construction of such a gaze fits the phenomenon noted by anti-heritage critics …

whereby the private property of an elite class becomes the pseudo-public, national "treasure" for everyone' (quoted in Dave 2000: 348).

Paul Dave observes:

> By contrast, Keiller's fictional witnesses establish an ambiguous viewing position around his carefully composed long shots and long takes of pastoral and urban heritage. Our awareness of the unseen narrator and his companion, Robinson, endows each image with the potential to act as a point-of-view shot – framings often include obstructions that are consistent with the type of fictional look being suggested. These shots imply that we are surveying private not public property, from a space that is specifically inhabited and vulnerable. In this way the secure, taken-for-granted public space that acts as a precondition of a public gaze acquires an unfamiliar presence – that of contested space only brought into existence by the efforts of invisible trespassers. (Ibid.)

The typical image accompanying the Narrator's references to the countryside, not unlike the city in *London*, is a fence, a bland metaphor for the barriers between those who enjoy rural pleasures and those who do not. The film also draws attention to those who challenge the privileges of the possessing classes, such as a group of anarchists protesting against property rights, and Greenpeace activists; at the same time, by revealing the small scale of the protests against the status quo and, by extension, of political dissidence in contemporary England, it testifies to the undiminishing power of the upper classes.

Keiller objects to the projection of England as a rural paradise to which everybody has access, irrespective of class, not only because it is false, but also because its purpose is to placate people, preventing conflict or even – to use a word with which Keiller appears to have a particular affinity – revolution. The following words of John Taylor perfectly express Keiller's views: 'The urgency of renewing the idea of the "imagined community" is so great, and the costs of failure perceived to be so threatening that, in the public realm of tourism, images of calm and contentment obliterate those of disarray and discord' (1994: 6). The dominant image of England as a static, rural paradise furthermore marginalises other types of heritage, especially working class and industrial/scientific heritage. Mentioning six films based on Jane Austen speaks for itself, and it speaks 'even louder' when compared to the absence of films based on literature on the working class made in a comparable period. Keiller also refers to the virtual silence surrounding one of the greatest English inventors, Alan Turing, who designed the first computer in the world. There were no monuments commemorating his achievements, nor films celebrating his life. This can be partly explained by the fact that he was gay and the victim of homophobia. Homosexuality, as with any transgression, does not fit comfortably with the image of England as a bastion of centuries-old traditions.

The second paradigm with which Robinson engages, which Dave identifies as 'cultural critique', links the dominance of the pre-modern, 'heritage England' of the aristocracy with national economic backwardness and decline. Their adherents, such as historians Anthony Sampson, Perry Anderson, Tom Nairn, Martin J. Wiener and Corelli Barnett, identify the bourgeoisie as the capitalist class and the aristocracy as the pre-capitalist class, and argue that

> there is an implied historical progression running from the aristocracy with its regressive 'rustic and nostalgic myths' of Englishness to the 'innovation', 'change' and 'energy' of a modern bourgeoisie. Also, capitalism is seen as a purely creative force that produces 'wealth' but only in circumstances in which it remains unhindered by 'checks' such as those provided by the longevity of the culture of the 'status quo'. (Dave 2000: 342)

Contrary to the supporters of the cultural critique who moan English backwardness, which they understand as failing to reach the ultimate stage of capitalism, in *Robinson in Space* Keiller suggests that England in the 1990s is not only a developed capitalist country, but that it has completed the transition to a higher stage of capitalism, typically described as post-Fordist or post-modern. At the same time, unlike Anderson or Nairn, who celebrate capitalism, he presents this accomplishment not as a success, but as a failure. He conveys the idea that England is advanced in its march towards capitalism by criticising another commonplace: that the North and South of England have very different characters – the South's wealth being based on a service economy and culture industry, while the North's on heavy industry. Keiller shows that in 1995, after sixteen years of Tory dominance, the North is largely de-industrialised due to the closure of coalmines and steelworks. Shopping centres, supermarket depots and high-technology business, producing mobile phones and computers, are now the main employers in Merseyside, Derbyshire and Lancashire, as they are in the South East. Moreover, in contrast to the past, there are now considerable similarities in the way industry is organised in different regions and types of businesses. It is suggested that the large old-style factories, often state-owned, with strong trade unions, were replaced by new types of establishments with fewer workers whose rights are undermined. These are often owned by foreign investors, usually North Americans, whose sole objective is to maximise profit, even at the expense of using devious practices. Robinson refers to a Canadian company, specialising in recycling scrap, which 'evangelises total team culture' by not paying workers overtime and persecuting trade union members. The foreign management practices are now applied even to such 'businesses' as prisons, detention centres for asylum seekers, private nursing homes and crèches (often owned by American companies), much to the disadvantage of those who are meant to be cared for there. Thus, it can be said that England, once a colonial power, allowed itself to be colonised, both economically and culturally, by its former colonies. The victims of this new, 'corporate colonialism' are mainly English working-class people (including a large proportion of underpaid intelligentsia). The upper classes, by contrast, profit from the deals with foreigners. The perception of the different parts of England being economically and culturally similar to each other results in the paradoxical impression that *Robinson in Space* represents a more homogenous object than that portrayed in *London*, where the focus was on the cultural and economic differences between various areas of the capital city.

Keiller contradicts the claim, perpetuated by successive Conservative governments, that English heavy industry was dismantled because it was unprofitable. On the contrary, he argues, supporting his assertion by official statistics, English coalmines, shipyards, ports and steelworks remained amongst the most profitable in the world. Hence, the film suggests that the shift from the old-style, Fordist-type industry to post-Fordist establishments was rooted in political motives, primarily the desire of the government and the section of society it upholds to weaken and fragment the English working classes. Obviously, no British government, even a Thatcherite one, was ever prepared to admit that it acted against its citizens' welfare. Instead, it 'manufactured consent', to use the famous expression coined by Walter Lippmann and popularised by Noam Chomsky (see Herman & Chomsky 1994: xi), to convince citizens that it acted for their welfare. We suggest that the stories about Martians landing in Surrey and other tales of the signs of extraterrestrial activities in England, apart from lightening the tone of Keiller's film, can be read as a metaphor of the conspiracy of the English upper classes against the ordinary people. In common with *London*, in *Robinson in Space* the author maintains that there is no antagonism between the old possessing classes – the royal family and the aristocracy, and the new possessing class represented by bankers, brokers and factory owners. On the contrary, they live in symbiosis and collaborate, often being the same people. The English system of education, dominated by Oxbridge, strengthens the links between 'old' and 'new' money. Again, as in *London*, the chief factor in this undesirable situation is the failure of the English Revolution.

By mirroring London in its economic, social and cultural structures, especially in the symbiosis between aristocracy and capitalists, rural life and city life, and the exclusion of a large part of population from enjoying the successes of English capitalism, England can be described as a particularly postmodern place. Its paradigmatic position in relation to postmodernity reveals itself especially in comparison with many post-communist countries, such as Russia, Poland and the ex-Soviet Republics, which also moved to postmodern capitalism, in a sense avoiding the stage of modernity associated with the values of the French Revolution (see Condee 1995).

Not unlike in *London*, where Keiller suggested that there is a time and space where the London status quo is abolished (the Notting Hill carnival), in *Robinson in Space* he depicts Blackpool as a place where the rules applied to the rest of England are reversed – an opinion that bears association with John K. Walton's (2004) ideas. Both Keiller and Walton perceive Blackpool as a welcoming and tolerant place, where ethnic minorities see their culture appreciated, celebrated, juxtaposed and mixed with other traditions, where gay people find refuge, where Scots feel at home as much as Englishmen, and where the sea allows for a change and renegotiation of identities. In an interview given to Patrick Wright, Keiller also maintains that Blackpool is a very modern place:

> The Illuminations were borrowed from the Kaiser's birthday celebrations, and the tower is borrowed from the Eiffel Tower; the company which became Jaguar began in Blackpool, and they used to make aeroplanes there. The trams are very Middle European. You can imagine that it's the coast of Bohemia, if you're looking for the coast of Bohemia... (1999: 231)

However, these features are also the reasons, to use Robinson's words, why Blackpool 'stands between us and the revolution'. Blackpool, in fact, prevents any large-scale revolution by allowing, although in the limited space of this seaside resort and the limited time of a holiday, those who are marginalised by the dominant strand of English culture to indulge in the sort of life which they could enjoy if the democratic revolution dreamt by Robinson happened, and was successful. In other words, the inclusiveness, egalitarianism and progressiveness of Blackpool act as a vent to their frustrations, and allow the rest of the country to remain reactionary, class-ridden, exclusive, corrupt and frozen in time. In Blackpool, as in Notting Hill, to paraphrase the words of Raoul Vaneigem, whom the Narrator quotes, 'a bridge between reality and imagination is constructed', a post-postmodern utopia created, thus preventing such bridges being built in the rest of England and lasting permanently. Watching Keiller's film one cannot help but wonder if Blackpool is not a product of the conspiracy of the English upper classes.

Keiller's outlook for his country is bleak: England will not change fundamentally, continuing to enjoy its status as a simultaneously archaic and postmodern country. Keiller's diagnosis seems very accurate when viewing *London* and *Robinson in Space* a decade after the first film was made, in the context of nine years of Tony Blair's government. This, in fact, proved to be unwilling or even overtly hostile to the project of weakening or dismantling those English structures and traditions, such as the monarchy, whose demise would make a French-style revolution possible, while at the same time creating the illusion that it is taking England into a new stage of its development, by emulating even further American policies.

Robinson and the Narrator: *flâneurs*, tourists, vagabonds, spies and dreamers

> The rhythms of the working day are set by the clock, and measures of time relate to measures of production. Tourists, along with the infirm and the unemployed, stand outside workaday time. But unlike other groups, tourists wilfully enter into the pleasures and dangers of time-travel. They seek to alter their relation to it just as they alter their relation to production … In its ideal form, touring is like dreaming. (Taylor 1994: 2)

In their travels through London and England, Robinson and the Narrator appropriate, or try to adopt, a number of 'travel identities', such as those of the *flâneur*, tourist, vagabond and spy, which allow them to explore the connections between these identities and test their limits. All these roles involve a certain distance from the places and objects visited, although the very type of distance plays an important role in determining each travel identity. For example, a tourist only visits the places of his interest, while having a home elsewhere. The *flâneur* is typically a resident, but feels different from both his fellow citizens and the tourists, as conveyed by the expression (taken from Edgar Allan Poe's story) that he is 'a man of the crowd', not 'in the crowd'. The vagabond has no permanent residence, but moves from one temporary accommodation and space of action to another. The spy gazes at people who do not want to be observed and at objects which are hidden, and conceals his true self from those whom he meets on his way. Moreover, he is often forced to appropriate several different identities and, consequently, his true personality is always displaced, while his adopted identity is constantly changing. The lack of permanence and, by the same token, a distance from the objects of his travel is also, albeit to a lesser extent, conveyed by the word 'traveller', which is sometimes understood as an 'umbrella' term, encompassing all the other identities of people on the move, and sometimes regarded as the antinomy of a 'tourist'.[3]

In his films Keiller acknowledges the gap between his travellers and the objects of their travel and conveys it by a variety of means. At the beginning of *London* the Narrator informs us that, although both he and Robinson are English and have lived in London for many years, they are detached from this city. The Narrator did not visit London for seven years, a time spent working as a ship photographer – an occupation encapsulating a solitary lifestyle. Robinson's lack of stability and detachment from his place of residence are rendered by his living in rented accommodation of poor standard in an undesirable neighbourhood, first in London (in *London*), then in Reading (in *Robinson in Space*), something which discourages him from leaving his flat and exploring his surroundings. Moreover, the nature of his jobs (in *London* he is a part-time university lecturer in art history, specialising in a subject of little interest for his employer, and of which he is the only specialist in his department; in *Robinson in Space* he works as a teacher of English as a foreign language, a job marked by short-termness and instability) precludes him from making lasting contact with his colleagues. His marginal social position is compounded by his homosexuality, which makes him vulnerable to the hostility of fellow citizens. Tacitly, Keiller suggests that in the political climate of the time his films were made (when John Major was prime minister) bigotry in England increased, making people like Robinson particularly insecure.

Robinson's and the Narrator's aloofness from the places they visit is also rendered visually and aurally. There is often a significant distance between the camera (identified as the place occupied by the travellers) and the object to which the Narrator refers in his monologue. As Paul Dave maintains, this suggests the difficulty of reaching or approaching a particular place and, more generally, the idea that England is an inaccessible country. Equally important is the fact that we do not see the main characters; neither do we experience the consequences of their actions. They remain hidden both from the audience and from people in the crowd and are ineffective, like spies or even ghosts. Moreover, the commentary accompanying the images suggests a significant gap between the completion of Robinson's and the Narrator's journey and its transformation into a film. Not only is it narrated in the past tense, with reference to events which must have taken place weeks or even months before, but it conveys some kind of fatalism. It feels as if, instead of embarking on the journey to learn about their city and their country, Keiller's protagonists travel to confirm what they already suspected.[4] The films are dominated by narratives of people and places that are unchanged or which cannot be changed by the intervention of the travellers, such as the Profumo scandal, recollected on the occasion of passing Cliveden, the impressive country house where John Profumo's affair with Christine Keeler began, and which was also the place of a meeting between Oswald Mosley and German foreign minister Joachim von Ribbentrop.

The passive character of their travel and, at the same time, their desire to transform the world is underlined by the motto of *Robinson in Space*, taken from the book by Raoul Vaneigem, *Traité de savoir-vivre a l'usage des jeunes generations* (*The Revolution of Everyday Life*, 1963–65):

> Reality, as it evolves, sweeps me with it. I am struck by everything and, though not everything strikes me in the same way, I am always struck by the same basic contradiction: although I can always see how beautiful anything could be if only I could change it, in practically every case there is nothing I can really do. Everything is changed into something else in my imagination, then the dead weight of things changed it back into what it was in the first place. A bridge between imagination and reality must be built… (Vaneigem, quoted in Keiller 1999: 1)

The most important identity which the Narrator and Robinson appropriate is that of the *flâneur*.[5] The concept of *flânerie* is by no means a simple one; it is embedded in controversy, which is understandable in the light of the fascination which this figure arouse in poets, novelists, sociologists, philosophers, authors as versatile as Charles Baudelaire, Honoré de Balzac, Theodor Amadeus Hoffmann, Emile Zola, Victor Hugo, Gustave Flaubert, Robert Musil, Jean-Paul Sartre, Marcel Proust, Charles Dickens, Edgar Allan Poe, Walter Benjamin, Siegfried Kracauer, Georg Simmel, Franz Hessel and Robert Park. They either cultivated *flânerie* themselves or described experiences of other strollers in European cities such as Paris, Berlin, London and Vienna, as well as abstract or imaginary metropolises.

The *flâneur* is strongly associated with the strolling of a fictional painter, Constantin Guys, through the modern Paris of arcades and department stores, as depicted in Baudelaire's essay 'The Painter of Modern Life', first published in 1863. Baudelaire's work provides a model with which other descriptions of *flânerie* are compared and on which the popular ideas about this activity are based. In the most commonsense approach, *flânerie* is marked by two characteristics: pleasure and purposelessness. The *flâneur* gawks with utter enjoyment at the magical spectacle of the city, for the sake of doing it; his pastime has no further purposes. For this reason, he is often regarded as a relative or descendant of an aristocrat or a dandy (Mazlish 1994: 49). However, various authors argue that the *flâneur's* pleasure of looking at the city and its crowds was never wholesale or uninterrupted. Even Baudelaire's *flâneur*, who is widely regarded as the closest to the model described above, as Bruce Mazlish argues, has an ambivalent attitude to the city's attractions. On the one hand, he 'marvels at the eternal beauty and the amazing harmony of life in the capital cities, a harmony so providently maintained amid the turmoil of human freedom … He delights in fine carriages and proud horses, the dazzling smartness of the grooms … in a word, he delights in universal life' (Baudelaire, quoted in ibid.). On the other hand, he rebels against the circumstances of 'universal' (meaning capitalistic) life as an existence in which 'monetary affections' thwarted all other sentiments (1994: 47). This is an important reason why the *flâneur* does not want to mix with the crowd, preferring to observe the metropolis from a detached and ironic perspective (ibid.).

With the passing of time, the area of the *flâneur's* enjoyment is diminishing, while the field of his disappointment grows. Walter Benjamin, who undertook the task of interpreting Baudelaire's comments on city life in the light of a new historical period, that of 'mechanical reproduction', and who was an ardent stroller himself, is a perfect case in point. As Susan Sontag observes, his *flânerie* is filled with melancholia and rebellion against the capitalist life which is structured, rationalised, standardised and, therefore, devoid of mystery (see Sontag 1980: 131–4). Keith Tester argues that, largely thanks to Benjamin's reading of Baudelaire, the *flâneur* is seen as a bygone figure:

> Benjamin's argument is that the rationality of capitalism and, especially, commodification and the circulation of commodities, itself defined the meaning of existence in the city so that there remained no spaces of mystery for the *flâneur* to observe. Capital imposed its own order on the metropolis as if from outside, like a natural force. Benjamin proposes that the hollowness of the commodity form and, indeed, the hollowness of the egoistic individuals of capitalism is reflected in the *flâneur*. *Flânerie* is a desperate attempt to fill the emptiness even though it is actually a final resignation to it. (1994: 13)

Benjamin's *flâneur* renounces his wandering in the city and, with the crowd of consumers, enters a department store to stray amongst the labyrinth of articles on sale. Tester maintains that the '*flânerie* which features in the work of Benjamin is soulless and truly empty' (1994: 14).

While some authors, including Benjamin and Robert Musil, maintained that the *flâneur* died with the modern city (see Tester 1994: 16), others, such as Susan Buck-Morss and Zygmunt Bauman, argue that in postmodern times, marked by the culture of spectacle, abundance and the intoxicating effect of free signifiers, epitomised by Disneyland, this figure proliferated, becoming an epitome of the consumerist attitude to life (Buck-Morss 1999: 331–74; Bauman 1994: 147–57; see also Friedberg 1997). At the same time, these authors agree that while *flânerie* still exists, or even is more widespread than in Baudelaire's times, it is markedly different from that which was described in 'The Painter of Modern Life'. In particular, it lost its reflexive and critical potential. Bauman even claims that today, in contrast to Baudelaire's times, it takes a heroic effort not to engage in *flânerie* (1994: 156). Yet not everybody agrees with the statement that the postmodern *flâneur* is the passive and manipulated consumer. Stefan Morawski argues that the very work of authors such as Bauman or Jean Baudrillard testify to the possibility of being a critical *flâneur* in the postmodern age; after all, they avoided being 'narcotised' by postmodern spectacles and managed to discuss them from a critical distance (1994: 186–8). We espouse this argument; the *flâneur* remains for us a critical, reflexive observer.

The second common assumption about the nature of the *flâneur* is that he is an epitome of idleness. It is worth mentioning here that the word *flâneur* is over four hundred years old. According to a 1808 French dictionary the term was first used to describe people without a stable position in the structure of feudal French society: vagabonds, criminals and homeless people (see Dzionek 2003). However, in the next centuries the connotations of the *flâneur* changed and nowadays many authors challenge the idea that the *flâneur* lacks a 'proper' occupation, largely because he needs to sell his work: his poems, paintings, essays, photographs or journalistic articles, to support himself or even pay his debts (see Sontag 1979: 133; Buck-Morss 1999: 306; Shields 1994: 62–5). Stefan Morawski conceptualises the *flâneur* as deputy of somebody who tries to make sense of the surrounding world and has a particular project in mind (1994: 183). He might be a philosopher, an artist or a scientist: a sociologist, painter, poet or photographer. Morawski suggests that the division between the *flâneur* and the artist/intellectual is often imaginary or internal: the *flâneur* is 'an extraction of the artist sent into the surrounding world to get to its guts' (Morawski 1994: 183). Rob Shields claims that 'the *flâneur* is the indulgent fantasy of *the writer not writing* but whose observing eye nonetheless transmits directly to the novelist's page' (1994: 64). No wonder many accounts of *flânerie*, including the classical works of Baudelaire and Benjamin, are interpreted as autobiographical and the borders of *flânerie* are blurred. The *flâneur* shares characteristics with other types of travellers, such as tourists, being described as a 'tourist at home, a native who feels partly homeless' (Morawski 1994: 184) and, as previously mentioned, vagabonds. Other related figures are the detective (who sheds light on the dark areas of the town), the spy or special agent (who observes the crowd), the photographer and painter (who are particularly interested in the visual dimension of the city), the journalist-reporter (who attempts to capture what happens here and now) and the scientist, such as a sociologist or ethnographer (who collects human customs and cultural patterns) (see Rignall 1989: 114–15; Buck-Morss 1999: 306). The slow pace of walking and living and the lack of a clear purpose pertain both to *flâneurs* and to dreamers or even daydreamers.

Overall, there are two aspects or dimensions to *flânerie*: an external/physical and an internal/moral, which can be described as the ethos of the *flâneur*. The external/physical aspect is defined by the fact that the *flâneur* walks through the city rather than using more sophisticated means of transport, as it is much more difficult to enjoy the spectacle of the city from the windows of a taxi or a tram. Secondly, he is interested in the spectacle of the city but preserves a critical distance from it. Accordingly, in their peregrination through the city, the two invisible heroes of Keiller's *London* decide to go to their chosen locations on foot. However, they cannot be *flâneurs* in the same way as Baudelaire, Flaubert or Proust, because, unlike Paris, London is not conducive to free and unconditioned strolling, due to such aforementioned factors as privatisation and the resulting lack of public spaces (especially in the city centre, where the model *flâneurs* spend most of their time), fencing, lack of security and excessive traffic.[6] To put it differently, the protagonists of Keiller's film cannot be successful *flâneurs* in London, because this is not a modern city. This opinion is supported by the Narrator's claim that when Robinson lived abroad he was an eager *flâneur*, only ceasing to be one upon his return to England.

Yet we suggest that the 'dead weight of things', to use Vaneigem's expression, which Keiller's heroes must overcome in order to become *flâneurs*, however unusual ones, testify to their credentials as performers of *flânerie*. For example, as a consequence of the difficulties of strolling through London, unlike Baudelaire and his followers, who walked in the centre of metropolitan towns, the *flânerie* of Keiller's protagonists is largely suburban, encompassing such places as nondescript borders between the city and the countryside and shopping malls, the postmodern descendants of the modern arcades, galleries and department stores. Moreover, although the Narrator and Robinson are not heroes of modernity, they are 'looking for that indefinable something we may be allowed to call "modernity"' (Baudelaire, quoted in Tester 1994: 6). In particular, the discourse on modernity informs their itinerary and is the main prism through which they interpret their travel experiences. This is rendered by their attempt to identify the moments in English history when their country entered or at least had a chance to enter the path leading to (European-style) modernity, and their visual traces in London, such as the monument of Charles I, as well as by their desire to follow the footsteps of the famous *flâneurs* who visited or had strong connections with the city, such as Edgar Allan Poe and Charles Baudelaire (whose mother lived in London). It is worth adding here that many accounts of *flânerie* consist of recreating the experiences of previous *flâneurs*; most importantly, Benjamin's writing is based on his research into Baudelaire's experience of Paris. Similarly, the Narrator and Robinson refer to Baudelaire as a theoretician of Romanticism and the way they recreate and elaborate Baudelaire's thoughts on this subject demonstrate the existence of a link between Romanticism, *flânerie* and modernism. All of them espouse Romanticism not as a particular literary style or a period in history, but as a mode of feeling or a mindset, defined by one's ability to look at oneself from the outside, as a figure in the romance, as somebody who does not have a firm identity, but waits to be 'written'. We argue that this is the way the *flâneur* looks at himself – as a palimpsest ready to be filled with images and stories he meets when strolling through his town, as somebody with a shifting identity, built from many disparate moments, who avoids fixation and commitment. Bauman describes the *flâneur* as somebody who is uncommitted and lives his life as a succession of absolute beginnings (1994: 139). Morawski observes that 'the *flâneur* does not idealise the contingency he encounters. The fact is that he is sunk in the fugitive and fleeting moments, but the string of elusive episodes does not reveal to him any deeper sense of being. The contingency of occurrences and opinions is observed and taken into account as related to social matrix' (1994: 184).

In line with this description, Keiller's characters typically move from one place to another before making any discovery (or at least acknowledging to the viewers that they made it) and the next stage of their journey bears little connection with the previous one. However, they hardly seem frustrated by this lack of coherence and life in perpetual presence. Instead, they cherish the most whimsical, unstable and least noticeable elements and aspects of human life, as demonstrated by their affinity for postcards, graffiti or strange road signs. Paul Julian Smith in his review of *Robinson in Space* makes an observation which is also appropriate to *London*: 'Neither nostalgic for the rural past, nor hopeful for the technological future, *Robinson* proposes rather that we pay patient attention to the present and cherish the enigmatic ephemera of everyday life' (1997: 44).

Moreover, Keiller makes his protagonists unwilling to come into closer contact with people whom they meet in their journey. Making lasting friendships or falling in love will jeopardise their position as eternal 'absolute beginners' and men of the crowd, changing them into men in the crowd or even those who risk becoming natives. This unwillingness or inability to engage with fellow passers-by is poignantly revealed in the episode of Robinson's meeting with a brotherly soul: a man who reads the works of Walter Benjamin.[7] Keiller emphasises that this incident is very unusual, as on the whole Robinson leads a solitary life and hardly meets anyone during his travels. Yet even the reader of Benjamin 'disappears from the picture' before Robinson can approach him, confirming the opinion that strollers shun close and lasting contacts. It is worth remembering that Robinson and the Narrator travel incognito and this status is strengthened by their invisibility; incognito being an important characteristic of the *flâneur* (see Tester 1994: 70). The concealment of his identity from the people 'in the crowd' allows the *flâneur* to achieve a better (less restrained and less structured) observation, and to more easily adjust his identity to any set of circumstances encountered during his journey.

Although the *flâneur* is a creature of modernity, in the sense of being born (or invented) in nineteenth-century Paris, and sharing similarities with such model figures of modernity as the dandy and the bohemian, he is also close to some postmodern concepts of subjectivity. One can notice a similarity between the condition of Robinson as a model *flâneur* and that of a schizophrenic, as described by Fredric Jameson: 'Schizophrenic experience is an experience of isolated, disconnected, discontinuous material signifiers which fail to link up into a coherent sequence' (1985: 119). Jameson uses the metaphor of schizophrenia to capture the condition of postmodernity: life which is quick and exciting, but lacking coherence and consequence, by extension devoid of any deeper meaning and, due to the belonging of this term to psychiatric discourse, pathological. The postmodern *flâneur* and its perfect embodiment in Robinson, despite many similarities, cuts much more dignified a figure than Jameson's schizophrenic, suggesting that one can operate in a postmodern universe, be strongly conditioned by it, but still preserve some independence and control over one's life and the 'game of discourses' in which one is plunged.

Another feature of *flânerie* relevant to Keiller's protagonists is circularity. Unlike the traveller, who might never reach again the place of his departure, the *flâneur*, in common with the tourist, always returns to the point where he began his journey. The same applies to Robinson and the Narrator when they roam through London: they travel from its centre, Whitehall, to the outskirts, visiting, amongst other places, Twickenham, Brixton, Vauxhall and the Docklands, and back again to Whitehall. The circular journey can be interpreted as a sign of their restlessness, disappointment with the place where they find themselves and desire to be somewhere else, while at the same time not being able to leave for good, due to such factors as lack of money, the urge to complete their project and, perhaps, their fatalism, as conveyed by the quotation from Vaneigem which accompanies their travels. In the last respect, *flâneurs* – and Keiller's protagonists in particular – are different from tourists, who are normally happy to be temporarily away from home and, even when they are not, do not experience total disappointment because they know that they will soon return home. Yet for Robinson and the Narrator there is no 'proper' home, no place to which they can belong, as testified by their living in places such as a ship or low-standard rented accommodation. Hence, in addition to *flânerie*, there is a touch of vagabond in them.

As we established, contrary to popular opinion the *flâneur* is rarely an idle creature who strolls for the pure joy of walking and gawking. Instead, he does this to collect material for a project embarked on by somebody else or by himself in a different capacity (as an artist, a writer or a sociologist). This is also the case of the *flânerie* of Keiller's characters; Robinson and the Narrator can be regarded as Keiller's 'deputies', providing him with the material for his project. We would like to describe them as 'scientific *flâneurs*', in the sense proposed by Edmund White:

> At the turn of the nineteenth century the scientific *flâneur* (a contradiction in terms, since *flânerie* is supposed to be purposeless) was Eugène Atget, an obsessed photographer who was determined to document every corner of Paris before it disappeared under the assault of modern 'improvements' ... Penniless and driven, Atget carried his tripod, view camera and glass plates everywhere with him, shooting all the monuments but also the fading advertisements painted on a wall, the dolls in a shop window, the rain-slick cobbled street, the door knocker, the quay, the stairwell, even the grain of the wood steps ... And he travelled beyond Paris, too, all the way to the empty, eerie gardens of Versailles and the ground of St Cloud ... Despite his irreproachable credentials as a documentalist, Atget came most into his own when photographing these pale gods and goddesses in marble, lining the unvisited *allées* of bare winter trees. (2002: 41–2)

In common with Eugène Atget, Robinson and the Narrator look at the city to document its present day, but also to carry out a critique of it, and to suggest how it could and should look in order to become an environment conducive to *flânerie*, as well as simply a better and happier place in which to be. Moreover, there is a 'scientific' intention in Robinson's and the Narrator's peregrination, as demonstrated by their frequent use of terms such as the 'project', the 'problem of London', as well as their conspicuous reference to scientific tools, especially historical accounts and statistical data. Furthermore, we can infer that the Narrator, like Atget, is a photographer who provides Robinson (and Keiller) with the images which we eventually see in the film. Firstly, at the beginning of *London* the Narrator introduces himself as somebody who worked for several years as a ship photographer. Secondly, as already mentioned, *London* feels more like a collection of photographs than a 'normal' film, and each view in the film can be interpreted as a subjective shot, achieved after overcoming numerous problems.

The identities adopted by Keiller's characters in *Robinson in Space* are more complex than those in the earlier film. This time they travel through England mainly using private cars; in this sense they cease to be *flâneurs*. However, the means of transport hardly affects the way they approach their subject – England. They not only travel through this country, but try to solve or at least elucidate the alleged 'problem of England' with the same seriousness and thoroughness with which they investigated London. This is testified by the quotations, even more frequent than in *London*, from various historical sources and statistical data to support particular points and the general hypothesis about the root of the 'problem of England'. Moreover, nothing in the film is photographed from the window of a moving car. When the characters find something of interest, they leave their vehicle, stay in a hotel and explore the surroundings for days on foot. No wonder that they refer to their project as a 'peripatetic study'. Again, we would describe them as 'scientific *flâneurs*'. At the same time, they convey a desire to be tourists, by deciding to see what tourists typically want to see in England, such as Oxford University, aristocratic houses, or Blackpool. However, as tourists they are atypical on several accounts. Firstly, contrary to the expectation that different categories of tourists choose different places of interest, according to their education and class background, their taste appears to be classless; despite their education and sophistication, they favour working-class Blackpool over any other place. Secondly, they treat with the same interest touristic places and those hardly mentioned in the tourist guides, such as the Midlands. Thirdly and most importantly, they cannot enjoy themselves as tourists, because – with the exception of Blackpool – they are aware that the attractiveness of places, which is displayed to tourists, conceals a more sinister side, which they are determined to reveal.

In addition, in *Robinson in Space* they become secret agents, hired by a mysterious agency, in this way confirming the previously mentioned link between *flânerie* and spying, and invoking the journey undertaken by Daniel Defoe (also accused of spying) described in his three-volume *Tour Through the Whole Island of Great Britain* (1724–27). A spy, not unlike a *flâneur*, but even to a greater extent, is excused for remaining at a distance, or at least for not exposing himself to natives and fellow travellers. Furthermore, being a spy involves seeing what is hidden to ordinary travellers and even to people familiar with what he spies on. The spy, as constructed or projected by Keiller, however, does not fulfil his objectives by physically overcoming the obstacles separating him from the places of his interest and looking inside them, searching for their hidden nature, but by analysing the meanings of what is widely visible, largely by comparing it to another well-visible object or situating it in a wider context of statistical data. In doing so, he follows a number of thinkers, regarded as precursors of postmodernism and close to *flânerie*, who privileged the importance of surfaces over the hidden essences or depths of things, including Oscar Wilde, whom he quotes as saying that the mystery of this world lies not in what is invisible, but in what is visible.

In particular, this method of 'spying' allows Robinson to reveal the hidden nature of English capitalism. As Paul Dave observes:

What begins to come into focus in Robinson's journeys around England is an understanding of capitalism that involves social relationships and effects far beyond the narrowly 'economic'. In this respect, the sequence showing the Queen gliding into the North West to give her blessing to its economic 'regeneration' by opening the Samsung plant at Wynard Park is instructive. It is edited in such a way that the announcement of her arrival anticipates her actual appearance and is relayed instead over a shot of local prison construction. Prisons – their privatisation and construction – form a motif in the film. Reminders of their omnipresence help to embed the abstract facts and figures of economic activity researched by Robinson and the narrator into a wider context of social relations marked by conflict and struggle. (2000: 344–45)

Hence, a 'travelling spy', as proposed by Keiller, does not differ from the tourist in regard to what he sees, only how he uses his perception. On the whole, Keiller shows that, if there is a difference between *flâneurs*, tourists, travellers, vagabonds and spies, this resides in their attitude to the place visited rather than in the character of the place itself. For example, somebody who is so disillusioned with England, as Robinson is, can hardly visit his country as a tourist. Similarly, people who cannot stand loneliness and distance from their own town, cannot become accomplished *flâneurs*. This suggests that the only travel identity open to all of us is that of a dreamer, who in his imagination transforms the objects which he encounters into their idealised versions.

chapter four
OUT OF EUROPE: WERNER HERZOG – THE CINEMA AS JOURNEY

> Humans are not made to sit at computer terminals or travel by aeroplane; destiny intended something different for us. For too long now we have been estranged from the essential, which is the nomadic life: travelling on foot.
>
> – Werner Herzog

The theme of travel in the work of Bavarian filmmaker Werner Herzog has often been discussed in the critical literature, but rarely as the main feature of his cinema. We suggest that Herzog's cinema is itself a form of journey and that it identifies with travel *tout court*. It is not surprising that Herzog's own 'lecture on the cinema' in his *Film Lesson* is devoted to 'Orientation in Film' and deals with the need of audiences for not losing their way, a topic that highlights the affinity between travelling and the cinema in Herzog's mind.[1] Similarly, when asked in an interview about opening a film school, Herzog suggested: 'If I did start one up you would only be allowed to fill out an application form after you had travelled alone on foot, let's say from Madrid to Kiev, a distance of about 5,000 kilometres' (in Cronin 2002: 15). Herzog himself is well-known for having walked from Munich to Paris during winter of 1974 in order to reach German film historian Lotte Eisner who was ill in the French capital – by walking all the way to Paris Herzog was convinced of saving her (see Herzog 1991). In 1984, he left Sachrang (the village of his childhood) and proceeded to walk along the border between West and East Germany, to promote the cause of the country's reunification.[2]

Many of Herzog's films represent travellers embarking on a journey; even when they do not do so, they are usually the outcome of a physical journey undertaken by the director himself, often to faraway and impervious locations. One could object that this does not make them straightforward examples of travel cinema; we claim that it does, because Herzog's films are not simply set in exotic landscapes, used as a backdrop or reconstructed where it is safe or easy to shoot. Herzog believes in going places, and in filming where the action unfolds, without compromises, no matter how difficult the situation. For this reason, he was often depicted by the press as a fanatic ready to endanger the lives of his crew and actors – however, Herzog insists that this fame is ill-deserved, and that he never ran unnecessary risks (see Cronin 2002: 175–90). Such an attitude was dictated, as is evident from his films and as the director has remarked (Cronin 2002: 176), not by a search for greater realism, but by the desire to capture the true 'spirit' of landscapes. The physicality and one would say the spirituality of the landscapes is so overwhelmingly important in Herzog's work that his films are real journeys to and through those sites. When watching Herzog's films one truly feels that 'cinema does not come from abstract academic thinking; it comes from your knees and thighs' (in Cronin 2002: 101). The director's interpretation of travel is very physical: it has nothing to do with tourism, rather with 'intense walking'.[3] Intensity seems to be afforded not only by the distance covered, but also by the walker's attitude. One example is provided by the pilgrims showed in both *Pilgrimage* (2001) and *Wheel of Time* (2003); their 'travel in prostration' (walking long distances while genuflecting at every second step, or walking on one's knees) transforms the journey into a true ecstatic experience, mixing pain and pleasure. Indeed, *Pilgrimage* is a case in point of our claim that Herzog's cinema is itself a form of journey: rather than being the account of a pilgrimage, the film is itself a pilgrimage to ecstatic landscapes, both physical and human (in the sense that the human face becomes an ecstatic landscape explored by the camera). As Herzog once stated, 'When you travel on foot with this intensity, it is not a matter of covering actual ground; rather it is a question of moving through your own inner landscapes' (in Cronin 2002: 282).

The presence of Herzog in a book on European travel cinema might seem questionable: most of his films, and practically all those which are explicitly about travelling, are set outside Europe, in faraway locations, including the Canary Islands, India, Tibet, Guadalupe, Africa, Australia, Mexico and Peru. We nevertheless believe that Herzog is essential to this volume, because his cinema remains strongly European even when it travels to the desert or the jungle. Many of his travellers are European (Fitzcarraldo, Aguirre, Stroszek, Roccia, Cobra Verde) and thus look at exotic landscapes from a European perspective. Indeed, the director claims that he is not just from Europe or Germany, but more precisely from Bavaria: 'It does not matter where the films were physically filmed. Geographically, I have travelled widely, but I do feel that all my films are not only very German, they are explicitly Bavarian' (in Cronin 2002: 23). In the same interview, Herzog names 'dreaminess and exuberance' as typical Bavarian qualities; he calls King Ludwig II 'the most imaginative Bavarian of all' and points to Fassbinder's films as another example of this 'baroque imagination' (ibid.). We suggest that Herzog's work is decidedly postmodern. We argued in chapter one that Herzog is a master of magical realism, for his interest in simpletons, 'idiot saints' and 'holy madmen', as well as miracles and 'ecstatic images'. His images are more 'true' than 'real', in the sense that they are staged but provide a poetic understanding of the reality portrayed – as Herzog suggests, 'only through invention and fabrication and staging can you reach a more intense level of truth that cannot otherwise be found' (in Cronin 2002: 253). We have also suggested that many of the critics who have discussed magical realism noticed its affinity with postmodernism, for instance for its aspiration to destabilise the reader/spectator, its distrust of rationalism and its interest in marginal characters and cultures. Herzog is indeed a director who dissolves character and narrative, concentrates on marginal, ex-centric subjects and cultures, questions civilisation, distrusts rational explanations, and can see the 'spirit' of things, proposing almost a New Age-type of mysticism. Indeed, as is clear from his films devoted to religious topics, the Bavarian filmmaker has an interest for primitive spirituality, which he associates with certain natural places, and which emerges from the act of travelling (of the kind he prefers, physical and extreme). Herzog himself in an interview put walking and spirituality together: 'I had a dramatic religious phase at the age of fourteen and converted to Catholicism … Also at the age of fourteen I started to travel on foot for the first time' (in Cronin 2002: 10). Walking and spirituality come together overtly in some of Herzog's films, for instance in *Wheel of Time* and *Pilgrimage*, but also *Invincible* (2001), in which strongman Zishe, a simple Jewish blacksmith, walks on foot the distance between his Eastern Polish village and Berlin, where he discovers his mission of being the new Samson in defence of his people against the raising threat of Nazism.

Herzog's vast filmography is made up of 52 titles to date; they can be categorised as features and documentaries, but the distinction is problematic, because his approach to authentic materials is not canonical and often stylised, and because many of his features present documentary-like – some say anthropological – aspects. The director himself dislikes the distinction: 'For me, they are all just films' (in Cronin 2002: 95). The great majority of them, we claim, constitute a form of travel in themselves, but in this chapter we will primarily concentrate on the films that are model samples of 'travel cinema', and for our purposes we will make no distinctions between fictions and documentaries.

From this body of films many themes emerge, which engage with different forms of travel and the ways in which they have been represented in art and culture. These include the pilgrimage (*Wheel of Time*; *Pilgrimage*); the colonial conquest and the journeys of the slave traders (*Fitzcarraldo* (1982); *Aguirre, der Zorn Gottes* (*Aguirre: The Wrath of God*, 1972), *Cobra Verde* (1987)); emigration (*Stroszek*); nomadism (*Wodaabe – Die Hirten der Sonne. Nomaden am Südrand der Sahara* (*Wodaabe: Herdsmen of the Sun*, 1989)); the pursuit of knowledge and memory (*Echos aus einem düstern Reich* (*Echoes from a Sombre Empire*, 1990));

escape and survival (*Little Dieter Needs to Fly* (1997); *Wings of Hope* (2001)); the 'going into the world' (*Invincible*); and extreme mountain climbing (*Gasherbrum – Der leuchtende Berg* (*The Dark Glow of the Mountains*, 1984); *Cerro Torre: Schrei aus Stein* (*Scream of Stone*, 1991)). Some of the cultural and philosophical concepts associated with these journeys are the sublime; orientalism; exploration; and adventuring. We will discuss most of these categories and perceptions of travel in this chapter, which we chose to structure according to the setting or destination of the protagonists' trips. The three places that most frequently resurface in Herzog's filmography, and which seem to us to constitute the true *loci* of Herzog's discourse on travel, are the mountain, the jungle and the desert.

It must be immediately noted that these locations, in the company of a few others, such as the sea, ice and the steppe, are among the key sites of the aesthetic sublime, and thus are prerequisites for the imperialist imaginary. They belong to that array of images that are inseparable from the orientalist tropes circulating in modernity, and their representation in Western art can hardly ever be considered as 'innocent'.[4] Indeed, several of Herzog's films deal with colonialism directly or indirectly – not surprisingly, numerous critics have discussed Herzog's work precisely in terms of colonialism and Romanticism.

The much-debated question of Herzog's Romanticism, which is particularly important for us in terms of his discourse on nature, is very complex both because the definition of the Romantics' attitude to nature is greatly complicated by the magnitude of their body of work and by the several national and personal variants of Romanticism; and because Herzog's *oeuvre* is itself copious and multiform, and thus not reducible to simple formulas. Several critics, analysing his most famous fiction films but also their much-debated production contexts, consider him as irredeemably belonging to the Romantic tradition, and/or as a neo-colonialist without respect for local environments and populations;[5] at times, they even trace Nazi overtones in his work.[6] We align ourselves with the critics who, conversely, rescued Herzog from these simplifications, for instance Brad Prager, who suggested that he does recuperate and play with romantic questions, but as part of 'a larger tapestry' (2003: 24). Prager convincingly shows how the director introduces ambiguity in his treatment of romantic tropes, and that the typical romantic image of the anthropomorphised landscape mirroring the character's or the artist's soul transforms in his films into the articulation of the vacuity of the subject itself: in Herzog, according to Prager, 'there is no "soul" for the landscape to mirror' (2003: 32).

In very general terms Romanticism is associated with a naïve longing for communion with nature. In an epoch in which the industrial revolution started to destroy large sections of European woodland and create an unprecedented artificiality in the landscape, people began to travel much more and to develop the myth of exotic lands and of nature in general. The Romantics' representation of the exotic and of nature was amply aestheticised. Nature was seen as a series of awesome views, to be enjoyed and pondered; sensitivity to nature was cultivated, and it was felt that to 'commune with nature' was morally improving. In German Romanticism, nature was often spiritualised, and even provided with a voice, as in the poetry of Novalis (1772–1801). The Romantics considered foreign countries as more colourful and sensual than their own; their vision of the exotic was often conditioned by the flourishing European colonialism, and their representation of the 'natives' and of distant lands was frequently stereotypical. Although Herzog is attracted to exotic landscapes and natural sights, and often engages with the representation of native populations and of colonialism, we feel that at least in a large part of his *oeuvre*, and certainly in the films that we will analyse below, he does not aestheticise nature, quite the reverse.

More specifically, the director has often been called an heir to the Romantics on account of the 'sublimity' of his sights, of what he calls 'ecstatic images' of nature. Superficially, these resemble Kant's 'dynamic sublime' (see Kant 1987). For Kant, the feeling of the sublime is provoked by a frightening nature, the observation of which initially suggests the subjection and vulnerability of humankind, but subsequently induces feelings of superiority or transcendence over nature itself. This process is induced by the observation of fearsome natural objects – massive rocks and mountain ranges, terrible tempests over the ocean, great waterfalls – but from a safe distance, so that we are not paralysed by fear, yet we intuit the danger. For Kant we experience the sublime also when we simply fantasise about measuring up against the omnipotence of nature. The first of these two processes could apply to the spectator of some of Herzog's films, who might experience the sublime by looking at frightening images of nature from his/her safe distance/proximity, this side of the screen. Obviously, this would be a vicarious experience to that of the director, who looks at the spectacle of nature from behind the camera – while being safe but close to the danger. The second experience of the Kantian sublime could instead apply to some of Herzog's characters, who sense and respect the might of nature, but fantasise of measuring up to it – it suffices to think of Aguirre who, as he states at the beginning of the narrative, is aware that the river will bring him to his death, and yet proclaims his supremacy on nature ('I am the Wrath of God … the earth I walk upon sees me and trembles'). Herzog's position on this second type of sublime and on the sense of superhuman greatness felt by some of his characters is one of understanding but also of condemnation, as testified by the failure of his travellers to reach their objectives, and sometimes by their death. For Herzog, human beings are not romantically larger or more powerful than nature;

as he said of Aguirre, 'he dares to defy nature to such an extent that nature inevitably takes its revenge on him' (in Cronin 2002: 79). This belief brings Herzog to an ironic position: the sublime is in his characters' eyes, so to speak; nature itself is impassive, is not for humans. This ironic position frequently finds expression in a final movement of the camera, which detaches from the protagonist and looks at him from above, dwarfing him in the landscape, and encircling him in a spiral movement, on which more below.

As regards the first type of Kantian 'dynamic sublime', we doubt that the director intends to propose naïve images of the greatness and frightfulness of nature for his spectators to observe with awe and wonder – as many critics implied by defining him a heir to Romanticism. In Herzog's direction there is no romantic striving for a mystic communion with Nature or Absolute Spirit (although there can be in his characters). Herzog's 'ecstatic images' are not melancholic and do not induce the audience to collectively share the 'nostalgia for the unattainable', as Jean-François Lyotard put it (1984: 81). We claim that this can be seen in the fact that nature is never beautiful or nostalgic in his films; it suffices to think of the rotting jungle in *Aguirre: The Wrath of God*, or the desert full of the debris of 'culture' in *Fata Morgana* (1971). The latter film, as discussed below, clearly shows that for Herzog there never existed a paradisiacal time of communion between Man and Nature. Such a mythical epoch (and the human nostalgia for it) is indeed a subject of ruthless irony in *Fata Morgana*.

Not only is nature hardly ever pleasant in his films, his most accomplished 'ecstatic images' are much more than a mere contemplation of the fearfulness of nature. They are staged, constructed images, whose dreamy quality is obtained by the framing, the choice of point of view, the camera movement and the editing, as well as by the sound and music. We share Alan Singer's view that irony is the essential aspect of Herzog's sublime, and that 'Herzog's mystic worlds finally always reveal the conditions of their viewing as their most oracular truth' (1986: 184), a concept to which we will return below. The director is very aware of the artificiality of this operation; famously, Herzog maintains that he 'directs' landscapes:

> I like to direct landscapes just as I like to direct actors and animals. People think I am joking, but it is true. Often I try to introduce into a landscape a certain atmosphere, using sound and vision to give it a definite character … Landscapes always adapt themselves to the situations required of them (in Cronin 2002: 81–2).

This is not to say that realism is not there – indeed, Herzog's shoots, as we have seen, exclusively in real settings. Interestingly, it is here that Herzog's sublime shows its postmodern rather than Romantic (nostalgic) character. By manipulating real landscapes or, in other words, by producing highly 'cinematic' ecstatic images of real settings, Herzog shatters realism and naturalistic belief, and – to borrow Lyotard's words on postmodern art – discovers the 'lack of reality of reality, together with the invention of other realities' (1984: 38). Herzog's cinema invents utopian or dystopian landscapes while, to use again Lyotard's words, denying itself

Fig. 9 Werner Herzog's *Fata Morgana* (Germany, 1971) © Werner Herzog Film

'the solace of good forms' – the consolation of a beautiful nature (and of a beautiful image) to gaze at. Furthermore, Herzog always shows that such landscapes are the result of the constructed nature of cinematic perception – a trait that links him to Lyotard's avant-garde. A perfect example of this operation is, once again, *Fata Morgana*, a film which proposes a hallucinatory vision of the real world, but always explicitly as the fruit of cinematic perception.

The vertical ascent: *Scream of Stone* and *The Dark Glow of the Mountains*

> I absolutely loathe adventurers, and I particularly hate this old pseudo-adventurism where the mountain climb becomes about confronting the extremes of humanity. I had some arguments with Messner about this. For a while he stylised his media persona on the concept of 'The Great Adventurer' and would make pronouncements that he was some kind of vicarious adventurer for the public. Me, I am waiting for the ridiculous act of the first one barefoot on Mount Everest. (Herzog, in Cronin 2002: 199)

As is well known, mountain ranges are among the most sublime landscapes for the Romantics, who described them with awe and wonder (see, for instance, Nicolson 1997). Thus, Herzog's interest in mountains is a catalyst for critical suspicions, particularly because several critics have pointed to the fact that Herzog's *Scream of Stone* is a film in the tradition of the German *Bergfilm* or 'mountain film', which flourished in the 1920s and 1930s, combined 'excessive melodrama, patriotism and death-defying mountain-top heroism' (Cronin 2002: 236), and was often invested of nationalist overtones. Herzog's feature presents neither excessive melodrama nor patriotism, but certainly a good dose of what could be defined as death-defying mountain-top (anti-)heroism.

Mountains are the principal setting of several films by Herzog - the 'documentaries' *Die Große Ekstase des Bildschnitzers Steiner* (*The Great Ecstasy of Woodcarver Steiner*, 1973), devoted to ski-jumping; *La Soufrière – Warten auf eine unausweichliche Katastrophe* (1977), on the announced explosion of a Caribbean volcano; *The Dark Glow of the Mountains*, on Reinhold Messner, shot in the Himalayan mountains; and the feature *Scream of Stone*, set in Peru. They also have important roles in other films, including *Aguirre: The Wrath of God*, which opens with the Spanish adventurers climbing down the slope of a mountain near Machu Picchu; *Herz aus Glas* (*Heart of Glass*, 1976), whose final sequence was filmed on Skelling Rock, in Ireland; *Fitzcarraldo*, whose protagonist notoriously pulls a boat up a mountain in the jungle; and the documentary *Wheel of Time*, which includes shots of the holy Mount Kailash, in Tibet.

Herzog's interviews describing the mountains in his films seem to indicate that he shares a Romantic idea of the sublime. For instance, Edmund Burke (1987) associated the feeling of the sublime elicited by mountains with fear of death, dismemberment, terror and darkness. Herzog says of the mountain featuring in *Scream of Stone*: 'Cerro Torre is the most dangerous, the most difficult and ecstatic mountain on Earth. There really is nothing like it anywhere. It is more a symbolic image of deadly fear than a mere mountain' (in Cronin 2002: 224). Mountains in his cinema generally have one of two connotations: either they are seen by characters as 'images of deadly fear', in line with the Romantic sublime; or as the sites of religious devotion and the presence of God, something that, again, could relate to the awe-inspiring Creator behind Romantic accounts of sublimity. For example, it is easy to see how the volcano in *La Soufrière*, spitting venomous gases and about to explode, is an image of fear for the filmmakers themselves, who are the only people left on the island (except some locals who show no fear of the volcano). Also the Alps in *The Great Ecstasy of Woodcarver Steiner* are seen in the light of the fear of death connected to ski-jumping, a feeling that is thoroughly discussed by the protagonist Steiner, although the film puts no (romantic) emphasis on the mountains themselves. The sense of sacredness attached to mountains emerges instead in some sequences of *Wheel of Time* and *The Dark Glow of the Mountains*.

Chloe Chard has shown how, in most eighteenth-century accounts, mountains are seen as geographical as well as symbolic boundaries – in particular, the Alps are seen as the border between the familiar (civilised) world and one in which 'the limits established by behavioural and moral rules are more easily disregarded than within the familiar' (1996: 125). In Herzog, mountains are never seen as symbolic boundaries exciting moral and behavioural transgression. Yet they can be seen as sublime in the Kantian sense, when they become the targets of a subjective gaze that transforms them into ecstatic images – such images are highly stylised moments of 'truth' in which, in Herzog's words, 'all the drama, passion and human pathos become visible' (in Cronin 2002: 93). At times, the vision is attached to a character who looks at the mountain (as happens more than once in *Scream of Stone*); other times it seems to derive directly from the camera, thus functioning as a sort of commentary on the characters' feelings (think of the final sequences of *La Soufrière* and *The Dark Glow of the Mountains*). These ecstatic images are the visualisation of human feelings – they are, in Herzog's words, inner landscapes, expressing either fear or reverence, or both.

It is necessary to distinguish Herzog's treatment of mountains in his films and the feelings of his characters when confronted with them. Whereas humans project their fears or spirituality on them, mountains as represented by Herzog's camera do not promote the idea of a Romantic unified, absolute subject; rather they reveal a rupture between nature and humankind. They are more often seen, in both narrative and visual terms, as a passive, even unpleasant natural scenario, as a raw physical presence which resists interpretation as well as assault. At times, they seem to possess their own 'spirit', which is nevertheless indifferent to humans. Westerners mainly use them as the setting of extreme travelling and physical activity. The very act of climbing up the mountain (or coming down from it, as is the case of Steiner) is the purpose itself of their journeys, which are extreme for different reasons: because the ramp of the ski-jumping is too fast (*The Great Ecstasy of Woodcarver Steiner*); because the mountain is about to explode (*La Soufrière*); because it is incredibly steep and swept by impossible weather (*Scream of Stone*); or because one is pushing a boat up the slope (*Fitzcarraldo*). The ambiguity of Herzog's position is that he admires the mountain climber for his insane determination and courage, but also exposes the futility and even ambiguous nature of his efforts. Alan Singer (1986) and Brad Prager (2003) have thoroughly explored this ambiguity in connection with two of his mountain films: *The Great Ecstasy of Woodcarver Steiner* and *Scream of Stone*. They have shown how Herzog reflects on both the supposed heroism of his protagonists and on the positioning of the camera as complicit in that heroism. We intend to reinforce their arguments through a study of the idea of travel constructed in *Scream of Stone* and *The Dark Glow of the Mountains*.

Scream of Stone opens at the world championship of indoor rock climbing, where journalist Ivan provokes a dispute between the winner Martin and eminent mountain climber Roccia (Vittorio Mezzogiorno). Roccia calls Martin an 'acrobat' and does not believe he could succeed in real mountaineering; Martin accepts the challenge to climb one of the most difficult peaks in the world, Patagonia's Cerro Torre. The expedition, which is also formed by Ivan, by Hans, Roccia's climbing partner, and by Katharina, his secretary and girlfriend, is stalled by Roccia who insists on waiting for favourable weather conditions. The group tries to kill time, only visited by a madman, 'Fingerless', a fan of Mae West, who claims he reached the peak and left four fingers on the mountain. While Roccia and Ivan go to acquire more provisions, Martin and Hans attempt the climb; Hans falls and dies, while Martin makes it back, claiming he reached the top. Frustrated Roccia decides to remain in Patagonia, and buys a hut at the base of Cerro Torre. Back in Munich, Martin develops a relationship with Katharina and enjoys for some time the fruits of his (dubious) success. Eventually, suspicious climbers challenge him on TV, and Martin accepts to scale Cerro Torre again, this time with a camera filming him. Ivan gets him a contract with an American producer, and everybody returns to Patagonia. With the cameras out of action because of serious weather conditions, Martin and Roccia attempt to climb the peak from two different sides.

Almost at the top, Martin falls and dies, while Roccia makes it, only to discover that Fingerless had already left his 'signature' on the peak.

Although partially disowned by Herzog for being his only film for which he did not write the script, *Scream of Stone* not only is not incompatible with the director's poetics, but also it is so self-reflexive that it functions as an interesting commentary on his *oeuvre* in general. Prager rightly notices how Herzog in this film curiously identifies with unscrupulous Ivan. Herzog, in fact, appears in the first sequence as the director of the television broadcasting of the competition, and when he disappears he is supplanted by Ivan. Prager contrasts this 'self-debasing' identification with 'the extra-textual synthesis of Herzog and Fitzcarraldo in which the combination afforded the director a measure of aggrandisement' (2003: 30). We go even farther and suggest that *Scream of Stone* is one of the most self-referential films by Herzog. The most obvious instance is the satire of televisual and cinematic production carried out through the stereotypical figures of the New York producer and the blonde 'personal secretary', Carla.[7] Yet the two most important self-reflexive moments are the sequence in which Ivan explains where the cameras should be placed on Cerro Torre in order to capture the best view of Martin's ascent; and when he directs the cameras on Cerro Torre itself. On both occasions, Ivan talks very much like the on-screen Herzog. Looking at the fake mountain slope of the indoor competition, Herzog asked his cameramen for certain shots and exclaimed: 'This is exactly what I need.' Looking at a paper-pulp model of Cerro Torre, Ivan similarly suggests: 'We need a camera here, there, here and here.' Both directors orchestrate a cinematic vision of a fake mountain, shot in a way that will make the audience feel (as Ivan suggests) 'as if they are climbing that mountain too' – and, we add, as if that mountain was 'spectacularly real'. Herzog here clearly reflects on the relationship between the artificiality of his cinema and the reality of its settings. He is famous for shooting in 'real landscapes' – but here he makes it clear that a real mountain is never to be seen in *Scream of Stone*, because all visions of it are mediated by the camera and are constructed through the choice of camera angle and the montage of image, sound and music. Ivan and the on-screen Herzog, in fact, mimic the off-screen Herzog, who claims to 'direct landscapes'; in other words, this is a strong and ironic reminder that what we are watching is a (Herzog) film of a mountain, and not a real mountain. This is stated again, but by purely visual means, in another self-reflexive sequence: during a longish 'ecstatic' shot of turbulent weather on Cerro Torre, the snow and mist hit the camera lens, clearly highlighting its presence. Also, we believe it is not by chance that the first climber to reach the top of Cerro Torre, Fingerless, is a fan of Hollywood cinema and of one of its most popular stars: 'his success makes a mockery of Roccia's accomplishment insofar as it is ultimately this Hollywood fanatic by whom he is bested' (Prager 2003: 31). Fingerless is also the antithesis, and therefore a mockery, of Herzog's typical 'visionary' hero – the 'holy madman' and seer who believes in his dreams, no matter how crazy, and because of his faith is somehow redeemed of his folly. Fingerless is not redeemed by his faith – his obsession with Mae West is futile and pathetic.[8] The true 'holy madman' should be the protagonist, Roccia; he does talk about a visionary dream – a train in flames going through a mountain range – but this is possibly the least remarkable dream that a Herzog character ever had (and, interestingly and unusually, Herzog chooses not to visualise it). Secondly, he is definitely not a seer. He states that if he believed that Martin truly reached the top he would leave Patagonia immediately; in the case of Martin he is right, but he fails to 'see' that Fingerless did reach the top, probably blinded by his own self-importance and ambition. The film's only Herzogian 'holy fool' is the old Indian woman who lives in the hut; she certainly is a seer – as is suggested by an eye-line match that ties her prophetic words 'the dead are coming back' with an image of Hans and Martin walking on Cerro Torre. Yet we suggest that her character is also strongly metafictional, for two reasons: because she is played by an icon of the spectacle, Mexican singer and actress Chavela Vargas; and because of her mystifying statement: 'They pay me to take me away in their pictures. Sometimes I ask myself, where do they get their money?' For Prager, this is a comment on tourism; we suggest it is a comment both on (neo)colonialism and on Herzog's cinema. The theme of colonialism had already been introduced in the film through the character of the owner of the hut bought by Roccia, whose grandparents came from South Wales in 1902. More interestingly, the old woman talks about being paid to be 'taken away in pictures', a reference not only to post-colonial tourism, but also specifically to Herzog's travel cinema as postcolonial tourism. Such self-irony is all the more abrasive against the backdrop of Herzog's aversion to 'tourism',[9] and of the whole history of accusations of neo-colonialism that have been made against him by the press as well as by several scholars. Therefore, Herzog is here extremely self-critical of both on-screen and off-screen components of his cinema. Such an attitude is particularly interesting, because it delivers critical insights in his 'travel discourse' and his treatment of mountains and hikers.

Despite his blindness, ambition and self-centredness, Roccia is ultimately more successful than Martin – the latter dies, while Roccia makes it to the top (if only to discover Fingerless' ice axe with Mae West's picture). We suggest that Roccia's partial success is due to the fact that he is constructed by the film as a walker – and we have already discussed the merits of 'intense walking' for Herzog. Martin's approach to mountaineering is, although it might sound paradoxical, sedentary. His indoor climbing resembles 'chamber mountaineering' and does not involve any travelling or walking. When the expedition is stationing at the base of Cerro Torre, Roccia is often seen walking and running to keep fit, whereas Martin is mainly seen sitting down, often playing chess. The chess metaphor suggests his static, intellectual approach to mountain climbing. Roccia, conversely, is characterised as more intuitive and physical, and as a walker – not only when he jogs, but also when he goes to acquire food for the expedition. After Hans' death, Roccia remains in Patagonia, a period that again links him visually with walkers and hermits (as Ivan himself remarks). He does not have a jeep parked outside the house, but a horse. When Ivan comes to see him, he brings him a copy of a Bruce Chatwin's *In Patagonia* – Roccia and the famous author/walker are thus deliberately associated.[10] Most significantly, when the competition between Martin and Roccia resumes and the two climbers start their ascent of the mountain, Martin is shown by the camera as already *in situ*, ready to start climbing, whereas Roccia is seen approaching the mountain from a distance, purposefully walking towards Cerro Torre in the middle of the snow.

The film, however, disowns Roccia, because his ambition is not 'pure' and selfless. He claims he wants to protect the integrity of mountain climbing against the 'acrobacy' of the new sport, and accuses Ivan to wanting to reduce climbing to a competition, but this is precisely what he does in the final sequences of the film – he climbs Cerro Torre against Martin and in competition with him, pushing him to his death (and himself to humiliation). Herzog condemns Roccia's climb because it is done for the wrong motivations – he does not climb for the pleasure of it, but to outdo others (whom he despises), as well as to achieve revenge for having been defeated both in sport and in sentimental matters.

The misdirection of Roccia's motivations can be seen *vis-à-vis* those of famous climber Reinhold Messner as portrayed in *The Dark Glow of the Mountains*. This comparison is authorised by the fact that the documentary was meant to function as a rehearsal for the fiction film, and that *Scream of Stone* is based on an idea by Messner himself. In the documentary, Messner is not in direct competition against other climbers (although indirectly he is, given that he finds pride in being the first to traverse two 8,000-meter mountains, Gasherbrum 1 and 2, in the same expedition). Not only is he not in competition, he is with another climber, Kammerlander, whom he clearly esteems, and talks of other climbers with solidarity and admiration. Nevertheless, Herzog is also critical of Reinhold Messner. The character emerges as deeply ambiguous, and so do his motivations. Messner spontaneously uses words such as 'addiction', 'obsessive' and 'morbid'; but when asked by Herzog whether he climbs because of a death wish, he denies this and naïvely states that he never had the desire to kill himself while walking up a mountain. Yet when discussing the expedition on the same Nanga Parabat in which his brother lost his life, he asserts 'I myself died in that expedition' and 'my life began anew after that tragedy'.

Consciously or subconsciously Messner identifies several motivations for extreme mountain climbing: self-annihilation and expiation; an addiction reflecting the corruption of society (because only members of advanced, degenerate cultures practice mountain climbing); the desire to leave a trace, prove oneself and express one's creativity. There are at least two types of masculinity that emerge from his words: one is a man weary of Western culture, who wishes to purge himself of his sins and those of his society, in a masochistic urge of self-annihilation and purification; the other is a man who is extremely conscious of his exceptionality (which he identifies with nerves, strength, endurance, an intuitive knowledge of the forces of nature, and a madness akin to that of artists and creative people). Herzog shows how these two images of Western masculinity merge in a being who proposes himself as a redeemer of the mediocrity of the masses and as a mass-mediatic neo-Romantic hero. While not being fully aware of his most obscure side, Messner is able to sense the complexity and contradictions of his motivations, and is aware that he came to embody a symbol of exceptionality in the eyes of the audience, who expect him to push the limits and risk death at every expedition – very similarly to ski-jumper Walter Steiner. In the film Herzog cruelly works towards stripping Messner of his superhuman greatness and self-esteem, as when he provokes his tears by questioning him about his brother's death, or when he films him bathing naked after the climb, and keeps asking him 'what was the point of this?' Visually, the film fully avoids the celebration of Messner's 'conquest' of the peaks – Herzog remains in the camp, and the few images of the ascent come from Messner's and Kammerlander's digital camera. The images are few and extraordinarily banal; we are given no panoramic shot from the peaks.

Messner represents a Western, postcolonial traveller/adventurer who exploits not the richness of newfound lands, but the exoticism of extreme and faraway locations in order to construct a mass-mediatic, self-conscious neo-Romantic myth. Herzog is fully aware of his potential complicity in the construction of such myth, and constantly highlights the presence of the camera and the practical details of filmmaking in order to stress that his portrayal of Messner is mediated rather than natural. The director also shows us the representatives of a different culture, Tibetans from 'the last village reached by a road', who walk to the mountain with Messner for much more basic needs – to earn money carrying his provisions. Whereas Messner talks of his own prowess and exceptionality, the Tibetan porters with their presence not only highlight his position as a neo-colonialist explorer in the age of mass media, but also offer a different view of mountain climbing. Herzog shows their tentative steps on the side of the crumbling mountain, under the weight of the provisions they carry; he comments that they are 'fearful of what has to come' and films them praying and dancing to the divinity that they sense in the mountain. The contrast is revealing, and is evocative of Herzog's final voice-over comment in *La Soufrière*: 'It is not the volcano that stays with me, but the neglected oblivion in which those black people lived.'

We suggest that there are two ways of going up a mountain for Herzog: one belongs to devout people from 'less developed' societies, who go to the mountain in pilgrimage (*Wheel of Time*) or for practical reasons (*The Dark Glow of the Mountains*). They revere and respect the mountain as a holy site, where the presence of God is felt. In the case of the pilgrims, their walking to the mountain and then up the slopes is all that matters – it is the meaning itself of the journey. The objective of their pilgrimage is twofold: to repent and be purified from sins; and to see and touch the holy place. Their way of ascending is by walking first towards the mountain, even from faraway locations, then up, going around in spiralling motion. The ascent of Messner's porters, although not done in pilgrimage, is equally careful and respectful, and associated to religious rites.

The second way is that of Western sportsmen and media stars who go up the mountain for ambition: Steiner, Roccia and Martin, Messner and his partner. It is well known that Herzog often explained the drive of the protagonists of *The Great Ecstasy of Woodcarver Steiner* and *Fitzcarraldo* with the same desire to defy gravity (see Cronin 2002: 96 and 188). The story of the friendship between young Steiner and a crow has also been discussed in terms of his desire to ascend and fly, as well as of the obscure side of Steiner's personality (see Prager 2003). Also Roccia in *Scream of Stone* has a meeting with a bird and the significance of the moment is highlighted by Herzog with emphatic music that speaks of the climber's identification with the falcon. Going up a perfectly perpendicular wall of stone reveals the same desire to defy gravity and fly. There is an idea of verticality associated to mountains in these films – going up straight (or coming down straight, as in the case of Steiner), in a way that is somehow inhuman. This inhumanity is exposed by the tragic outcome of some of the expeditions, as well as by the anti-climax of most of these films' endings: once the protagonist is on top of the mountain, he is confronted by the vacuity and absurdity of his accomplishment. What next?; after going up one can only come down, or even fall down. The spiralling camera that accompanies some of the endings mimics the idea of vertigo and a plunge into the abyss – like the recurring spiralling shot of Martin's fall from Cerro Torre in *Scream of Stone*.

The distinction between the two types of mountain climbers is not absolute. The Western mountaineers, Herzog suggests, aspire to be somehow like the native devout climbers (or the way they perceive them); they portray themselves as hermits or seers, in contact with nature, more similar to birds than to humans. Although acknowledging the exceptionality of their will, their ability and endurance, Herzog strips off their motivations and reveals their virile, neo-colonialist ambitions of conquest and primacy, as well as their skilful exploitation of the media in the construction of an image of neo-Romantic heroes. In this, Herzog also reflects on the dangers run by his cinema on mountain climbing of becoming postcolonial tourism and myth-making.

Ultimately, Herzog condemns the approach of European climbers. Their 'vertical ascents' are amply dictated by ambition. That which partially saves them is the walking component of their activity. This is clearly demonstrated not only by the success of Roccia over Martin which, as we have claimed, is due to his walking abilities; it can be seen with particular clarity in the finale of *The Dark Glow of the Mountains*, in which Messner describes his dream of walking until the end of the world: 'I just keep walking for decades, maybe for ever, without looking back or ahead, with no destination. I keep walking until the world just stops.' In this walk, 'the climbing part does not matter anymore, what counts is just to keep going and going and going'. Herzog suggests that he has exactly the same dream.

If the 'climbing part' is tied to the ambition of the vertical ascent, the walking reveals its component of horizontal and progressive self-annihilation – the walker travels with few possessions, and neither looks back, progressively detaching from people and things, nor looks ahead, planning or dreaming about the future. This hermitic condition is perhaps the expression of spirituality without religion, which seems to come from a disappointment with and rejection of the neo-capitalist present and the colonial past of Western society. Yet the impossibility of this dream and of ever attaining innocence for Western European travellers is revealed by some details of their imagined journey: Messner would like to be accompanied by 'pack animals and a few porters', the symbols of colonialist adventuring, and Herzog by a dog (a Husky) and two leather saddle bags, emblems of lonesome frontier conquest. The innocent primitivism aspired to by Western European walkers is only a chimera.

Going around in circles: *Little Dieter Needs to Fly* and *Wings of Hope*

> For me, jungles have always represented something as an intensified form of reality, though they are really not particularly difficult challenges. A jungle is just another forest, that is all. It is the myth of the travel agencies that they are dangerous places, full of hazards. (Herzog, in Cronin 2002: 86)

The meanings attached to the forest and the jungle in the history of Western culture have been multiple, although the most frequent association is probably with primitivism, with the opposite of society and civilisation. As Lutz P. Koepnick recalls, in a myth told by Gianbattista Vico in *New Science* (1744), the forest is the place where civilisation began, in a clearing in which a group of giants took residence – thus 'the origin of Western civilisation lies in the attempt to draw boundaries between the space of human dwelling and the forest' (1993: 134). The forest has also been construed as a space that lies beyond the law, particularly in the Middle Ages: 'the law of identity and the principle of non-contradiction go astray in the forests … The straight line becomes a circle. Or the law of gender is confused. Be it religious, political, psychological, or even logical law, the forests, it seems, un-settle its stability' (Harrison 1992: 63). Koepnick also recalls the portrayal of the forest offered by René Descartes, who 'compared the workings of scientific reason with a straight walk through a dense forest' (1993: 150). The forest offers to Des-cartes 'a fertile training ground to prove and exhibit the full capacities of scientific reason and human determination over nature' (1993: 151), and accompanies the emergence of the science of forestry, 'inaugurated in Germany in the latter half of the eighteenth century and built around the figure of the forest geometrist and his mathematical approaches to straighten out the diversity, randomness and irregu-larity of natural forests' (ibid.). As the above Herzog quote reminds us, the jungle has also been and continues to be constructed as a site full of deadly hazards in narratives, in films, and in the Western tourist industry.

Herzog's two most famous films set in the Amazon jungle are *Fitzcarraldo* and *Aguirre: The Wrath of God*. Most of the existing literature on Herzog's cinema, in fact, concentrates on these films, which are in all probability his two most famous. Some critics have focused on their much-publicised production contexts,[11] some-times putting forward very harsh allegations of neo-colonialism: 'Having already made *Aguirre: The Wrath of God* in the Amazon … Herzog returned, determined to force his way in and carve out his dream's vision, and stealing thousands of Indian souls in the process' (Davis & Jenkins 1985: 8). Other critics have con-centrated on the texts. John E. Davidson, for instance, has claimed: 'Despite its nominal critique of European colonising projects, the notion of culture at work in *Fitzcarraldo* advances a neo-colonialist logic. While composing his admittedly striking images for cinematic culture, Herzog re-maps the land, captures the beau-ty of nature on film, and exploits the native people' (1994: 69; see also Davidson 1993). The analysis of the jungle in Herzog's films proposed by Koepnick is more subtle. The author demonstrates how these films' accounts of colonialist sylvan politics evolve from *Aguirre: The Wrath of God*, which focuses on 'colonialism's struggle with its own invention of South America as mere nature' (1993: 139), to *Fitzcarraldo*, whose protagonist 'enters the Peruvian rain forest as a direct descen-dant of German eighteenth-century foresters and their scientific methods' (1993:

152). Overall, Koepnick suggests that the jungle in Herzog is 'a text that frustrates all hermeneutic efforts from the outset; with course brutality, the chaotic diversity of the rain forest exposes the systematic inappropriateness of Western routines of cognition and ordering' (1993: 135).

Here, we are particularly interested in the depiction of the journey through the jungle, rather than in the representation of the rain forest itself. Instead of delving once again into the much debated question of Herzog's relationship with colonialism in his two most famous jungle films, we prefer to tackle a different, and neglected, topic: the journey of survival through the jungle. Our analysis will focus on two 'documentaries', *Little Dieter Needs to Fly* and *Wings of Hope*.

In *Little Dieter Needs to Fly* and *Wings of Hope* the jungle, respectively of Vietnam and Peru, is the difficult environment that the unlucky protagonists have to traverse in order to escape death and make a return to civilisation. The protagonist of the first film is Dieter Dengler, a German-born pilot whose plane came crashing down into the Laotian jungle forty minutes into his first mission in Vietnam. Captured by guerrillas and handed over to the Viet Cong, Dengler endured severe torture before his escape into the jungle and finally to freedom six months later. The protagonist of *Wings of Hope*, Juliane Koepke, was the seventeen-year-old daughter of two German biologists working in an ecological site in the Peruvian jungle, when her airplane crashed in 1971, killing her mother together with ninety other passengers. Juliane was the only survivor of the disaster, and miraculously emerged from the jungle twelve days later.

In both films a German-born person is confronted with the jungle and with a dangerous journey of survival through it, thus these films' gaze on the jungle is European, precisely as in *Fitzcarraldo* and *Aguirre: The Wrath of God*. Nevertheless, the contemporary setting means that European colonialism no longer is the immediate topic. *Little Dieter Needs to Fly* has to do – through flashbacks – with American imperialism, with the Second World War and Germany's Nazi past; *Wings of Hope* is more detached from history and politics, although the presence of Juliane in the jungle and her dealings with the local populations have colonial reverberations and echoes of both Tarzan and Robinson Crusoe. Despite the inevitable historical and cultural connections, though, we claim that these two films are eminently self-reflexive and that their main theme, especially in *Little Dieter Needs to Fly*, is the role of the jungle and of the journey of escape not in Western culture as a whole, but more modestly in fiction cinema, and in Herzog's cinema in particular.

Narratives of survival can be either set in a single location, in which the protagonist is stuck (as in Robinson Crusoe), or entail a dangerous journey; often, the two possibilities coexist, as in the recent *Cast Away* (Robert Zemeckis, 2000).

When it is built around a journey, the narrative of survival employs the mechanisms of suspense and surprise afforded by the trip, and encourages a strong identification between spectator and protagonist. Rather unusually, in Herzog's two films the events are not narrated directly, as in a fiction dramatising the protagonist's adventures, or in a traditional documentary alternating interviews with the survivor and re-enactments of the events, played by actors. In these films, in fact, the protagonists go back with Herzog and his crew to the jungle and recount their adventurous escape in the settings in which the real events unfolded. This choice, which can certainly appear bold and excessive in terms of the painful recollections that it caused to the protagonists, was explained by Herzog as follows: 'The German television network wanted me to film re-enactments of the events Dieter was talking about, the kind of stupid thing you can see on television worldwide. I hate this kind of stuff so much and thought it better that Dieter do it all himself' (in Cronin 2002: 167).[12] At the opposite of the fictional re-enactment, which usually tends to produce a sense of naturalism and identification, corroborated by the knowledge that the events truly happened, this form places a greater emphasis on the activity of narration itself, as well as on the staging – many years have gone by and the 'actor' is now middle-aged, thus no naturalism is achieved. Moreover, at times the voices of Dieter and Juliane are replaced by Herzog's voice-over, which narrates the events for them. This attracts attention to the identification between director and protagonists, an identification that Herzog himself suggests during the films. In the case of *Little Dieter Needs to Fly*, both the director and protagonist are Germans who, at the time of filming, resided in Northern California; Herzog also stresses how both himself and Dieter grew up in war-time Germany, where they experienced 'real hunger', a detail that is far from being trivial, given that, for Herzog, it is probably because of his upbringing that Dieter managed to survive the jungle. In the case of *Wings of Hope*, the connection between director and protagonist is revealed by Herzog himself in an early sequence: he also was in the Lima airport on Christmas Eve in 1971, trying to reach the set of *Aguirre: The Wrath of God* out in the jungle, and was scheduled on the plane on which Juliane flew.

The identification between the director and his protagonists is strengthened during the films by the fact that both Dieter and Juliane, while in the jungle, at some stage 'become' a filmmaker and direct some local men, who turn into actors: in *Little Dieter Needs to Fly* they follow Dieter's instructions and play the guerrillas who escort the protagonist through the jungle; in *Wings of Hope* Juliane asks a man accompanying the troupe to lay down in her place and show the position in which she found herself when she came to after the accident. These self-reflexive instances of role reversal not only put the actor in control, but also place emphasis on the idea of staging and of cinematic fiction. *Little Dieter Needs to Fly* is particularly fecund in this sense. An extremely ironic film (starting from its title), it uses an array of heterogeneous materials, including archival footage from Vietnam War air raids and allied World War Two bombings over Germany, reconstructed wartime images, photographs of young Dieter and his family, still and moving images taken after Dieter's escape, sequences from a ludicrous 1967 US military survival training film, as well as images of Dieter in the present, in which Herzog impudently mixes reality and fiction (some sequences, as Herzog himself admitted, are staged, for instance the opening one of the tattoo shop). This assortment of visual materials and discursive registers is coupled with a whimsical use of music in a soundtrack which adopts – often producing stark ironic contrast with the visuals – Belá Bartok, Glenn Miller, Wagner, Dvorak and Bach, as well as 'primitive' world music such as Tuva Singers and Oay Latlyé. This mix breaks the effect of naturalism and realism. Some 'original' footage looks so unreal that one wonders whether it is real or reconstructed; some present-day sequences are clearly scripted by Herzog and staged, like the one of the jellyfish in *Little Dieter Needs to Fly* (and the evidently false ones of Juliane's dreams in *Wings of Hope*).

All these self-reflexive, realism-breaking devices serve at least two purposes: their first aim is to cool down the material, in *Little Dieter Needs to Fly* with decidedly ironic effects, in *Wings of Hope* to ease the human misery caused by the memory of the disaster. In fact, the main difference between *Little Dieter Needs to Fly* and *Wings of Hope* resides in the approach of the director, which is ironic and often critical in the first case, more emotional and personal in the second. This is not only because Herzog was booked on the airplane that crashed and was filming *Aguirre: The Wrath of God* very near to where Juliane was fighting for her life, but also because, as he says at the beginning of the film, he (exactly like Juliane) 'was not out for adventure, war, or self-imposed dangers' – whereas Dieter Dengler clearly was.

The second purpose of the self-reflexive devices is to reinforce the idea that what we are watching is not reality (something quite extraordinary, given that these films are supposedly two documentaries), thus that this is not the jungle, but the jungle as a (Western) cinematic set. In the same way as he referred to the 'mountain film' in *Scream of Stone*, with these films Herzog alludes not only to the important heritage of the forest in German culture, but also to one of early cinema's most popular genres, the so-called 'jungle melodrama':

In turn-of-the-century Nickelodeons weary industrial workers thrilled vicariously to the adventures of intrepid white explorers as seen through intrepid European cameras. Hollywood soon embraced this genre. Over a seventy-year period the studios produced more than 49 Tarzan movies. Later, in the 1950s and 1960s, productions such as *Mogambo* (1953) and *Hatari!* (1961) rediscovered 'the jungle melodrama', this time shot in technicolor and cinemascope on exotic African locations. (Moore 1990)

The fact that Herzog's jungle is a set becomes at times particularly tangible, as in the sequence in which Dieter recalls when a Viet Cong amputated the finger of a villager guilty of stealing his engagement ring. Dieter tells the story while standing next to a local and pointing to his finger and, noticing that the man is a little anxious, he gently reassures him: 'Don't worry, it's just a movie.' The fact that these are cinematic jungles becomes very evident also in *Wings of Hope*, when Herzog inserts some images of *Aguirre: The Wrath of God*'s Spanish expedition down the river and states in voice-over: 'We were fighting our way through the journey as she in the very same days was fighting for her life.' The jungle is an exotic stage on which the battle for survival of a white Westerner is performed and filmed by a Western director for a Western audience.

In both films, Herzog shows excerpts of other films about survival in the jungle: in *Little Dieter Needs to Fly* from a US military training film from the late 1960s; in *Wings of Hope* from a B-movie precisely based on Juliane's experiences. Both excerpts present a highly-fictional and humorously exaggerated version of the survival trip, in which the jungle is seen as an extremely (and unrealistically) dangerous place full of hidden hazards, including an invisible human enemy, thirst, hunger and evidently fake injuries (in the military film); wild and dangerous animals including insects, crocodiles and snakes (in the B-movie). The heroes of these films are remarkably stereotypical: a handsome, well-built, cool and overconfident US soldier; and an impressionable, clueless, scantily-dressed blonde teenage girl. By including this footage, Herzog points to and criticises the way in which the jungle and the journey through it have been represented by so many jungle melodramas (not only Tarzan but also war films, including the *Rambo* cycle), and by the media and tourist industry more in general.

At the opposite of these stereotypical narratives, *Little Dieter Needs to Fly* and *Wings of Hope* show that the jungle is dangerous, but not in a clichéd way. The dangers come from not knowing nature and animals; from being severely wounded; from not having even the most basic gear (shoes, a knife) and food to eat; from being chased by the enemy (in *Little Dieter Needs to Fly*). The main danger, though, is that of the loss of orientation: the jungle is represented as a labyrinth in which it is very easy to lose one's way. Dieter and Juliane do not attempt, as Fitzcarraldo did, to superimpose a map on the jungle (see Koepnick 1993), thus defeating/straightening the thick and impenetrable woodland, as an eighteenth-century forester. Both know that the only hope not to lose one's way in the jungle is to find and follow a stream. This knowledge comes to Juliane from experience; to Dieter from intuition ('I knew water was the only thing that would make me survive'; 'I thought: this is our highway to freedom'), but also from a vision of his father (who had died in the Second World War), standing in a river and pointing him in the right direction. By walking in the middle of or navigating down a watercourse, if this becomes large and deep enough for boats, one will eventually find human beings. Nevertheless, the form of journey afforded by the river through the jungle is not very different from the route through a labyrinth. This is best seen in *Wings of Hope* when the camera lifts in the sky to show the stream that Juliane found and followed for days, revealing its convoluted route though the trees. This stream, Herzog tells us, was too small, and would have never led Juliane to people. Next to it, the camera shows us another river, the right one, so close and yet invisible to Juliane. Thus, the journey through the jungle along a watercourse is portrayed as going around in circles, like travelling in vain. As Robert Pogue Harrison suggested, in the forest 'the straight line becomes a circle' (1992: 63). It is only out of luck and perseverance that, eventually, both Juliane and Dieter met people, and people who were willing to save them.

The 'going around in circles in the jungle' has also been analysed by Dana Benelli in relation to Herzog's *Aguirre: The Wrath of God*. For Benelli, going in circles does not exclusively belong to the jungle, but also to other settings – her analysis also refers to Herzog's *Lebenszeichen* (*Signs of Life*, 1968). Circles in Herzog's films represent for Benelli the repetitiveness associated with civilisation, the 'meaningless passivity' and 'vitiating containment', 'entrapment' and 'madness' of the human condition (1986: 95). In *Aguirre: The Wrath of God*, she notices examples of the figure of the circle: 'A whirlpool strands a raft of men and it is claimed that they are sickened by going in circles. The next morning they are dead. At film's end Gaspar's last journal entry states: "I can write no more, we are going around in circles" in another whirlpool' (1986: 96). For Benelli, it is the civilisation that the Spaniards carry with them through a catalogue of its emblems ('guns, animals, slaves, women, royalty and religion') that weighs them down, making them unable to generate new responses to the unknown environment of the jungle. Aguirre is the one who 'breaks the circle'. For him, 'the river provides release from the fate of failed civilisation' and 'offers resources for willed action' – but, for Benelli, he fails to see that 'its course still remains bounded, contained, within the killing landscape of the jungle. In Herzog's universal scheme society's grip on the individual may be broken, but not nature's' (1986: 98). We have already seen how, for Koepnick – and we agree with this second reading – the problem is not that the river is part of 'the killing landscape of the jungle'; the jungle is not in itself a killing landscape, but a landscape that Aguirre looks at through his colonial gaze, as a Western construction: 'Floating on the open river, yet in fact circling in the dense forest of their imperial visions, they project feelings of fear and terror onto the physiognomy of the jungle' (1993: 141). As always, Herzog's primary interest is that of the point of view, of the perspective through which the characters, the camera and the audience via the camera, look at the world.

Whereas Aguirre and Fitzcarraldo are, more or less tragically, defeated (Aguirre dies and Fitzcarraldo loses his boat), both Dieter and Juliane are successful and survive the jungle. We argue that the main difference between Aguirre and Fitzcarraldo on the one hand, and Dieter and Juliane on the other, lies in their gaze on the jungle, on which more below, rather than in their moral or physical characteristics. For Herzog, in fact, the journey of survival through the jungle requires an exceptional willpower, something that all four characters, fictional and real, have. Aguirre's and Fitzcarraldo's determination is self-evident and notorious. Dieter's willpower is connected by Herzog to his early experiences (including enduring hunger in wartime and having a particularly violent boss when working in Germany in his youth), but also to his outstanding determination, as seen when he immigrated to the US following his dream of becoming a pilot. Juliane for Herzog inherited her own willpower from her father, who immigrated to Brazil following his dream to study the jungle, and who, after the landing, crossed the entire continent on foot. In both cases, Herzog thus puts the journeys of emigration of Dieter himself and of Juliane's father in a very favourable light; it is the endurance built in difficult journeys that becomes useful in the jungle. In other words, in the jungle as on mountains, the inclination and ability to walk 'intensely' is necessary for a successful journey in difficult natural settings.

Another feature that all four characters share is that their presence in the jungle is an act of defiance. Fitzcarraldo in particular defies the laws of nature, with his absurd project of pushing a boat up and over a mountain; also Aguirre is construed as one who rebels to and challenges nature. His identification with the sun and with God has been pointed out by several critics. His project of marrying his own daughter to give birth to the 'purest dynasty on the earth' is certainly a form of rebellion to the primordial laws of human society. Despite Dieter and Juliane ostensibly having little to do with these characters' arrogance, we suggest that their presence in the jungle is also the result of an act of defiance of nature. We have already highlighted how in Herzog's cinema the desire to fly is connected with an insane will to defy gravity, which can be achieved through ski-jumping or extreme mountain climbing (what we have called the 'vertical ascent'). In these two jungle documentaries, Herzog constructs air travel as 'unnatural'. In *Little Dieter Wants to Fly*, the protagonist's desire to fly even from the film's very title is constructed as excessive (childish, irrational), as well as connected to devastating air raids, both on Germany and on Vietnam. In *Wings of Hope*, Herzog addresses the question of the fear of flying (and of falling from the sky), and calls the airplane disaster the 'nightmare of each and every one of us'. Several critics noticed how many films by Herzog include the theme of the fall:

> In the opening of *Aguirre: The Wrath of God* the expedition moves downward out of the fog/clouds. Later Pizarro and Aguirre confer by the river and both refer to the journey ahead as 'downhill' (a direction linked to death/mortality by Aguirre's preceding observation that 'no one can get down that river alive'). (Benelli 1986: 93)

These falls are sometimes represented through spiralling movements of the camera – in *Wings of Hope*, for instance, Juliane describes her own fall from the sky towards the jungle as a spiral, and the camera enacts the movement while she talks. The spiralling plunge is a direct consequence, almost a punishment for the act of defiance, for wanting to defy gravity and fly – or 'vertically ascend', as happens to Martin in *Scream of Stone*.

Given that all four characters seem to share certain features (exceptional determination and willpower, and a tendency to defy natural laws), what truly differentiates them is their gaze on the jungle, their 'sylvan policy'. Earlier we pointed to the fact that, although European colonialism is not the most direct reference of *Little Dieter Needs to Fly* and *Wings of Hope* as it is of *Aguirre: the Wrath of God* and *Fitzcarraldo*, the trips to the jungle of Juliane and, in particular, of Dieter (and, given the identification between Herzog and his protagonists, of the director himself) give rise to questions of neo-colonialism and interference. Dieter's and Juliane's gaze on the jungle is, inevitably, a Western one. Juliane is a distant descendant of German eighteenth-century foresters. She is a scientist, something that Herzog clearly emphasises, for instance to justify her 'emotional detachment'. Yet her sylvan policy is not the one of the forest geometrists adopted by Fitzcarraldo – she lived in the jungle ever since she was a child with her parents, two biologists, in an 'ecological observatory'. Far from being an *enfant sauvage*, a little Tarzan, she was raised to respect and observe the jungle. It was her scientific and empirical knowledge of the jungle that saved her.

Dieter Dengler's case is obviously more ambiguous, but Herzog strengthens his protagonist's credentials by suggesting that he joined the army not for militarism ('I never wanted to go to war', he states) but for his immense desire to fly and for naïvety (seemingly, the fact that there were people who suffered and died only became clear to Dieter when he was held prisoner), and by showing how – in spite of his daunting experiences in the jungle, which he never recalls in sombre or self-pitying tones – he developed a great liking and respect for it, for Vietnam and for its people. Dieter is constructed by Herzog as an 'accidental soldier', who does not consider himself a hero. Yet the film is divided into four chapters, whose titles – 'The Man', 'His Dream', 'Punishment' and 'Redemption' – suggest that for Herzog Dieter was ultimately guilty and his vicissitudes in the jungle were a sort of retribution for the perversity of his dream.

Despite some neo-colonial echoes that their figures unavoidably trigger, Dieter and Juliane are represented as people who do not feel superior to nature or to the natives, who have an empirical knowledge of woodland (not only Juliane but even Dieter, who comes from the Black Forest), and who do not superimpose their imperialist vision on the jungle. Notwithstanding the exceptionality of the two walkers, their journeys have nothing to do with adventuring but with basic survival. Yet Herzog is clearly aware of the fictional, staged component of telling the story of a survival trip, of the thick layers of cultural meanings attached by Western culture, and by its cinema, to the jungle and the journey through it – and of the contribution brought by his films to this system of representations.

Nowhere to go: the desert in *Fata Morgana*

> My time in the desert is part of a quest that has not yet ended for me, and even though we were in a car, the spirit of our journey was like one made on foot. (Herzog, in Cronin 2002: 50)

Herzog filmed several fiction features and documentaries in Africa: *Die Fliegenden Ärzte von Ostafrika* (*The Flying Doctors of East Africa*, 1969), *Auch Zwerge haben klein angefangen* (*Even Dwarfs Started Small*, 1970), *Fata Morgana*, *Cobra Verde*, *Wodaabe: Herdsmen of the Sun* and *Echoes from a Sombre Empire*. Some of these films involve travelling – for instance, *Wodaabe: Herdsmen of the Sun* concentrates on nomadic people who roam the desert, *The Flying Doctors of East Africa* shows an organisation of German doctors who fly to patients in remote locations, and *Echoes from a Sombre Empire* follows journalist Michael Goldsmith's journey to the Central African Republic, where he was held prisoner under the dictatorship of Jean-Bédel Bokassa. However, *Fata Morgana* is the film that here most interests us, being more distinctively a road film – a journey through the desert, despite the lack of characters travelling.

The film was shot initially in Kenya, Tanzania and Uganda, then in the Sahara desert, from Algeria to Niger, in Central Africa (Ivory Coast, Mali and Cameroon), and finally in the Canary Islands. It is organised in three chapters: 'Creation',

'Paradise' and 'The Golden Age'. In the first chapter, the voice of German film historian Lotte Eisner reads passages from the sacred book of the Quiché Indians of Guatemala, *Popul Vuh*, about the failure of the first creation, after which the gods decided to wipe out the humans and start again. In the two subsequent chapters, Herzog reads texts that he wrote, which sound as 'increasingly absurd parodies' of *Popul Vuh* (Cleere 1980: 16). Music as diverse as Händel, Couperin, Mozart, Blind Faith and Leonard Cohen is played, reaching that effect of dissociation between visuals and soundtrack (both voice and music) typical of Herzog's cinema.

Fata Morgana is a case in point of our assertion that landscapes in Herzog are usually not viewed in a romantic way. The desert and lands in the film do not speak of mystical union between Man and Nature, rather of a rupture, of incommunicability, and of death. The landscapes of *Fata Morgana* have nothing to do with films on the sensual exoticism of the desert as seen by Westerners, including *The Sheltering Sky* (Bernardo Bertolucci, 1990) or *The English Patient* (Anthony Minghella, 1996). They do not have to do with primitivism either – Herzog does not adopt an anthropologist's perspective to show us uncontaminated, primeval lands; rather he looks with a clearly cinematic eye to a post-cultural, polluted environment.

At a superficial level, if we read *Fata Morgana*'s desert in terms of the title of the film's first chapter, 'Creation', and of the *Popul Vuh* narrative, the desert is constructed as the site of an unfinished act of creation, a creation gone badly wrong. This theme would indicate that the film is set in a primordial time, or outside time altogether. Yet many factors disallow this reading; some are elements of the *mise-en-scène*, objects insistently framed by the camera which are the signifiers and debris of Western society – carcasses of airplanes, buses and cars; burning petrol wells; pipes, barrels, shacks. Other elements belong to the cinematography, like the music accompanying these images, which is not 'primitive' or timeless, but is the identifiable expression of different epochs of Western culture, from classical music to pop. Furthermore, the constant presence of the camera undermines the naturalism of the representation. The camera is made visible in many ways: people whom the filmmakers meet always perform for the camera, speaking directly to it, holding out animals before the lens, or simply looking into the lens and walking towards or away from it. Once, we see a man filming with his own camera. In the last chapter of the film, while a bizarre couple play together in a gaily decorated bar, Herzog's voice-over states: 'In the Golden Age man and wife live in harmony … Now, for example, they appear before the lens of the camera.' This self-reflexive comment not only interferes with the naturalism of the representation by reminding us that we are watching a film, but also draws attention to the fact that the mythical tripartition of the film is a parody, that the 'man and wife of the golden age' are risible objects of the cinema's gaze.

We suggest that Herzog's desert does not come before or at the beginning of time, but after time – to the extent that *Fata Morgana* can be seen as an apocalyptic science fiction film. Interestingly, Herzog went to Africa precisely with the intention of making one, and only changed his mind on location:

My plan was to go out to the southern Sahara to shoot a kind of science fiction story about aliens from the planet Andromeda, a star outside our own galaxy, who arrive on a very strange planet. It is not Earth, rather some newly discovered place where the people live waiting for some imminent catastrophe, that of a collision with the sun in exactly sixteen years ... But from the first day of shooting I decided to scrap this idea. (In Cronin 2002: 47)

As Herzog himself admits in the same interview, *Fata Morgana* retains much of the first idea:

I liked the desolation and the remains of civilisation that were out there, things that added to the science fiction idea. We would find machinery lying in the middle of the desert – a cement mixer or something like that – a thousand miles from the nearest settlement or town. You stand in front of these things and are in absolute awe. Was it ancient astronauts who put these things down here? (In Cronin 2002: 50)

Fata Morgana's desert is that which has been left after civilisation – a post-atomic landscape that Herzog would call 'embarrassed' or 'offended' (in Cronin 2002: 49). The director takes us through such a landscape on a journey that has nothing to do with the 'getting lost' and 'going primitive' so typical of literary and cinematic Western travellers (as happens to Kit in *The Sheltering Sky*). Although we never see the filmmakers, their presence is constantly highlighted; the camera is often placed on a car – more specifically, 'on the roof of our VW van' (ibid.) – which travels for long stretches of time, always in the same direction, from left to right. These tracking shots are not 'panoramic vistas' but create the strong feel of a cinematic journey.

After the vertical ascent of the mountains, and the going in circles in the jungle, Herzog's trip through the desert is under the sign of endless horizonality. The long left-to-right tracking shots convey a sense of travelling, but without going anywhere. The trip has no beginning, no destination and no end. The camera pauses several times, to look at people, conurbations surfacing from the desert, signs of the human presence, remains of animals rotting under the sun, relics of cars and airplanes, or mirages. The recurrence of similar encounters along the way removes their value of special, unique events. Both the human presences and the emergences of isolated objects are so bizarre and meaningless as to resemble optical illusions, and fall into the same category as the mirages that Herzog's camera captures. There is a strong lack of purpose and destination; by travelling horizontally, sometimes slowing down or even stopping, no improved knowledge, no superior understanding of the desert's landscape is achieved. The same sense of disorientation is conveyed by some panning cameras. The 360-degree pan is a trademark of Herzog's cinema, but here when the circle is completed we do not find the same landmarks of the beginning, conveying the impression that it is not possible to find one's way, to understand the geography of the place. We suggest that this impossibility has nothing to do with the idea of a mysterious, exotic, 'other' land – it has more to do with a lack of sense. As Herzog's voice-over twice recites in the 'Paradise' section, '…there is landscape even without deeper meaning'.

The impression of lack of meaning and disorientation is also conveyed by some aerial shots, which go in the opposite direction to the tracking shots from the van's roof, from right to left. The gaze performed in these aerial shots is not an imperial one and has nothing to do with the vista from a vantage point much exploited in colonial travel literature – that which Mary Louise Pratt (1992) has called the 'monarch-of-all-I-survey scene': 'Seen from an elevated, detached vantage point, the alien space is at once rendered as a beautiful painting and stripped of its threatening otherness, as well as produced as colonial space, unlocked for the metropolitan devices of subordination and exploitation' (Koepnick 1993: 243). Far from conveying the domination of the landscape, the aerial visions in *Fata Morgana* produce at least two consequences. On the one hand, they strengthen the sense of travelling; on the other, with their right-to-left movement, they reverse the left-to-right motion of the tracking shots from the car, somehow undoing and negating all which that vision had produced. Furthermore, these aerial visions, despite the supposed vantage point, do not shed any clarity on the configuration of the landscape; at the opposite, they augment the confusion by showing a land with indistinguishable features – desert, sea or ice, we do not know what we are looking at. The landscape that we are shown is not transformed into an aesthetic artefact and dominated by a human eye – it is an unattractive, meaningless, indistinguishable land that could well be the setting of a science fiction film about a post-atomic era.

Travelling through the eye of the camera

All the films considered in this chapter portray natural settings such as mountains, jungles and deserts, and instances of travel through them. The meanings of and goals behind the journeys here described vary significantly – from the desire to defy gravity to self-punishment; from pilgrimage to escape and survival; from the ambition to excel and become a media star to the ironic observation of an offended landscape. All these travels have to do with the borders and limits of humanity, and with the encounter between various forms of civilisation and the primitive or the non-human. Rarely do they delve into the romantic desire to commune with nature – a nature that seems mostly oblivious to men. At times, ecstatic natural images are produced, either as seen from the perspective of a character, or as a direct commentary from the director. Herzog observes his characters' feelings on nature: those of white male Europeans who propose themselves as mass-mediatic neo-Romantic heroes like Roccia and Messner, whose ambition is to defy gravity and conquer mountain tops; and those of less aggressive and ambitious Western-ers, like Juliane and (to a lesser extent) Dieter, who are just seeking escape and survival and look at nature as a labyrinth that needs to be deciphered. When he observes nature directly rather than through the eyes of a character, as in *Fata Morgana*, Herzog chooses the perspective of an alien, who looks on the chaos of an unfinished creation or a post-human place, without finding the solace of beauty.

These films' main similarity lies in the director's engagement with the question of the point of view. In all of them, Herzog's discourse on nature and on travelling coincides with his interest in the cinematic vision. It is the point of view of the characters or of the filmmaker on the landscapes through which they travel that shapes the journey and determines its success or failure. Werner Herzog never fails to highlight that his landscapes are cinematic, and to reflect on his own cin-ema as travel on the border between culture and nature.

SECTION TWO Geographies

chapter five
POSTMODERN NOMADISM: ENFORCED ROOTLESSNESS AND OPPOSITIONAL MOTION

The tension between sedentariness and nomadism is commonly placed at the on-set of accounts of the history of civilisation. The birth of settlements and societies is closely intertwined with the passage from cattle-breeding to agriculture, from a nomadic lifestyle to one tied to the land and the fixed abode. Nomadism, there-fore, is embedded in the experience of sedentariness; it represents its antecedent and preparatory phase, as well as its antithesis.

Since the 1980s, the terms 'nomad' and 'nomadism' have been frequently used in the critical discourse to describe alternative ways of existing, of experiencing life in contemporary Western societies. For some thinkers nomadism has become the epitome of postmodern subjectivity itself, and there is a strand of postmodern theory which endorses and promotes 'nomadic thought'. The theorists who more readily identify with this strand are Gilles Deleuze and Félix Guattari. Reacting against the constrictions of Freudian psychoanalysis and of the liberal philosophi-cal tradition, Deleuze and Guattari theorised alternative subjectivities, in radical opposition to the mainstream capitalist and patriarchal society. 'Nomadism' for them comes to exemplify a subjectivity which is unanchored to any specific his-torical formation; 'deterritorialisation' is a mode of resistance, a radical counter-practice. Being a nomad means, in this context, to resist the constricting and regi-menting structures of Western society, in all the spheres, including the economic, social and sexual spheres. The desert, the typical environment of nomads, is de-scribed by the authors as a space which is empty, liberating and marginal, because it escapes the rigid 'striation' of culture, money and society. The desert is therefore a margin for linguistic, cultural and political experimentation.

Inspired by this thinking, other critics have developed ideas linked to nomadic deterritorialisation. Caren Kaplan has summarised some of these positions:

> Dominic Grisoni celebrates nomad thought as a link between 'street politics' and philosophy, signifying the abandonment of established codes and meth-

ods. Rosi Braidotti proposes a 'new nomadism' in which ideas function as 'ruses and mobile, specific strategies, which are resistant to systematisation' in order to develop 'multiple, transverse ways of thinking women's becoming'. Braidotti terms this new feminist subjectivity 'interconnected nomadism'. Teshome Gabriel has theorised 'nomadic aesthetics' in relation to black independent cinema, arguing that the figure of the nomad spans diverse cultures but symbolises universally the 'lifestyle of a free people'. (1996: 91)

'Nomadism', as much as 'exile' and 'diaspora' – terms with which we will engage in the next chapter – has thus come to refer to a generalised, universal poetics of displacement, usually described in positive, liberating terms, rather than as the product of specific anthropological and historical conditions. In this sense, Kaplan is right to suggest that 'Euro-American recourse to the metaphors of desert and nomad can never be innocent or separable from the dominant orientalist tropes in circulation throughout modernity' (1996: 66).[1]

We acknowledge the dangers of producing a form of neo-colonialism by a-historically and a-critically adopting terms such as 'nomad' and 'nomadism' to refer to current counter-practices and lifestyles within Western postmodern society. We will nevertheless use them, primarily as terms that aptly evoke the opposite of dwelling in a sedentary and permanent manner, but also that suggest lifestyles which significantly differ from experiences of emigration, relocation or exile. In this chapter, we wish in fact to refer to the demise of sedentariness and rootedness not as a phenomenon that produces migrations,[2] but different forms of inhabiting a territory and of moving within its boundaries. The use of these terms allows us to allude to and engage with ideas developed by thinkers such as Deleuze and Guattari, but also Michel Maffesoli, Zygmunt Bauman and Mario Perniola. It is our intention to use these terms as much as possible without romantic or neo-colonial hues, in order to define a socio-historical experience that is not always or necessarily liberating and elective, but often imposed and dictated by economic and socio-political changes. On the other hand, we will also engage with forms of resistance to mainstream society and ideology that manifest themselves in terms of radically different, oppositional lifestyles, and which have more in common with a nomadic than with a sedentary existence.

Many Western European films could have figured in this chapter: for instance the landmark *Sans toit ni loi* (*Vagabond*, 1985), directed by Agnès Varda, a chilling but sympathetic observation of the last weeks in the life of a homeless young woman who camps on the roadside of the French province and eventually dies of cold; Federico Fellini's *La voce della luna* (*The Voice of the Moon*, 1990), a story of harmless madness and of male friendship developing on the road on the backdrop of a contemporary, vulgar Italy; Manuel Poirier's *Western* (1997), a distinctive road movie also about a male friendship developing between two vagabonds, one Spanish and one Russian, this time in Brittany; and *Drôle de Félix* (*The Adventures of Felix*, 2000), by Olivier Ducastel and Jacques Martineau, in which the protagonist takes a road trip to Marseilles to track down the father he has never met. Yet we have decided to concentrate on four films, two of which were produced in Italy and two in France, which overtly explore different but related aspects of the phenomena of enforced or voluntary vagrancy connected to socio-economic change: Gianni Amelio's *Il ladro di bambini* (*The Stolen Children*, 1992), Laurent Cantet's *L'Emploi du temps* (*Time Out*, 2001), Agnès Varda's *Les Glaneurs et la glaneuse* (*The Gleaners & I*, 2000) and Nanni Moretti's *Caro diario* (*Dear Diary*, 1994).

Amelio and Cantet: the loss of stability and meaning

This section is devoted to *The Stolen Children* and *Time Out*, two road films that in focusing their attention on fictional travellers explore the effects of the widespread loss of stability and meaning in Western Europe, a phenomenon affecting first of all the sphere of work, but also of shared values and of private feelings and relationships. *The Stolen Children* paints a landscape of socio-economic uncertainty and cultural homogenisation, which we will describe through Bauman's ideas on the postmodern vagabond. *Time Out* looks at the decline of a traditionally masculine form of movement: commerce; ideas coming from Michel Maffesoli's work will help us to understand this film's portrait of a novel figure of itinerant worker. Adopting a very pessimistic stance, Amelio's and Cantet's films draw attention to the contemporary deterioration of the working environment and to the generalised social decay. The films' protagonists are all losers; their wanderings simply take them to their final humiliation and defeat.

The Stolen Children: vagabonds and tourists in the homogenised landscape

> Today, towns like Catanzaro or Matera are substantially similar to Turin and Milan. You can travel transversally, north to south, east to west, and absolutely nothing changes. You see the same things, hear the same words, and come in contact with the same feelings and the same mythologies. (Amelio, in Volpi 1995: 139)

As Pauline Small has suggested, Gianni Amelio's *The Stolen Children* is 'characterised by an intense awareness of Italy's cinematic past', and 'is a film that takes Italian film as its theme' (1998: 151 and 166). Small traced in the film the intertextual presence of Visconti's *Rocco e i suoi fratelli* (*Rocco and His Brothers*, 1960), of Rossellini's *Roma città aperta* (*Rome, Open City*, 1945) and of De Sica's *Ladri di biciclette* (*Bicycle Thieves*, 1948).[3] Amelio retells, in a new socio-political context, themes that were central to those films, and particularly to *Rocco and His Brothers* – the emigration to Northern cities and the disappearance of the old native village; the mutation of the relationship between town and country; the transformation of the father/son relationship.

The Stolen Children in fact presents a reversed migration – the protagonist, Antonio, is a *carabiniere* from Calabria who lives in Milan and travels back to the South, first to Reggio Calabria and then to Sicily. Amelio directly evokes *Rocco and his Brothers* by setting his second scene in Milan's railway station, the same Stazione Centrale in which Visconti's film began, with the Parondis' arrival from Lucania. As Small has suggested, Antonio's trip may be read as that return home which in *Rocco and His Brothers* was only imagined by the two younger brothers, Ciro and Luca. As Ciro had already guessed, though, the native village, the *paese*, was already transforming in the 1950s and in the process of disappearing. As if to confirm this, in *The Stolen Children* Antonio mentions that nobody lives in his native village any longer, since most people have either emigrated or built new houses by the sea. Small aptly discusses the phenomenon of the physical disappearance of the *paese*, as well as that of its persistence in the emigrant's make-up: 'the *paese* has gone but it remains as an illusion, perhaps a necessary one, to those who struggle to find a sense of identity in a constantly shifting and changing world' (1998: 157). It is worth here repeating Stuart Hall's opinion on the nature of the 'lost object' that the native place acquires in the construction of diasporic identities:

> It is because this New World is constituted for us as place, a narrative of displacement, that it gives rise so profoundly to a certain imaginary plenitude, recreating the endless desire to return to 'lost origins' ... And yet, this 'return to the beginning' is like the imaginary in Lacan – it can neither be fulfilled nor requited, and hence is the beginning of the symbolic, of representation, the infinitely renewable source of desire, memory, myth, search, discovery – in short, the reservoir of our cinematic narratives. (1990: 236)

Yet Amelio's film is deceptively about a reversed migration, a return to the lost origins (of the character, of Italian cinema). *The Stolen Children* does retell *Rocco and His Brothers*; this retelling, nevertheless, cannot be read exclusively in terms of the internal emigrations of the 1950s and of their legacy in today's Italy, but more generally with reference to the existential condition that characterises postmodern Italy as well as other European countries. The society painted by Amelio is – to

Fig. 10 Gianni Amelio's *Il Ladro Di Bambini* (*The Stolen Children*, Italy, 1992) © Rizzoli Audio-visivi S.p.a.

borrow Small's words – 'a constantly shifting and changing world'; however, while in the 1950s it still made sense to struggle to 'find a sense of identity', in today's Italy (and Europe) this goal is unachievable and meaningless. Identities, in fact, are more and more diasporic, somewhere 'in between', as Hall would say, decidedly unstable and constantly renegotiated.

Luciano and Rosetta are brother and sister who live in a poor peripheral area of Milan with their single mother, who for some time has been organising the prostitution of the eleven-year-old Rosetta. When their mother is arrested, the two children are sent by the authorities to a religious orphanage in Civitavec-chia, near Rome. Two *carabinieri*, one of whom is Antonio, are ordered to escort them by train, but in Bologna station Antonio's partner goes absent without leave. When the institute refuses to accept the children, Antonio, covering for his part-ner, accompanies the brother and sister to their next destination, an institute in Sicily, their native region. The trip is longer than expected: Luciano suffers from asthma and cannot travel continuously. Antonio slowly transforms from an escort into both a father-figure and an idealised boyfriend. The trio stop several times to rest, first in Calabria at the roadside restaurant of Antonio's sister; then, after a local woman has recognised and exposed Rosetta, by the sea in Sicily where they enjoy a liberating swim; and subsequently in Noto, where Antonio catches a robber and, at the headquarters of the local *carabinieri*, is accused of kidnapping the children and is under suspicion of abusing Rosetta. The last stop is Gela, in a neglected square surrounded by high-rise apartment buildings where Antonio parks the car to get some sleep before handing the children to the institute the following morning.

The journey lasts four days and five nights, travelling first by train, then by bus, by ferry and by car. The stops are Milan, of which we only see the train station (but previously we were shown Luciano and Rosetta's destitute quarter); Bologna, of which, once again, we only see the station, where Antonio's partner leaves the train; Civitavecchia, with its train station, a bar, the institute for orphans, and the port from which Antonio calls his partner; Rome, of which we are shown a gritty square behind Termini train station; a national road in the area of Reggio Calabria, where Antonio's sister and grandmother live, in an unfinished building that is both a restaurant and a home; a hotel in Marina di Ragusa, where they spend the night, and a beach where, the morning after, Antonio lets the kids swim, and where they have a meal in a restaurant by the sea; here, they meet two French tourists with whom they move to Noto; and finally they reach Gela by night.

One critic has rightly noticed that 'the backward journey, from north to south … portrays an Italy that by now is without roots, without a horizon and without the will to fight, without people and without guides' (Cattini 2000: 116). It seems the description of a desert, a place where people are rootless and keep travelling like nomads. Amelio chose as the settings of his film a long series of those spaces that Marc Augé has called 'non-places': sites of stopover and departure, such as train stations; places of eternal lingering, as the destitute no-man's-lands around them; ports, with their departing ferries; vehicles – train corridors and carriages, ferry decks, the inside of a car; and places of passage and travel, such as railway tracks, national roads traversed by heavy traffic, and viaducts entering towns. These are places where people do not reside but only pass through, without even noticing the difference between one spot and the next, because of the lack of landmarks indicating a change of setting. The characters' trip is long, but not as long as that of Rocco's family, of whom the Milanese exclaimed: 'And where is this Lucania they come from? Africa!' As Amelio has repeatedly stressed, Lucania and Lombardy today are much the same. In this Italy, the characters travel rather easily, and when they get off their trains, destinations are always at a walking distance, as to recon-firm that space is now compressed and all places are within easy reach. Music and human voices on the soundtrack are given a homogenising function: throughout the journey, we hear the same popular Italian songs playing from radios and tapes, and southern dialects are spoken also in Milan, in Bologna and in Rome. Very little landscape is shown. As Amelio has explained, the Italy described in *Rocco and His Brothers* no longer exists:

The landscape itself, from north to south, presents similar characteristics … It is not by accident that there are very few point-of-view shots of the landscape, like, from Rossellini onward, is almost 'natural' to do when filming a journey by train, by car, or motorbike … The point-of-view shot as image of what the traveller sees. Mine was not a narrative or a stylistic choice, but because the places, in my opinion, look too much all the same, they no longer are truly different. (Quoted in Volpi 1995: 139–40)

In the homogenised landscape, in the constantly shifting desert, Antonio, Rosetta and Luciano truly are three vagabonds, in the sense attached to this term by Zygmunt Bauman:

Wherever the vagabond goes, he is a stranger; he can never be 'the native', the 'settled one', one with 'roots in the soil' … The early modern vagabond wandered through the settled places; he was a vagabond because in no place could he be settled as the other people had been. The settled were many, the vagabonds few. Post-modernity reversed the ratio. Now there are few 'settled' places left. The 'forever settled' residents wake up to find the places (places in the land, places in society and places in life), to which they 'belong', no longer existing or no longer accommodating; neat streets turn mean, factories vanish together with jobs, skills no longer find buyers, knowledge turns into ignorance, professional experience becomes liability, secure networks of relations fall apart and foul the place with putrid waste. Now the vagabond is a vagabond not because of the reluctance or difficulty of settling down, but because of the scarcity of settled places. Now the odds are that the people he meets in his travels are other vagabonds – vagabonds today or vagabonds tomorrow. (1996: 29)

None of the three characters has solid roots: the children were born in Sicily, but immigrated to Milan, where they lived detached from their origins a life devoid of quality in a neglected suburb. Their family did not offer any solidity: their father left very early on, and the mother sunk so low as to organise the prostitution of her young daughter. More so than to the crisis of the family, their experience reflects the end of the family, the transformation of the family from a private hub of love and solidarity into a business that commodifies its members and becomes a mirror of the external, consumerist world. Antonio too is rootless: he emigrated from Calabria to Milan, and this move changed him so much that, when he returns home, he is clearly at odds with his relatives. His rootlessness is exacerbated because his village no longer exists: everybody left, either to emigrate, or to build on the coast. The new settlement, seen against the myth of the abandoned village of Antonio's childhood, inspires a true *horror vacui*. The half-finished houses on the two sides of a roaring state road are impotent in creating a sense of community and maintaining ties with the past. The spread of illegally constructed buildings along coastal areas, so common in the years during and following the economic boom, is a powerful symbol of the changed realities of the country, of the loss of values and traditions, both moral and aesthetic, which was an effect of the pervasive greed accompanying the Italian boom. The unfinished buildings also convey a sense of lack of permanence and durability. Antonio does not belong here anymore; but even his belonging to the *Carabinieri* proves to be only a deceivably permanent condition.[4] 'It's a secure job', he says to the superior who interrogates him in Noto, but Antonio's future as a *carabiniere* is deeply compromised by his behaviour with the children. In fact, his gun and identification card, which along with the uniform form the symbols of his job, are taken away.

Before being reprimanded in Noto, Antonio had promised Luciano that they would stick together. Yet this elective family is not going to last – after being accused of kidnapping the children and of abusing Rosetta, Antonio knows that there is no future for the three of them; even the children guess it quickly, when their putative father sets off in silence to take them to the orphanage. Family, community, jobs, feelings – nothing seems stable and durable. Not even love is likely in this Italy. On the beach at Marina di Ragusa the three travellers meet two French girls; Antonio agrees to give them a lift to Noto. One of them seems attracted to him, and Luciano asks him if he is going to become her fiancé. Antonio 'sensibly' replies that there is no point in asking her for her address, since 'tomorrow morning they'll be gone'. In order to cope with a constantly shifting world the best strategy is, as Bauman suggests, to avoid fixing one's identity, to remain a vagabond.

The other characters whom we encounter are also either vagabonds or tourists. The former are represented by the several businessmen boarding the trains, but also by the many people we see lingering in the areas around the stations, as well as the orphans in the Civitavecchia institute, who lack the stability of a family and a home. The tourists are embodied by the many young people with rucksacks in the stations and on the trains, by the strollers on their bicycles near the beach in Sicily, and by the two French tourists.

By taking a leisurely break at the beach, and then by joining the two French girls in their trip, Antonio, Luciano and Rosetta's status of vagabonds transforms briefly into that of tourists. The soundtrack confirms the metamorphosis, with the Italian version of a famous pop song – 'I look for a bit of blue, I dream of California...' This short experience is, to borrow Bauman's words, 'a pleasant feeling, a tickling and rejuvenating feeling, like letting oneself be buffeted by sea waves' (1996: 29). In their tourist phase, all three characters are rejuvenated – Luciano and Rosetta look and behave like children for the first time, and Antonio seems fresher, lighter and happier. Being a tourist, however, implies having a house somewhere – something that none of the protagonists has. Houses are totally absent from the film: Rosetta and Luciano's poor apartment was transformed by their mother into a brothel. When Antonio gives the address of the barracks in Milan to Rosetta, who wants to send him a postcard, we cannot but think that his residence is a far cry from a true home. The other houses are a surrogate home, the orphanage; the flat that a *carabiniere* friend of Antonio's shares with a colleague in Rome, and which has the strong un-homely feel of a bachelor's house, only amplified by its location near a heavily-trafficked viaduct; the unfinished building in Calabria, which is so scruffy that Antonio's sister complains: 'We are camping, like the Albanians, actually worse', thus comparing her family to exiles and refugees. Even the hotel where Antonio and the children sleep on their way to Sicily has windows and balconies that open onto a loud state road, highlighting its function as a place of passage.

After their short tourist break, the characters soon return to their condition of vagabonds, and this time, Antonio in particular, with an even clearer consciousness of their status. Amelio has stated: 'You cannot assign to the journey of my protagonists a meaning that can recall, even superficially, that of *Rocco and His Brothers*. In this return trip one cannot find a weight or an "ideological" meaning' (in Volpi 1995: 139). The ideological significance of Rocco's south-to-north journey no longer makes sense today; and neither does the reversed migration. The north-south route travelled by Antonio is not a trip back home – not even to a missing, disappeared home. Antonio's journey is true vagrancy, a vagabondage without horizon and without destination, without purpose and without achievements, in a desert-like land where 'settled' homes, jobs, relationships and places no longer exist.

Time Out: merchants and adventurers in the late-capitalist market

Vincent, the protagonist of *Time Out*, is an executive who, having become unreliable, was fired by his company after fifteen years. We learn of his discharge only gradually, because the film opens with Vincent on the road, behaving as if he still had his job. Rather than confessing the truth, Vincent keeps up the pretence and spends his days driving around, eating in roadside cafes and sleeping in his car. Living with his wife and their three children in a French town not far from the Swiss border, Vincent invents that he got a new job with the UN in Geneva. He convinces his proud but controlling father to lend him money to buy an apartment there, but uses the cash to purchase a jeep. Then he persuades some friends to invest their savings in a scheme connected with his job, and again uses the money to get by. One day he is approached by Jean Michel, who smuggles counterfeit watches and designer goods from Eastern Europe; first reluctantly, then excitedly, he joins his venture. In the meantime, his wife, who was suspicious all along, finds out the truth. Vincent crumbles, dumps Jean Michel and, to avoid a confrontation with his father, drives away in the night. The film closes with Vincent taking an interview for a new job, for which his father has recommended him.

Laurent Cantet's *Time Out* has been described as a continuation of the director's previous *Resources humaines* (*Human Resources*, France 1999), a film that also dealt with the theme of job loss, but looking at a whole community of workers rather than at one individual's drama (see Kemp 2002; Vincendeau 2002). In this description, the film's distinctive dimension of road movie is understated. An overwhelming section of screen time is devoted to travelling, specifically to Vincent's driving along highways, city streets and countryside roads. We believe that Vincent's travelling is an essential component not only of the character, but also of the filmmaker's analysis of work, of society and of lifestyles in contemporary Europe.

Vincent's travelling can be divided into three phases. At first, it is aimless and joyful; we see him following the routes of invented appointments with non-existent clients, using his mobile phone to call home from a parking lot, competing in speed with a train travelling on a roadside railway, stopping to eat at a diner, and sleeping rough in the passenger seat. This first phase conveys the feel of leisurely, juvenile tourism, and is in fact visually associated with it: in an early sequence, Vincent is in a parking lot, and a bus full of children on an outing stops and unloads its cheerful passengers. Vincent is playing at being on the road – as confirmed by his childish pleasure at racing with the train, or by the sequence in which he eats in a playground full of children. In this phase, Vincent has been out of a job for about a month or two, but has continued to leave the family home daily, often staying out at night. This behaviour is dictated, firstly, by his fear of telling his wife, as well as his domineering and exigent father. It is also suggested, though, that he wilfully avoids being at home with his wife and children: Vincent, in fact, could easily keep up the pretence without staying away so much from his family. Furthermore, it is suggested that he does it for pleasure, in order to be able to be on the road – being behind the wheel, driving while listening to the radio and singing, traversing towns and rural landscapes, stopping at diners and petrol stations seems to be very pleasant and fulfilling for Vincent.

After this early, short phase of leisurely roaming and playing at heading south for important appointments in sunny Marseilles, the second phase of Vincent's travelling is overall much less pleasurable. In order to increase and somehow institutionalise the time he spends on the road, away from home, Vincent invents that he took up a post at the UN in Geneva. His travelling becomes a commuting, from his French family home, where he spends weekends and holidays, to Geneva, where he spends the 'working week'. This second phase constitutes a border crossing: Vincent moves from concealing his dismissal to constructing a new, fake identity; from lying to his family to lying to friends and strangers; from doing something reproachable to doing something illicit. This phase involves border crossing also in literal terms: Vincent is shown approaching the customs between France and Switzerland with some tension and expectation – he is not asked to stop and drives through with some relief. He finds himself, literally and metaphorically, in another country, and his life on the road changes. Initially, the travelling is not unpleasant; we see Vincent driving alongside the lake in the evening, then approaching expectantly the UN building in the morning. After having spent some time there, gathering information, he drives into the mountains, leaves the car and walks in the snow, reaching an abandoned hut, where he studies the documents he has collected. As Ginette Vincendeau has suggested, 'the majestic, forbidding mountains encase his solitude while the snow echoes his emotional coldness' (2002: 30). Additionally, the trip into the mountains, with their open, imposing landscape, visually links the film to North American road movies, as well as to westerns. As already suggested, and as several critics have indicated, the road movie is a direct descendant of the western (see Roberts 1997; Watson 1999; Laderman 2002: 23–34). Vincent's trip, not surprisingly, owes much to typical elements of this genre, primarily the lonely male hero who rejects domesticity and roams around looking for fortune, often in illicit ways, but also for the pure enjoyment of travelling. As Vincendeau rightly suggested in her interview with Cantet, 'the life Vincent invents for himself, his roaming abroad while keeping his family back home, is a very masculine fantasy … Through a lot of the film he inhabits the great outdoors, traditionally a masculine space in cinema, while Muriel is always confined at home' (2002: 32). This masculine space of the great outdoors is precisely the space of the frontier, constructed by the western, and transformed into the highway by the Hollywood road movie. At a certain point the two genres visually coalesce: a crane shot shows us from above Vincent testing his new jeep's speed and steering power in a wasteland, as if he were taming a wild horse.

Vincent's voice-over, reading out loud and learning by heart documents about the UN activities in Africa, covers much of the travelling of this second phase, which is increasingly associated with a demanding occupation. Vincent is only pretending that he has a job, but this is shown to be very hard work, and all the fun of travelling progressively vanishes. Slowly his car, from being a vehicle of freedom and liberation from the constraints of a dull working life and of family duty, turns into a novel office, and is in fact now constructed as a closed, suffocating environment. Fewer shots are devoted to filming the outdoors through the windscreen, and more are dedicated to framing Vincent in the car, behind the wheel, with the mobile phone placed in good evidence next to the steering wheel. His phoney business brings him to spend more and more time in hotel halls, meeting his clients, or in the car talking to them on the phone. Paradoxically, Vincent has escaped a constraining, unsatisfactory job, only to create for himself another one.

We believe that Vincent is an operator as well as a victim of the new market – which is characterised by abstraction and by an absence of material goods, and in which the object of the exchange is never seen, is an intangible construction. Vincent's quest and his rejection of his former job are dictated by his desire to be a merchant, in the traditional, old sense of the term: one whose job is somewhere in between exchanging or selling goods, and travelling and exploring. In the line with an ancient tradition, Vincent is almost a descendant of Marco Polo, the Venetian merchant of the Middle Ages who travelled to China and whose journey was both that of a businessman and of an explorer and an adventurer. As Michel Maffesoli (1997) reminds us, the travelling merchants were nomadic elements who conjugated movement with the flux of exchanges, and who were among the main agents responsible for the original 'circulation' of goods, peoples, ideas and cultures, on which any social system is based. The activity of merchants combined the circulation of material goods with that of ideas and feelings, because of their being in movement, of their being 'strangers' and explorers. In the reality of the late-capitalist market, Vincent is an outsider. His old job was that of the financial advisor – one inscribed in a purely abstract economic scenario, in which there is no exchange of material goods but of data and figures. The only part of his job that agreed with him was travelling. He confesses to Jean Michel: 'I love to drive. When I first started working, driving was my favourite part. Alone in the car, thinking about nothing, smoking a cigarette and listening to the music, I could go on for hours. I think the only thing I really liked about my job was the driving.'

The pleasure of driving for Vincent is more than a symptom of alienation, of his desire to detach from the world and stay in the protective, enclosed environment of the car. We suggest that Vincent is actually excited and fulfilled by being on the road, by travelling and exploring, as part of the ancient profession of the merchant. This is made very clear by the type of job that he invents for himself, as a UN officer involved with African countries – and which is as close to the exploration of new continents as it could be in Vincent's case. It is in the third phase of his travelling, however, that this idea finds confirmation. Involved by Jean Michel in his business, Vincent becomes exactly what he always wanted to be, a merchant and an adventurer, carrying real (although counterfeit) goods along dangerous roads, in exciting night-time trips across borders, making money but also meeting people and establishing human contacts. Behind the wheel, en route towards an unguarded borderline, Vincent rediscovers the excitement and pleasure of driving and of being on the road, and finally, for the first time in the film, becomes able to share his thoughts, memories and feelings with another human being. It has been noted that the intimacy that grows between Jean Michel and Vincent, particularly in the sequence in Jean Michel's bedroom, could suggest homosexual overtones (Vincendeau 2002). It certainly intimates the camaraderie of male co-travellers, who wash and relax together after an adventurous trip, who count the money they have made through their courage and adventurousness and who confess to each other secrets about their lives.

Despite his evident pleasure and satisfaction, Vincent is not capable of keeping up this role. When his wife discovers the truth, he leaves Jean Michel and returns home. At the news that his domineering father is coming to confront him, Vincent jumps in his car and drives away into the night, refusing to answer his relatives' phone calls. It is suggested that he may just keep driving, but when he stops and leaves the car we even imagine that he may commit suicide. Instead, the last sequence of the film shows him at a job interview, faking the desire to take up the challenge of a new position.

As in a traditional western, and in so many road movies, it is the woman (as wife, but above all as mother of the hero's children), who stops the protagonist from his dangerous but rewarding wanderings and brings him back to the sedentariness of domestic life, of social ties and work, and above all to his role of father – one which is given extreme importance in the film. Vincent's problem, as Cantet has noted, is his paradoxical 'desire to be elsewhere, to experience a certain precariousness and … to preserve what brings him equilibrium, namely his bourgeois family life' (in Vincendeau 2002: 32). The tension between sedentariness and nomadism, between domesticity and male freedom, is again shown to be at the core of the road movie. In order to be able to live an unbound life on the road, the male hero should reject the stability of a married, bourgeois life (as Jean Michel did). Vincent is unable to do it, something that clearly depends on his faltering masculinity. Controlled by his father, on whom he depends emotionally and economically, Vincent is presented by Cantet as a son incapable of freeing himself from the embrace of his parents, as a husband who shuns his wife's company, and as a father incapable of communicating with and of educating his son. His castrating father is indicated by the film as a major culprit in Vincent's weakened masculinity, which is only briefly restored to him by a replacement father, Jean Michel. We nevertheless suggest that the abstract characteristics of the late-capitalist market and of work in contemporary society are ultimately responsible for the 'diminishing masculinity' that affects Vincent, a character who aspires to be the hero of a manly, itinerant adventure in the great outdoors, but who, for historical reasons, is unable to realise his dream.

Varda and Moretti: oppositional movement, alternative filmmaking

In this section we consider two films that have much in common: both are semi-documentaries that deliberately adopt and continually display the contingent point of view of their directors; thus, while offering critical observations on contemporary society, they are also portraits of their makers – obliterating the border between self-portrait and portrait of the world. Furthermore, both films are road movies, suggesting that movement, intended as the opposite of fixation and sedentariness, allows the development of oppositional artistic and social discourses and personal lifestyles. *The Gleaners & I* is a 'wandering road documentary' that addresses the question of people moving at the margins of the late-capitalist society, either as a choice or as an imposition, as well as being a self-portrait of Agnès Varda. *Dear Diary* is only apparently more disconnected from our theme of mobility deriving from socio-economic change. In this film, in fact, Nanni Moretti firmly positions himself at the margins of and in opposition to contemporary society. We will analyse the first episode of *Dear Diary*, 'On My Vespa', with reference to strollers such as the modern *flâneur* and the situationists of the 1960s, but will update these images of urban travellers by engaging with ideas on the 'transit' developed by philosophers of postmodernity. In both cases, the theoretical framework is that of Deleuze and Guattari's concept of oppositional nomadism, of living 'smooth' in the 'striated' space of society.

Although Varda and Moretti paint a very negative portrait of contemporary Western European society, in their films they are both capable of seeing a way out, and propose nomadism as a successful oppositional practice. Both directors display a moderate optimism, although their critical attitude and their ability of discriminating between different positions remain lucid and vibrant.

The Gleaners & I: picking through a society's surplus

On this type of gleaning of images, of impressions, of emotions, there is no legislation, and in the dictionary gleaning is described figuratively as an intellectual activity. To glean facts, acts and deeds, to glean information. And, for forgetful me, it's what I have gleaned that tells me where I have been. (Agnès Varda, *The Gleaners & I*)

Varda's *The Gleaners & I* was generally analysed as a documentary on people who live on the fringes of capitalist society, in overtly oppositional ways or as a result of extreme poverty; on people who salvage the refuse of society in order to recycle it, or to produce art; and on Varda herself – a self-portrait of the artist as an old lady (see, for instance, Rosello 2001). Although these perspectives are obviously correct, we believe that, first and foremost, *The Gleaners & I* is a road movie. As Varda herself suggested, hers is a 'wandering road documentary' (quoted in Darke 2001: 30). Movement is central to Varda's film in many interrelated ways, and the oversight of this component results in a simplification of its project. The type of movement represented and produced by the film is, indeed, a wandering and a roaming, which we will read in terms of postmodern nomadism.

The film starts at home – at Varda's home – but leaves it straight away. Varda is constantly on the road in order to make her film, often returning home, only to leave it again right away. Most of the screen time is indeed devoted to the outside – to travelling, or to filming places visited by the filmmaker. The camera is often placed inside the car or a train, and films from behind the windscreen – we are given many moving sights of rural or seashore landscapes, of cityscapes (rows of houses, streets), trafficked highways, and skies. The movements performed by Varda, by car or by train, are multiple and ample. The first stop is Paris, the Musee d'Orsay, where Varda views Jean-François Millet's famous painting, *Les Glaneuses* (1857). Next she drives northbound, to the Museum of Arras, in order to view another famous painting of a gleaner, Jules Breton's. Then she drives south of Paris, to the region of Beauce, the 'granary of France', between the Seine and Loire rivers, to look at the disposing of tons of edible potatoes that do not match the commercial, standardised size, and to interview a first-class chef, who also happens to be a gleaner. Then, again by car, she is off southeast towards a famous wine area, Burgundy, where she interviews wine growers at Beaune and Pommard. Next, Varda goes further south, to Avignon, to interview a lawyer about the practice of gleaning, then north again to the Ile-de-France, to Sannois, where she meets an artist who uses waste salvaged from the streets. In the meantime, we are told but not shown, Varda even travelled to Japan, then returned home to deposit her souvenirs. Back en route, she goes to Viry-Noureuil (Picardie) to see the much visited Jardin Fantastique by Bodan Litnanski, who builds 'totem towers' with debris, and whose wife calls him 'an amateur', then to talk to an established artist who also uses salvaged materials, Louis Pons. Next stop is the island of Noirmoutier, in Normandy, to talk to people who glean oysters, and then south again to the Jura region, to Apt, where we see a family picking grapes in an abandoned vineyard, and then to interview a descendant of Etienne-Jules Marey. Next, Varda is on a train leaving Paris, slowing down when passing the waste collection centre of Ivry, and finally arriving in Prades (Auvergne), where a group of wandering youth were accused of damaging the trash cans of a supermarket. Back on the train, Varda goes to meet a white man who has lived for ten years eating food out of rubbish bins, then a black man who lives with an old Chinese and also salvages both food and objects from the streets. At Villneuve sur Lot (south again) Varda shows us an exhibition of old fridges now filled with all sorts of objects; in Arles (Provence), she looks at a man who watches the river in the early hours of the morning. Then she is off to interview apple growers in the Rhône valley. Back in Paris, she investigates the people who search in the remains of the street markets, and meets a biologist who lives in the *banlieue*, sells magazines during the day, and does voluntary language teaching for immigrants at night. The film's last stop is Villefranche, to dig out of a museum's storeroom a painting of gleaners by Hédoin.

Varda's journey is not a linear, clear progression from place A to place B, nor is it a circular trip, from A back to A. The journey is asymmetrical, almost illogical: rather than exhaustively exploring each area, it is made up of many comings and goings, and frequently returns to the same or nearby areas. The movement is a repeated north-south-north-south one, like the swing of a pendulum, and similar in a sense to the movement of the lens cap of Varda's handheld DV camera, which in a curious sequence swings back and forth at the rhythm of a jazz piece. The film's movement is clearly suggestive not of a trip, but of a roaming, of a wandering, dictated by an internal, secret logic. The home is not clearly marked as a place of departure (we do not see Varda leaving her house at the onset), but as a place of many departures and returns, and is not geographically located – something which interferes with and diminishes its function of anchoring and of permanence in place and time. We suggest that Varda's home and many other homes in this film are represented as places of passage, as well as shelters and storage rooms. For instance, when Varda goes to Japan, we do not see images of her intercontinental journey but are shown its souvenirs – images and objects that the artist gleaned and brought back with her, which add to the collection in her house, and project new meanings onto things and images that were already there. Her house is, in fact, constructed as a deposit of objects/images, in which even a stain of dampness on the ceiling becomes a picture (several different pictures). In Varda's life, the film suggests, home is the place to which to return, in which to position the journeys' souvenirs in meaningful ways, and from which to depart again in search of more gifts and mementos. The home is thus an anthology (or an encyclopaedia, an image that often returns in the film) of souvenirs, the signifier of our trips, the memory of where we have been. Other people met by Varda, be they artists or ordinary people, treat their houses in similar ways. This is at least the case of two artists, Louis Pons and the young white man who goes around at night on his bicycle to salvage objects for his paintings. The latter is asked by Varda whether his place is indeed a shelter (from emptiness), and she also describes it as a 'cave'. Also the black man who lives with the old Chinese accumulates objects in the house; his guest describes him as a 'migrating bird', who comes and goes, who leaves but always returns; the man describes himself in similar terms – 'I wander around'.

As well as moving in space, Varda's film performs a movement in time, as is often the case in road movies, particularly those in which the journey has strong metaphorical meanings. Varda's own form of gleaning is mainly connected to durable objects, rather than to perishables such as foods. The only edibles she brings home are heart-shaped potatoes picked from a pile of tons of rejected produce. Instead of cooking them, Varda films them, over and over again. Towards the end of the film they reappear, covered in sprouts and wrinkles; the filmmaker comments: 'I like filming rot, leftovers, waste.' The potatoes have turned into images, first of hearts, then of the passing of time, of decay; similarly, everything else Varda brings back from her trips also turns into images – a clock without hands, two chairs, the postcard of Rembrandt's self-portrait from Japan. True, they are objects in their own right, and Varda's DV camera, placed very close to them, often produces a tactile effect, so that we almost feel as if we could touch them and experience their physicality. However, it is only an impression of texture, and all we have is images, which become souvenirs of a journey, of Varda's (and the camera's) 'having been there'. In particular, the handless clock is a strong image of the passage of time, or the refusal to acknowledge it, or even of the end of time – Varda's own image, motionlessly moving behind the clock, highlights both the idea of the passage of time and of the freezing of it.

The sense of travelling in time, and salvaging images from it, is conveyed also by the theme of Varda's research into old-time gleaning, which is carried out by interviewing people who remember the time in which this activity was commonly practised, and by an iconographic investigation, which uncovers and digitally re-produces artistic images of gleaning and gleaners from the past. The sense of the passage of time, and of the desire to record it and, perhaps, stop it, is also clear from the director's interest in filming herself, her thinning hair, her wrinkly hand, which, as she highlights, suggests that 'the end is near'. With her film, Varda is making a self-portrait – producing images of herself in time, filming 'death at work'. She suggests this directly, when she compares what she is doing to Rembrandt's self-portrait. Significantly, most images of Varda's hand appear during a trip on the motorway, during which she plays at 'catching hold' of big trucks, and reminisces about her childhood games and juvenile excitement of being on the road. The journey is, as we have claimed, not only a travelling in space, but also in time; images of the past are instigated by and emerge from images of the present, come to the fore and activate clusters of memories as well as insight into the future and the ephemeral nature of things. Movement is, thus, the movement itself of life, from past to present, from childhood to adulthood, to maturity and to death. This is, also, how the pioneer of cinema Etienne-Jules Marey comes into the film – apparently by chance, another fortuitous gift of the mobile activity of gleaning, in truth because he belongs in this film (as Varda suggests of another chance en-counter, the one with a painting of the gleaners found in a salvage sale). Marey's photographic and filmic experiments in capturing the essence of movement (and therefore of time) constitute the actual prehistory of filmmaking, not simply in a chronological way, but in conceptual terms. Beyond his scientific dream of discov-ering the secret of movement, as Varda suggests, that which remains of his work is images, beautiful images of perishable bodies in motion. Varda's making of a self-portrait in this film is not a marginal activity, secondary to her documentary on gleaning and gleaners, but is itself a form of gleaning, of salvaging images. As Mireille Rosello suggests, filmmaking, as well as art in general, is portrayed by Varda as the activity of capturing images that 'were left behind, images that no one had seen. Varda plucks images from a reality where others had seen only banalities or ugliness'. (2001: 32).

Another way in which movement is central to the film depends on the activity of gleaning itself. Varda travels around in order to pick images, and ultimately make her film on gleaning which is also her self-portrait; similarly, gleaning is an activity that requires being on the move, roaming, and ultimately rejecting sedentariness. For the purpose of our analysis, we will consider here simultaneously the activities of gleaning for food, either in the country or in the city, and of salvaging garbage, for either recycling or for artistic ends, because they share the same humble ges-ture of bending one's back and stretching one's arm to pick up something from the ground. In spite of the partly romanticised gaze that Varda casts on old and new gleaners and on their activity, gleaning is ultimately described as a difficult and hard, although rewarding, occupation. One of the aspects of the hardship of glean-ing is connected to mobility. Successful gleaning involves a patient search, both for sites and for the objects of interest; it requires information (sometimes in the form of a map with details about the sites and times for disposing old objects, or of a tide table), knowledge (of the territory, as well as of the law and codes of practice), perseverance (it usually requires returning to the site several times) and even luck (many are the chance encounters). In order to glean – images, objects, foods – one has to leave the house and go about. More than the figure of the vagabond, who incessantly moves from place to place, progressing in space, that of the nomad is of use here. Gleaning is the opposite of cultivating the land, of accumulating, of ownership; but is also distant from the idea of migrating and changing places. It is closer to the lifestyle of the nomad, as described by Deleuze and Guattari:

> The nomad is not at all the same as the migrant; for the migrant goes principally from one point to another, even if the second point is uncertain, unforeseen, or not well localised. But the nomad only goes from point to point as a consequence and as a factual necessity ... Whereas the migrant leaves behind a milieu that has become amorphous or hostile, the nomad is one who does not depart, does not want to depart, who clings to the smooth space left by the receding forest, where the steppe or the desert advance, and who invents nomadism as a response to this challenge. (1986: 50–1)

Nomadism for Deleuze and Guattari is a certain way of being in space:

> There is ... a significant difference between the spaces: sedentary space is striated, by walls, enclosures and roads between enclosures, while nomad space is smooth, marked only by traits that are effaced and displaced with the trajectory ... The nomad distributes himself in a smooth space, he occupies, inhabits, holds that space; that is his territorial principle. (1986: 51)

If nomadic space is smooth, sedentary space is striated by the organising principles of money, work, road building, farming and housing.[5] Contemporary gleaners in France are seen by Varda in a light similar to Deleuze and Guattari's nomads: gleaning is the response to a challenge, an oppositional practice. Gleaners 'live smooth' in a striated space, both urban and rural. The agricultural space of contemporary France, for instance, is shown by Varda as striated by all-powerful machines that maximise production and harvesting. Yet these machines have faults and leave behind a surplus of 'unpicked' produce, as much as the machine of the capitalist EU market produces a surplus of 'unsellable', oversized or misshapen produce. Thus, a smooth space is created within the striated space, where the practice of gleaning can flourish as a response to the challenge of poverty and unemployment. The city for Deleuze and Guattari is the striated space *par excellence*; however, it is also the space from which smooth space is put back into operation:

> The smooth spaces arising from the city are not only those of worldwide organisation, but also a counterattack combining the smooth and the holey and turning back against the town: sprawling, temporary, shifty shantytowns of nomads and cave dwellers, scrap metal and fabric, patchwork, to which the striation of money, work or housing are no longer even relevant. (1988: 481)

Like nomads in the city, Varda's urban gleaners pick foodstuff, appliances and various objects from the surplus of product that is discarded and left behind in the sites of street markets, in domestic or commercial rubbish bins, on the side of roads and in public dumps – once again, their gleaning is a response to the challenge of poverty and unemployment, which flourishes in smooth, interstitial places where surplus is abandoned. Some of Varda's interviewees, though, practice gleaning as a form of active resistance and opposition – the most outspoken being the man in green boots, who declares: 'I am an activist, salvaging is a matter of ethics for me'; but also the young biologist who commutes every morning to sell newspapers and glean food, and in the evening teaches French to immigrants in the Parisian *banlieue*; the group of young homeless in Prades, who adopt an alternative, nomadic lifestyle; or the pickers who state they do it because they do not want to see fruit and vegetables go to waste. The artists as well, more or less overtly, glean for oppositional reasons. Varda's own form of artistic gleaning produces counter-cinema – by using a cheap, lightweight medium Varda made a non-mainstream, non-art-house, political film which denounces poverty and the suffering of people left behind by a society that authorises waste on a mass scale. Her film is also an example of 'women's cinema' – as Rosello convincingly shows, Varda 'questions both the cultural definition of female beauty and the cultural imperative that makes beauty mandatory in our representational universe' (2001: 34). Varda is well capable of drawing distinctions between practices of contemporary gleaning – some glean objects to use in their art; some glean for the pleasure of it; some glean as an oppositional practice; others glean because they are poor and starving. 'I never forget', proclaims Varda. 'They got to roam around to kill the hunger', shouts a rap song on the soundtrack.

Dear Diary: a nomadic transit in the city

> I don't know, I can't understand. I may be nuts, but I love this bridge. I need to cross it at least twice a day. (Moretti, in 'On my Vespa', *Dear Diary*)

Nanni Moretti's *Dear Diary* presents an unusual structure in three sections, 'On My Vespa', 'Islands' and 'Doctors', corresponding to three chapters of the eponymous diary, which the author is shown handwriting during the film. The film adapts the fragmentary and diverse form of the diary to cinematic language, therefore presenting a mix of autobiography and critical distance, private confession and commentary on public affairs. This linguistic and narrative mix makes *Dear Diary* (and its sequel *Aprile*, 1998) a unique film, one which apparently does not compare to anything else. And yet the imprint of the cinema of Roberto Rossellini and of the theories of Cesare Zavattini are strong in the film. Whereas Rossellini's lesson emerges in the film's attention to reality and in its moral attitude towards life and its contradictions, a series of elements vividly recall Zavattini's most extreme ideas: the conveyed feel of 'a day in the life of Nanni M.'; the shadowing of a real person for a day; the use of the camera as a pen, as a light and (at least apparently) inexpensive medium that allows free movement; and the creation of a cinema that talks of real and individual feelings, ideas and experiences, as in Zavattini's utopian project of the *Cinegiornali Liberi* ('Free Newsreels'). Even more importantly, in the 1950s Zavattini claimed that the diary, intended as 'the attempt to offer to the judgement [of the spectator] oneself, the others and everything worth telling', is 'the most complete and authentic expression of the cinema' (1979: 71–2). The filmmaking in *Dear Diary* is consistent both ideologically and aesthetically with Zavattini's cinematic language. A critic pointed out that the presence of Zavattini in *Dear Diary* becomes apparent in the film's movement:

The physical movement translates the necessity of discovering other dimensions, other destinations, thus of transcending the level of the appearances in order to seize something deeper. Those small intervals, in which the camera follows the character from afar, renovating Zavattini's theory of the shadowing to uncover other dimensions of reality, are in this sense significant. (Marangi 1999: 22)

Movement is very evident in the first 'chapter', an urban journey in which Moretti rides his Vespa in August around Rome, unusually deserted because of the summer vacations. The camera follows the filmmaker, who rides aimlessly through the empty streets, squares and bridges of the capital, gazing at the houses, fantasising on his passion for dancing, discussing films and talking to casual passers-by (including actress Jennifer Beals and filmmaker Alexander Rockwell). The second chapter is based on an actual trip: Moretti goes to the Eolie Islands looking for a peaceful place to work, but then incessantly moves from one island to the next, as he cannot find what he is seeking. The last and apparently more static chapter may be seen as Moretti's journey from one doctor to the next, in search for the right cure for a tormenting itch: as one critic noticed, '*Dear Diary* is a kind of road movie, from a quarter to another, from an isle to another, from a doctor to another' (Gili 1994: 12). We will limit our enquiry to the first chapter, 'On My Vespa', which presents the most fitting material for the discussion of our topic – urban nomadism.

The pervasive presence of motion in *Dear Diary* was noted by more than one critic. Flavio De Bernardinis (1998) has suggested that the film be read in the light of Mario Perniola's (1998) theory of the 'transit'. Observing that our society has lost both the idea of the past and that of the future, both the concept of fatherland and that of utopia, Perniola suggests that we live in a state of becoming, of movement lacking precise direction, of a shifting in which nothing reaches its destination. This movement is, for the philosopher, a 'transit', a passage from the present to the present (given the absence of past and future), a movement from the same to the same, which is nevertheless the opposite of fixation and the failure to transform. De Bernardinis suggests that *Dear Diary* be viewed as being pervaded by the dimension of the transit, because the film 'proceeds through imperceptible shifts, tiny returns, microscopic accelerations', and because it celebrates *atopia*, which is 'the negation of place as destiny, as absolute destination, as metaphysical objective' (1998: 128 and 130).

Although agreeing in general terms with this reading, we argue that an important distinction must be drawn between the first and the other two episodes of the film. In 'Islands' and in 'Doctors' a purpose and a destination of the travel subsist: in the first case, it is the right island (which does not exist); in the second case, the right diagnosis and the right cure (which do exist). In both cases, there is something to be learned from the journey, as can be seen by the two following entries of Moretti's diary: 'Dear diary, I am happy only at sea, sailing from the island I've left to the one I'm going to' ('Islands'); 'Dear diary, I have learnt that in the morning, before breakfast, it's healthy to drink a glass of water' ('Doctors').

Whereas it is not possible in our opinion to call 'Islands' and 'Doctors' instances of pure transit, 'On My Vespa' presents a totally different trip, in this case a true transit. Moretti's ride through Rome is not a journey proper, as there is no departure (the filmmaker is first seen when already in motion) and no true destination (even if at the end of the 'chapter' Moretti does stop at the site of Pasolini's murder, this too is a detour in the filmmaker's peregrinations, and no real ending of the episode). 'On My Vespa' elects a permanent inclination to dislocation, to the detour, and to fluctuation. Furthermore, there is nothing essential to be learnt from the journey – only a lengthy list to be drawn of pleasant things to do.

Moretti's attitude in this episode is self-indulgent and almost hedonistic, and the relationship with the city is so positive and pleasurable that it makes us think of modern *flânerie*. The modern *flâneur*, as we saw in the chapter devoted to the films of Patrick Keiller, is 'a man of the crowd but not in the crowd', a stroller who visits the various locations on foot, who enjoys the spectacle of the crowds and gazes at people but who also wants to keep a distance, refusing to engage with others, and who gawks at the city simultaneously as a miniature world or landscape, and as an interior or apartment. Moretti does show some characteristics of the modern *flâneur*, for instance he enjoys the spectacle of the crowd (in the episode in which

Fig. 11 Nanni Moretti's *Caro diario* (*Dear Diary*, Italy, 1994) © Sacher Film

he looks with pleasure and envy at the group of dancers); nevertheless, he is generally more interested in the city in architectural terms than in its inhabitants: the
landscape he gazes at is one of houses, squares, bridges and buildings rather than
of crowds – and in fact his journey takes place in the middle of August, when
Rome is almost deserted. Also, despite the fact that he suggests to a passer-by that
he will always 'only feel comfortable with a minority', he does seek contact with
people, rather than keeping at a distance. Furthermore, whereas the *flâneur* is both
attracted to and afraid of the city, Moretti is fully comfortable and optimistic.

Moretti's ride bears more direct similarities with the detours of the situationists in Paris in the 1960s. Guy Debord and his friends practiced their 'psychogeo-
graphic' detours in the city, or in specific quarters, which became novel urban
landscapes, lands of playful and dream-like adventures and encounters. The playful and even oneiric side to Moretti's journey is evident – it suffices to think of
his paradoxical, almost surreal exchanges with the film critic he tortures by reading to him his fanatic prose, or his encounter with Jennifer Beals and Alexander
Rockwell, or his general light-hearted and humorous attitude. Moretti's trip does
not reach the unfamiliar and disorienting results of the situationists' detours; he
always knows very well his way around, the names and history of the areas he
visits and the routes to follow, and never appears disoriented and surprised. On
the other hand, he does perform a sort of research on the various areas of the city,

and reflects – as the situationists did – on the sensations and feelings that different urban areas elicit, without simplistically connecting them to the affluence or deprivation that characterise them. For instance, he visits an area that has the fame of being ugly and depressing, Spinaceto, and finds it surprisingly pleasant. In another instance, he acknowledges the inexplicable attraction that the Flaminio Bridge exercises on him. Moretti's interest in the architecture of Rome does not derive from purely aesthetic concerns: some of the buildings are beautiful, other ones much less so. His route is not rational, but follows a secret logic and the attraction exercised by places; his journey traces a true 'psychogeography' of Rome. In this landscape, like the situationists, Moretti has absurd, surreal encounters, and even plays, for instance, at being a filmmaker who is scouting locations for making a musical on a Trotskyite pastry cook in the conformist Italy of the 1950s.

There is an apparent distinction between Moretti's journey and those of the situationists. While the latter wanted to make art – they wanted to create *situations* through playing with architecture, time and space – Nanni (as a character) simply wants to enjoy the pleasure of riding his Vespa through his city while gazing at it. However, Moretti in truth travels in order to produce art – he transforms his journey through the city into a film. In voice-over Moretti exclaims: 'What would be great is a film just of houses, panning shots of houses!' – and that film is indeed made. Nevertheless, there is no intention to produce an avant-garde cinema of poetry in Moretti, or in transforming his life in a work of art – his attitude is much more modest and self-ironic than the situationists.

Both the *flâneur* and the situationists were walkers, only distinguished by the speed of their pace, leisurely in the case of the *flâneur*, variable but faster in that of the situationists – as Debord wrote, 'the *dérive* is a technique of the rapid passing through different locations' (quoted in Ghezzi & Turigliatto 2001: 29). Moretti, instead, does not walk, but rides his Vespa. We suggest that, whereas the *flâneur* and the situationist are figures of modernity (despite being more recent, the *dérive* is a true modernist avant-garde activity that has much in common with Surrealism), Moretti is a postmodern traveller. His journey is best described as a nomadic transit through Rome – in the sense attached to the term (and already addressed above) by Deleuze and Guattari. The fragmented and dispersed contemporary urban space can be seen simultaneously as alienating and frustrating (as seen in the episode of the traffic jam in *Dear Diary*'s 'Doctors'), and as positive and liberating, because its same fragmentation can offer spots in which different lifestyles may be developed. We refer once again to the difference between smooth space and striated space: the first being typically nomadic, the second sedentary. The organising principles of money, work and housing make of the city the striated space *par excellence*, but Deleuze and Guattari suggest that there are two forms of urban nomadism that allow 'smooth' living in the urban space: the first is the 'sprawling, temporary, shifty shantytowns of nomads and cave dwellers, scrap metal and fabric, patchwork, to which the striation of money, work or housing are no longer even relevant'.[6] The second is the transit: 'For example, a stroll taken by Henry Miller in Clichy or Brooklyn is a nomadic transit in smooth space; he makes the city disgorge a patchwork, differentials of speed, delays and accelerations, changes in orientation, continuous variations...' (Deleuze & Guattari 1988: 481–2).

It is the second form of urban nomadism that Nanni engages with. Rather than producing it by strolling, he mobilises himself and his gaze by riding his Vespa. The scooter, which in films such as *Noi due soli* (Marino Girolami, 1952), *Roman Holiday* (William Wyler, 1953) and *Poveri ma belli* (Dino Risi, 1957) had already proved its potential in the Roman space, is the (distant) urban relative of the Harley Davidson immortalised by *Easy Rider* as the ideal means to cross in total freedom the wide open spaces of North America. Moretti's Vespa produces both the sense of personal freedom, playfulness and enjoinment, and the lack of restrictions, suppleness and lightness of the gaze. This gaze is both human and mechanical: the first image of the opening chapter, after that of the hand writing the diary, is an objective/subjective shot of the camera, which travels forward in a street; a few seconds later, Moretti on his Vespa comes out from behind the camera, becoming its personification, and begins to travel forward. The camera, from now on, will either follow him (including him in the frame, and thus performing that shot which is sometimes defined as a 'semi-subjective') or replaces his gaze (performing a classical subjective shot). The filmmaker on his Vespa appears as a true materialisation of the camera. The 'filmmaker's mobilized gaze' (Marcus 1996: 239) – and that of the camera behind him – makes the city 'disgorge a patchwork, differentials of speed, delays and accelerations, changes in orientation, continuous variations'.

This smooth transit in the otherwise striated city can take place for two reasons: because the city is deserted for the summer holidays, thus no traffic is seen in the streets and the Vespa enjoys complete freedom of movement (so much so that it can even 'dance'); and because Moretti has deliberately become a postmodern nomad, in the oppositional sense of Deleuze and Guattari. Moretti's elective nomadism is highlighted by his gear (he almost never takes off his helmet and dark glasses, which show his status as a biker – with its associations of freedom and mobility), and by his ideological position in a society in which he is in agreement only with a minority. Even his choice of an old Vespa as a means of transport is an ideological statement, and shows Moretti's self-elected marginal position. His habitual critical attitude towards the homogenised capitalist society is not diminished by his cheerful, *flânerian* mood; contemporary Italian films and film critics,

American movies, high house prices, the decadence of Rome's socio-physical environment, and the shameful 'monument' in memory of Pasolini all become targets of his satire. In the eyes of the urban nomad, Rome becomes supple, soft, almost marginal, thanks to the choice of areas rarely seen on screen, and almost non-Italian, thanks to a soundtrack dominated by world music.

chapter six
EAST MEETS WEST: THE POST-COMMUNIST DIASPORA

'Diaspora' – as much as 'nomad' and 'nomadism', terms explored and used in the previous chapter – is a problematic expression endowed with a long history and used in different and sometimes contradictory ways in contemporary theoretical and critical discourses. The archetype of all diasporas is of course the scattering of the Jews after the Assyrian, Babylonian and Roman conquests, but the term has also been attached to more recent scatterings of peoples, including Armenians, Africans, Chinese, Indians, Irish, Greeks, Lebanese, Palestinians, Vietnamese and Koreans (Chaliand & Rageau 1995); Caribbean peoples and Sikhs (Cohen 1997); Turks, Haitians, Mexican, Nepalese and Albanians (Van Hear 1998). Commonly, 'diaspora' denotes displacement from a centre, from a homeland: 'Diasporas are the result of the "scattering" of peoples, whether as the result of war, oppression, poverty, enslavement or the search for better economic and social opportunities, with the inevitable opening of their culture to new influences or pressures' (Woodward 1997: 304). Nicholas Van Hear suggests three minimal criteria that characterise diaspora: 'First, the population is dispersed from a homeland over two or more other territories. Second, the presence abroad is enduring, although exile is not necessarily permanent, but may include movement between homeland and new host. And third, there is a kind of exchange – social, economic, political or cultural - between or among the spatially separated populations comprising the diaspora' (1998: 6).

Diaspora has much in common with the term 'exile'; both experiences may be either enforced or self-imposed, and are often the result of violence or a threat. 'Yet, despite their close affinities, in recent usage *diaspora* often lacks the pathos of *exile*, a term that is never without a deep sense of woe' (Peters 1999: 20). Whereas exile usually implies a missing home, and an intense longing to return to it, diaspora may connote a way of living far from home without fostering the will to go back. Furthermore, whereas the condition of exile can concern a single person, diaspora is always collective and suggests a network of real or imagined relationships between compatriots.

As much as nomadism, both diaspora and exile are often used in contemporary theoretical and political discourses, having been invested by metaphorical meanings and much romanticised. All these concepts 'are often invoked of late as alternatives and antidotes to the totalling character of Western society and thought' (Peters 1999: 17). Whereas nomadism has for some become the epitome of postmodern subjectivity (Deleuze and Guattari 1986 and 1988; Braidotti 1994), many usages of exile have an unambiguous modern slant which has been deconstructed, for instance by Caren Kaplan, who has explored the strong component of imperialist nostalgia in Euro-American constructions of exile (1996: 33–40). 'Diaspora' is also used as a metaphor of identity in contemporary debates – as in Stuart Hall's 'diasporic identities'.

> [Diaspora] is an extra-national term which contributes to the analysis of intercultural and transcultural processes and forms. It has an extra – though disputed – currency in contemporary political life as part of a new vocabulary that registers the constitutive power of space, spatiality, distance, travel and movement in human sciences that were once premised upon time, temporality, fixity, rootedness and the sedentary. (Woodward 1997: 329)

It is within this framework that we are going to employ 'diaspora' as a term that calls attention to the historical and experiential rift between homeland and place of residence, as well as to the challenge that the diasporic condition brings to the modern political forms and meanings of citizenship.

In this chapter we are going to address the phenomenon of what we call the post-communist diaspora – the scattering of Eastern Europeans after the fall of the Berlin Wall and the crumbling of the Iron Curtain. Whereas in the previous chapter we used the terms 'nomad' and 'vagabond' within the context of postmodern discourse, thus intentionally furnishing them with metaphorical meanings, here we adopt the term 'diaspora' to refer to a historical phenomenon rather than to a metaphorical construction. Nonetheless, because we take the end of Communism as one of the principal factors that have greatly increased movement in this continent in the past three decades, we see the Eastern European travellers depicted in our films also as an expression and as a symbol of the extreme mobility that characterises postmodern Europe. In addition, the diasporic condition implies a 'suspension' of one's identity, a position of difference both from one's homeland and from the host country (Laguerre 1988: 9), and therefore easily becomes, like exile, the epitome of the generalised postmodern condition of rootlessness. We will nevertheless strive to avoid the risk that the symbolical component of the concept may obliterate historical, gender, class and socio-economic differences. The use of the term 'diaspora' will allow us to highlight several elements of this phe-nomenon: the displacement from a bygone centre, both intended as home(land) and as centre of power; the search for a new home in the host country, while main-taining a condition of difference; the challenge brought to the idea of nationality and of citizenship.

As well as in terms of diaspora, we will also read the post-communist scattering in terms of emigration, looking at issues such as legal and illegal border crossing and national and European immigration policies on the one hand and, on the other, motivations to emigrate, private experiences in the host country and the negotiation and redefinition of identities. In this context, we shall adopt and adapt the perspective, deriving from Max Weber's studies on migratory movements in the Eastern provinces of Prussia in the 1890s (1984; 1993), which 'traces at the origins of the migratory movement an *individual* gesture of refusal, the claim of the right to secession and escape from the prevalent patriarchal organisation ... which becomes a social process inasmuch as it presents itself as a *mass* experience' (Mezzadra 2001: 48).[1] In other words, we will concentrate on the *individual* and private component of this process of scattering, while at the same time considering it a *social* migratory movement.

The post-Berlin Wall scattering: a new migration?

Research on recent migratory movements in Europe has greatly increased. This growing body of work suggests the idea of a novelty factor, encapsulated by the widely used expression 'new migration'. This is identified with a set of movements that are prevalently seen as the result of a series of social, economic and political transformations which took place in the last twenty to thirty years. The events principally referred to as causes of the new migration are the impact of *glasnost* through the Eastern Bloc, the end of the Cold War, the fall of Communism, and the disintegration of the Soviet Union. Other parallel and contributory factors which have been widely identified are the advent of post-Fordism, with the decline of the manufacturing industry, the shift to a service economy, the growth of disor-ganised capitalism, of neo-liberal economy, and of globalisation; the strengthening of the European Union, the disappearance of some customs and borders (while other borders strengthened after the collapse of the Berlin Wall), the diffusion of a common currency, and the formation of a single market; conflicts such as those in the Balkans, which have made refugees of many and have reconfigured whole geographical areas; and the growing poverty of the Third World.

Some scholars question the 'novelty' of the post-1989 European migrations. Many of these movements should be contextualised and read as a continuation or strengthening of patterns which had been at work for some time. This is the case, for instance, of the expulsion of ethnic Turks from Bulgaria. In 1989 more than 300,000 ethnic Turks who had long been settled in Bulgaria were obliged to leave the country as the result of a failed attempt at cancelling their Turkish identity and assimilating them to the majority Slav society. One of the largest European mass exoduses since the end of World War II, this diaspora was in fact part of a process of emigration that started with the collapse of Ottoman rule in the Balkans: 'successive waves of Turkish emigration occurred, peaking in the first part of the twentieth century and in the early 1950s, when what was effectively a forced mass exodus was instigated by the Bulgarian authorities. The still larger expulsion of 1989 thus had ample historical precedent in the turbulent Bulgarian migratory order' (Van Hear 1998: 118). Similarly, the emigration of Jews and ethnic Germans from Russia and the return of ethnic Russians from the Transcaucasian and Central Asian Republics have been occurring since the 1970s (Codagnone 1998). Other movements in post-Berlin Wall Europe are instead truly 'new', for instance the mass emigration of Albanians to Greece and Italy after the demise of the communist regime, or the flight of refugees from the war in the former Yugoslavia, or the migrations from capitalist to ex-communist countries (for example, after 1989 many Poles returned to the motherland from Australia and Germany).

Although in some cases the migratory movements to and within Europe were accelerated but not necessarily caused by the fall of Communism, many factors induce us to look at them as 'new migration'. First, the collapse of the Eastern Bloc and the opening of the borders between East and West are estimated to have triggered the migration of up to four million people in Europe between 1989 and 1994. At the same time, the outbreak of ethnically motivated wars and so-called 'ethnic cleansing' have precipitated the expulsion and flight of an estimated five million refugees from the territory of the former Yugoslavia alone (see Koser & Lutz 1998: 1). These numbers justify the use of the term 'new'. Furthermore, we are confronted with a novel geography of migration in Europe, both in the sense of new countries of origin (for instance Yugoslavia) and new countries of destination, both in Southern and Eastern Europe (for instance Russia, Italy, Greece). Scholars also speak of new types of migration, with an intensification of short-term and transit movements, as well as the 'regional' migrations in the Europe of free movement of employees, capital and services. Consequently, commentators talk about an increasingly wide range of migrant subjects, including highly-skilled workers, clandestine migrants and asylum seekers – and 'an important overall comment is that together they embody an increasing polarity in migration flows … manifested by a bipolar distribution according to skills, occupation and income' (Koser & Lutz 1998: 2). The feminisation of migration is another novelty factor: whereas in the past migration was essentially a male phenomenon and woman followed the man as a member of his family, the new migration is characterised by a mobilisation of women who travel alone leaving their families behind or who are the main stimulus in the relocation of their relations.

Although not always 'new', the post-Berlin Wall migratory movements are certainly 'newly relevant', to use the expression suggested by Cristiano Codagnone (1998). The end of Communism not only put in motion people from outside and inside Europe, but also impacted on the socio-geographical aspect of the continent, and ultimately on the idea of Europe itself. Therefore, the importance of the discourse on migration in the current political discourse is paramount. As the East/West boundary dissolves, and the North/South boundary becomes the main divide, 'in Europe we are witnessing a redefinition of the organisation of territory and borders established in the first half of this century' (Montanari & Cortese 1993a: 229); processes of construction of the frontier – both in geopolitical terms and in terms of national identity – have greatly intensified. Migration policies and immigration control are at the core of the current political agenda in many European countries, and in the European Union itself. The new migration has raised waves of alarm in many European societies, often causing the resurgence of racism and nationalism. The attention currently given to the issue of illegal immigration 'also stems from a moral panic among politicians and parts of the population … The "illegal immigrant" has become a social symbol for immigrants who supposedly abuse welfare arrangements (social security, housing, education and health care), commit crimes and jeopardise the employment of established citizens' (Engbersen & van der Leun 1998: 200). At the same time, Western Europe is caught in a 'conflict of interest and of policy' typical of industrialised societies – 'between maximising labour supply (and flexibility) on the one hand and protecting a nation's cultural integrity on the other' (Fielding 1993: 42).

Through the analysis of relevant films, we intend to highlight and discuss two main aspects of the new migration, and specifically of the post-Berlin Wall diaspora: the challenge to the twentieth century concept of citizenship, based on the once prevalent experience of sedentariness and rootedness; and the role of the frontier in the post-communist diaspora.

The crisis of home: seeking love and bread in Fortress Europe

Two films about the new migration, the international co-production *Code inconnu: Récit incomplet de divers voyages* (*Code Unknown: Incomplete Tales of Several Journeys*, 2000) by Austrian filmmaker Michael Haneke, and the British-produced *Last Resort* (2000) by Polish-born director Pawel Pawlikowski, identify and confirm the existence of some of the novelty factors listed above: for instance, the feminisation of migration flows – both films concentrate on women travelling from Eastern European countries: Maria, a Romanian who twice leaves her home and family back in Romania to travel to Paris, in the hope of making some money; and Tanya, a Russian single mother who comes to Britain with her 10-year-old son Artiom to meet her English 'fiancée', who does not even show up at the airport. Also, the categories of travellers that these characters embody: the refugee (although an 'accidental refugee') in the case of Tanya, who decides to seek political asylum in order to gain time and try to contact the man she came to be with; and the clandestine migrant in the case of Maria. We will analyse and compare the post-Berlin Wall journeys of these two new migrants; in particular, we will look at how these two films construct the idea of the journey as tension between home and away, but challenging the old conception of home as well as of citizenship.

Most road movies are deeply concerned with the theme of home:

> Typically, the road takes the traveler away from home. Sometimes, the road leads to a new home, as in frontier narratives or tales of emigration. As often, in various kinds of escape and travel narratives, the road just leads away – away from boredom, or danger, or family, or whatever it is that produces the desire or need for something called 'away' as opposed to the place called 'home'. While it provides an escape from and an alternative to home, and home can be 'anywhere and everywhere' on the road … the trope of the road still requires the concept of home as a structuring absence. (Robertson 1997: 271)

Whereas in most films about immigration the road takes the traveller from the old home to a new home, these two films show that home no longer exists in the sense of a permanent hub. According to many observers, including Anthony Giddens (1990), Stuart Hall (1992) and Zygmunt Bauman (2000), in postmodernity it is impossible to find anything solid, and we are all condemned to decentredness, fragmentation and fluidity; these two films, in our opinion, accordingly subvert customary representations of home, although adopting different strategies in their construction of spatiality and mobility.

Code Unknown: the home as (incomplete) journey

At the beginning of *Code Unknown* a deaf child mimes a feeling or situation which her friends must decipher. The other children's unsuccessful attempts at decoding the mimed scene are expressed in the language of signs, which to non-hearing-impaired spectators is equally undecipherable. Subtitles name their conjectures:

'alone'; 'hiding place'; 'gangster'; 'bad conscience'; 'sad'; 'imprisoned'. It is tempting to adopt this list (exclusive of 'gangster', a hypothesis which makes the girl smile for its absurdity) as a guide to try to make sense of the rest of the film. The narrative is in fact one to be deciphered, consisting as it is of fragments of blandly interconnected stories regarding five main characters: Anne, a French actress, who tries to further her career in the cinema and the theatre; her war-photographer boyfriend, Georges, who comes and goes from Kosovo; Georges' younger brother Jean, who resists his father's plan to retire and leave him the family farm in the North of France; Maria, a Romanian illegal immigrant who begs in the Parisian streets; and Amadou, a teacher of deaf children, originally from Mali. The expressions 'alone', 'sad' and 'bad conscience' can easily apply to many of the characters, in tune with the film's modernist critique of life in Western society and the impossibility of communication among people. We are more interested in taking up the two spatial hypotheses put forward by the children, those of 'hiding place' and 'imprisoned', and explore them in relation to the theme of this chapter: the post-communist diaspora and the new migration. We will argue that *Code Unknown* associates and equates the seemingly contradictory concepts of travel and home, and that the film's most striking achievement is its use of different elements of the *mise-en-scène* to construct a peculiar type of space, of which motion and transit are fundamental components. Although it cannot be described as a traditional road movie, this film is about travelling, as its subtitle confirms. It explores life in terms of tension between movement and sedentariness, between travel and home, of a series of transits from place to place – and these stations can be sites of passage, of shelter, as well as of entrapment. Ultimately, the impression that *Code Unknown* conveys is that there is not much difference between travel and home, because home is also seen as transit, as lack of permanency.

Place is on different levels an important factor for most of the characters in this film, and the question of home – absent or present – is essential and yet contradictory for all of them. Young Jean oscillates between the family farm, which he clearly perceives as a place of entrapment, and the external world, seen instead as freedom. He runs away twice: the first time he goes to Anne in Paris, looking for a hiding place, but she denies him protection claiming that her apartment is not big enough; the film does not follow Jean's second journey away from home. Anne shares her apartment with her boyfriend when he is in Paris, and fluctuates between her home and the stage or set as places of belonging. Her apartment functions as a temporary shelter, where she sleeps and rests; the stage and set are at first characterised as her true space or even home, but they are soon shown as sites of entrapment and control, in which Anne is scrutinised by (often invisible) people and by cameras. The entrapping quality of these places becomes self-evident in the scenes of the audition and then shooting of the thriller, in which Anne is captured in a windowless room transformed into a gas chamber by a maniac who wants to watch her die.[2] Even her apartment is slowly shown to be an insufficient or inadequate shelter for her, since here she is reached and disturbed by the desperate screaming of a child living next door (another character who is literally imprisoned in her own home) and even receives from under the door an anonymous letter asking for help. Although distressed by these incidents, Anne does not act and in the end will attend the funeral of her little neighbour. Her sentimental relationship adds to the transitory feel of her home: Georges, in fact, only transits from Anne's apartment during the pauses between his trips to Kosovo, and claims at some point to prefer being in war areas, where life is 'less complicated' than at home.

Amadou lives in a pleasant-looking apartment that he shares with his large family, but also for him home is not associated with sedentariness and rooted-ness, rather with transit and tension between places, as in Hall's diasporic identi-ties – Mali as the fatherland and France as the place of residence. Amadou is never seen pondering about going back, but his edginess and heightened sense of dignity are the result of this tension, of the awareness of his 'incomplete belonging' to the host country. When he is maltreated by the police for defending Maria, his mother goes to a compatriot, an advisor and seer, who claims that someone disapproves of Amadou mixing with white people and wants him to return. 'Return where?' his mother asks. 'Home, to the land of his ancestors' is the reply. Although Amadou's mother takes this possibility as ridiculous, her husband later in the narrative ac-tually decides to return to Africa, in a journey back home which has an unclear ending – as a relative argues, others have gone but have not come back, and have formed new families there.

Contrary to Georges, who goes to war-torn Eastern Europe looking for that 'simplicity' he cannot find at home, Maria goes to Western Europe in search of bread. She is a member of the new migration: a transient illegal migrant, while her husband stays at home with the children she resides in the Western host country, France, only for brief periods. She has been in Paris for four months without find-ing work, and has become a beggar – her 'place' in Paris is a spot in a street, in front of a shop whose owner barely tolerates her presence. When Jean passing by throws a paper bag on her lap, with a mindless and insulting gesture, Amadou, who hap-pens to witness the scene, intervenes and tries to force Jean to apologise. This is the beginning of an argument that attracts the attention of the police and ends up with Jean being dismissed and Amadou and Maria being escorted to the police station. Maria, who is without documents, will be repatriated. Back in Romania, she finds her family moving into an unfinished house which, with its bare walls, highlights once again the lack of permanence of home and which also contrasts sharply with

Anne's fully-furnished Paris flat. Having being back only shortly, Maria is offered the opportunity to return to Paris with four other compatriots, hidden in a German truck. Once again in Paris, her hopes to inherit from an acquaintance a work permit as a newspaper seller quickly vanish, and she is left to despair over the shame of having to beg in the street once again. In a brief and dark night-time sequence we are shown the place that she shares with her compatriots; the ambience – possibly an attic – is not clearly visible, and listening to the characters signing together we actually wonder whether we are in Paris or back in one of the unfinished buildings of the Romanian sequences. Even her old 'work place' is gone: when Maria goes back to her street, she finds that it is now occupied by another woman. She walks back and forth, and then chooses a new spot in front of a different shop; she carefully lays down her newspapers and sits. The owner of the shop comes out to peer at her and goes back inside; shortly after two menacing men come to talk to Maria. We see the scene from the distance, and cannot hear the dialogue (the soundtrack is now covered by the drums of the deaf children continuing from the previous sequence). Maria gets up and leaves, accompanied by the menacing gaze of the two men. Whatever the meaning of this sequence, the result is, once again, the loss of a fixed place for the character, whom we leave roaming the street.

Because it is constructed as a place of conflict and transience, home in *Code Unknown* is somehow itself a form of journey – where journey is intended as a non-concluded tension between here and elsewhere, as transit from place to place. Such a situation is shared by all the characters in the film – the new migrants like Maria, who are trying to move around in 'Fortress Europe' to improve the life condition of their families, but whose right to do so is not recognised; those who belong to a prior migration, and are therefore French citizens, but whose identity card does not have the same importance as that of a white French person, as in the case of Amadou; and those who have all the rights, and primarily the rights of residing and of moving freely, even across frontiers. Nevertheless, the 'full' French citizens in *Code Unknown* are, as much as the migrants, also looking for hiding places; they often feel imprisoned, and their moving around is compulsive, without destination and almost pointless. The idea of 'citizenship' – traditionally seen as the condition of being endowed with the rights to reside, work and travel – is undermined by the subtraction of meaning from the concepts of 'residence', 'work' and 'travel'. *Code Unknown*, although careful at distinguishing between characters on the basis of census, ethnicity, gender and wave of migration, clearly points to the existence of a new society in which the old Western bastions of national and personal identity have been undermined and replaced by a void, a fragmentation of experience and a diffuse awareness of the increasing ambiguity of the real and of the lack of codes to interpret it. In this society, sedentariness and rootedness have lost their meaning and have been replaced by movement, which is often senseless and inconclusive. Seen in this perspective, the idea of Fortress Europe looks like an expression of the nostalgia for fixity, in the face of a fluidity that repositions us all and gives us all a diasporic identity.

Last Resort: the futility of escaping home

Whereas Maria in *Code Unknown* travels to Paris in search for bread, Tanya in *Last Resort* goes to Britain looking for love. The distinction is fundamental – Tanya's journey defies the commonplace expectation by which Easterners travel to Western countries lured by the wealth of the capitalist world. The same could be said of the Swedish *Lilja 4-Ever* by Lukas Moodysson (2002), which shows a Russian girl going to Sweden in search of love. Although economic reasons certainly came into Tanya and Lilja's trips (the Western fiancées' perceived wealth must have played its part in the process of falling in love), the trips in these films are romantic quests, which is usually seen as a privilege of the prosperous Westerners. This is not the only commonplace subverted by *Last Resort*; Tanya's journey is unusual also because of the way in which it is represented, as stasis rather than movement, as hiatus rather than progression. As much as *Code Unknown* does, *Last Resort* also describes the journey as tension between home and away, but it does so by challenging and reassessing the standard conception of home (and therefore also of journey).

After landing in Stansted, when she realises that her British fiancée, Mark, is not in the airport waiting for her, Tanya decides to claim political asylum, in the hope of gaining time and look for him. Tanya and Artiom, her son, are transported to Stonehaven, a gloomy seaside resort, in which many others are held while their applications wait to be processed. Tanya and Artiom are assigned a grim apartment in a high-rise building, overlooking an abandoned amusement park, and are given food vouchers to buy unpleasant food in the local eating place. Tanya tries unsuccessfully to contact Mark through the only functioning public phone of the area, outside which people are constantly queuing. Apparently, Tanya and Artiom are free to move around – in truth, they are constantly under surveillance through cameras which are installed everywhere. They try to leave, but the station is 'closed until further notice'. Tanya and Artiom befriend the manager of the amusement arcade, Alfie, who helps them redecorate the flat, and even begins to date Tanya, who in the meantime has discovered that Mark has no intention of ever seeing her again. Tanya declares that she made a mistake when she claimed asylum, but is told that it will still take months to process her application to be repatriated. Alfie, though, finds a way to help Tanya and Artiom to escape.

Les Roberts (2002) has analysed in detail the three main zones through which Tanya moves with her son Artiom: the zone of arrival and departure (London Stansted Airport); the zone of transition (between airport and holding area); and the zone of stasis (Stonehaven). He rightly states that all three zones are characterised by an 'absence of agency in movement'; the characters, in fact, 'are *conveyed* through the airport on the shuttle car, *processed* by the immigration officials, *despatched* by the police and *delivered* to the holding area' (2002: 80). The film, although it describes a journey, actually insists on lack of movement and on the 'long periods of waiting and enforced sedentariness' (ibid.) for the characters, in this way subverting the idea that travel is a linear trajectory from departure to arrival. *Last Resort* is a film about a journey, yet it conveys a general sensation of lack of motion, which often provokes frustration in the protagonists. We claim that this approach to travel is characteristic of European road cinema, which is much more sensitive to the detour and the lingering than the majority of Hollywood road movies. Paired with this static conception of travel is an original construction of the idea of home, which we now want to explore.

Roberts notices that *Last Resort* makes ample use of those spaces that Marc Augé has called 'non-places': liminal zones of lingering, 'of sedentary and transitory experience', which – contrarily to utopia – exist but don't contain any organic society (2002: 79). He points to the fact that 'home' itself is ultimately a utopian construction, and thus cannot exist in spatio-temporal presentness. This argument is particularly relevant when looking at narratives of migration, in which the journey is often set in motion precisely by a utopian desire for a new home, and is frequently marked by the sense of irreparable loss of the former home. Roberts insists on the utopian nature of home as structuring absence (2002: 83–4), but also ascribes to home an experiential fullness when suggesting that Tanya's journey is inscribed in the polarity home/non-place: similarly to Augé's passenger through non-places, 'Tanya's desire to leave the resort becomes a desire to retrieve an experiential and phenomenological sense of being-in-the-world' (2002: 83). This sense is clearly attributed by Roberts to what came before the trip – home, which is therefore seen as the opposite of non-place.

The film does suggest through its narrative the existence of 'an experiential and phenomenological sense of being-in-the-world' linked to a stable home(land), for which Tanya craves while in the non-place of Stonehaven; yet we suggest that, by means of visual and verbal devices, *Last Resort* actually undermines this idea. Firstly, we are never shown 'home': the film begins and ends with the same, mirror sequence of Tanya and Artiom travelling on the airport shuttle. Many road films avoid showing the location of departure and of return, but in this case the repetition (with variations) of the same sequence typifies the two characters as 'travellers', almost detached from an outside reality, even more so because of the way in which they are framed. In both the opening and the closing sequences we see Tanya and Artiom on the shuttle, which enters the frame from the right and travels left through a tunnel, until it emerges from it. The camera is placed in a way that erases the presence of the shuttle, and pushes Tanya and Artiom 'outside', as if they were travelling in a motionless and magical way, suspended mid-air. In particular, while the first sequence has a diegetic soundtrack (with the airport announcements on the loudspeaker), the last sequence is accompanied by extra-diegetic, dream-like music; when the shuttle exits the tunnel, the two characters are invested by an unrealistic bright light, which submerges them until they disappear and the camera fades on white. Moreover, the two characters are travelling in the same direction in both sequences, thus the impression of repetition rather than of return (homecoming) is conveyed. Not only is Tanya and Artiom's home(land) erased by these sequences, but even the two characters themselves disappear from the screen, as if their existence materialised only in the act of travelling.

The unreal quality of Tanya's 'home' is confirmed later through verbal devices – Tanya's description of it to Alfie places it in the realm of the imaginary: 'I grew up in the forest, in a house with three women: me, my mother, my grandmother and my grand-grandmother.' This matriarchal home in the forest is marked as a place of solitude, madness and repetition: 'Everyone made the same mistake: married with the wrong man … and all life looking for love.' After this statement, Alfie asks her: 'Are you still looking for love?' Tanya replies: 'This is why I am here.' 'You found it now', is Alfie's reply.

Although Alfie has fallen in love with her, and she seems equally taken by him (and Artiom supports their relationship), Tanya will ultimately decide that she does not want to stay: 'I have to stop dreaming. I have to go back and start my life', she declares. This decision is puzzling and contradictory; in fact, there is no home in Russia for Tanya to go back to – she can only return to the solitude and madness of her mythologised origins. Her decision thus reveals the opposite of what she affirms – that she does not want to find a home, to transform a non-place like Stonehaven into a place in which she can have love and develop ties with an organic community, but that she rather wants to go on travelling and dreaming, as if she knew that 'home' is a utopia that can not be achieved in our times – and certainly not in Stonehaven.

The border after the Iron Curtain: Italy as new door to the East

Although it remains distinguished from it, the experience of the frontier, which shapes conceptually as well as practically the figure of the migrant, tends today to merge more and more often with the experience of diaspora ... What interests here is to draw attention to the consequences of the merger between frontier experience and diasporic experience for the specific form of 'belonging' which characterises the migrants: marked by a distance, which is a constituent of migration, from the country and 'culture' of the origins, it rarely becomes unconditional adhesion to the host country and its 'culture' and development of an aspiration to naturalisation. (Mezzadra 2001: 74)

In this section we wish to examine the relevance of the question of the frontier in the phenomenon of the post-communist diaspora. In order to reach conclusions of some relevance, we will concentrate on one case study, Italy, and will examine how the issues of the redefinition of the frontier with the East and of border-crossing in both eastbound and westbound journeys are represented in recent Italian films. In the past decade, Italy has become, together with other Mediterranean countries (Greece, Spain, and to a lesser extent Portugal) one of the main doors of immigration to the EU, from Eastern Europe as well as from Africa and from the Far East. 'This is explained partly by [its] location ... partly by the residual effects of African colonial influences, and partly by inadequate methods of surveillance and control. It is this last feature which accounts for Italy's current reputation as the "soft underbelly of Europe"' (Fielding 1993: 50). Furthermore, Italy, along with Greece, has become 'the second pole of attraction of the fluxes coming from Eastern Europe, after Germany' (Campani & Carchedi 1998: 16). This novel status is reflected not only in the emphasis placed on immigration in the current national political discourse, but also in the proliferation of Italian films that take Eastern European characters as their protagonists.[3]

Historically, Italy is a country of emigration, so much so that it is possible to talk of an Italian diaspora. 'In just one century [from the 1870s to the 1970s] a total of about 25 million Italians ... emigrated, almost 12 million to countries outside Europe' (Montanari & Cortese 1993b: 276). A steady drop in Italian emigration was recorded since the early 1970s, and in 1972 Italy achieved a positive emigration balance. Although immigration to Italy started in the 1970s, it was only after the collapse of Communism that the inflow became significant and a matter of concern to the public and the political establishment. At first, Italy was slow in reacting and no 'formal steps were taken to try to control the phenomenon effectively, and increasingly large groups were allowed to settle in the territory illegally' (Montanari & Cortese 1993a: 221). In 1982 and then in 1986 foreigners were given the opportunity to legalise their position, although this happened only to a small extent. In 1989 it became compulsory to have a residence permit. A law of February 1990 contained 'provisions for political asylum, the entry and residence of non-EC citizens, the legalisation of the position of non-EC citizens and stateless persons already in the State territory' (Montanari & Cortese 1993b: 281). Between 1990 and 1996 – the period covered by our four films in this chapter – the influx from Eastern Europe increased five fold: 'At the end of 1996 [those from Eastern Europe] represented approximately one fifth of the total number of foreigners in Italy – 22.8% (of a total of 1,095,622 immigrants) – registered on the basis of the residence permits' (Campani & Carchedi 1998: 20).

Given this historical context, the question of the frontier is of great relevance in contemporary Italy. Although the proximity of Eastern Europe was politically and also culturally relevant in the past, only after the fall of Communism did it become an issue of paramount importance. The frontier with the East has become an arena for the redefinition of the Italian identity, as well as of the European identity at large. The use of troops along the southern coastline, the patrolling of the sea and the police controls at the northeastern borders have intensified ever since the first landings of boats carrying Albanian refugees, and are an indication of the importance of the frontier both in geopolitical terms and in the current discourse on safety and on citizenship.

We will now consider how four recent Italian films describe the frontier with the East. Two of these, *Il toro* (*The Bull*, Carlo Mazzacurati, 1994) and *Lamerica* (Gianni Amelio, 1994), depict journeys of Italians to neighbouring post-communist countries; *Elvjs e Merilijn* (Armando Manni, 1995) and *Vesna va veloce* (*Vesna Goes Fast*, Carlo Mazzacurati, 1996), conversely, describe the frontier from the perspective of Eastern European characters illegally travelling to Italy. Although set in different regions and telling diverse stories, they are informed by a similar agenda, highlight similar problems and reach similar conclusions.

Il toro and *Lamerica*: the East as new frontier

In *Il toro*, before being made redundant, Franco had worked for nine years at the leading Italian farm of bulls for reproduction. Exasperated by his former employer's refusal to pay him his redundancy, Franco steals Corinto, the best bull in the farm, and persuades his friend Loris, a farmer in economic difficulty, to put the animal on his truck and drive with him to Hungary. Despite the lack of a document, they manage to cross the Yugoslavian border, but then run the risk that Corinto be killed and given to eat to a group of starved Croatian refugees. After a short break in a local farm, they reach a gigantic Hungarian farm, where they hope to sell Corinto to Sandor, with whom they had business dealings ten years earlier. However, Sandor is no longer the director of the cooperative, which after the fall of Communism was bought by English businessmen. These find out that

Corinto was stolen and refuse to buy it. Franco then offers the bull to a dodgy Italian businessman, but is derided by him and his local business partners. On their way back towards the Italian border, Loris and Franco get lost and end up in a cooperative where the farmers recognise Corinto and offer to buy it in exchange for 300 cattle.

In *Lamerica* Fiore and Gino, two Italian businessmen, come to post-communist Albania in 1991 with a view to buying a state-owned shoe factory at a bargain price, taking advantage of the financial chaos reigning in the country. In order to fulfil the requirements of the contract they must find an Albanian partner. They come across Spiro Tozaj, mentally ill and alone in the world, who spent thirty years in a prison camp doing hard labour. On the eve of the appointment at the Ministry of Industry Spiro disappears and Gino goes after him. This quest takes Gino all over a devastated and starving Albania. The purchase of the factory falls through and Gino is arrested and charged with corruption. After the police confiscate his passport, his only chance of returning to Italy is to pay his passage on one of the ships leaving for Bari with a load of illegal emigrants. On board he comes across Spiro, who now believes he is aboard a ship en route for America, where a future of work and well-being awaits him. Spiro dies during the trip (see O'healy 2004).

The crumbling of the Iron Curtain meant for the post-communist countries an abrupt and often traumatic assimilation to capitalism. Open for the first time to Western investment and business, the East in the 1990s became a true new frontier for Europe. A movement that can be defined as neo-colonial involved Western investors, entrepreneurs and, in some cases, conmen going East to take advantage of a situation which was perceived as being in transformation, and which was believed to offer new opportunities of an economic and, in some cases, not-so-legal nature. After years of closure and constraint, post-imperialist Europe had at its disposal a new land to colonise. *Il toro* and *Lamerica* make of this question one of the foremost characteristics of both their narrative and their cinematography. In terms of narrative, the clearest example is offered by *Lamerica*, whose Italian protagonists are soon revealed to be two conmen who plan to divert funds of the European Community thanks to a phoney business. They arrive in Albania by boat, almost in the footprints of the Italian Fascist colonisation – to emphasise this connection, the opening titles of the film run on an old newsreel that shows the landing of the Fascist troops in 1939; immediately afterwards, we see the two characters' arrival in the port of Durrës. Gino and Fiore behave from the start as veritable neo-colonialists: they look with arrogance and contempt at the starved Albanians who surround them and who are trying to embark for Italy, and in their first dialogue with local functionary Selimi portray themselves as saviours of a Third World country incapable of making it unaided. Their contempt and scorn for Albanians is patent, as much as their ignorance: 'It's the head that you don't have, the brain … How the hell is it possible that you're dying with hunger? All this land … all the petrol you have … the water, the sea, these fields…' Even the much more pleasant and civil protagonists of *Il toro*, who are in truth two losers, the victims of the fast changes imposed on the economy of the Italian northeastern regions by neocapitalism, go to Eastern Europe to place stolen goods which could never be sold in Italy – the idea being conveyed is that they take advantage of a confused situation which escapes control and creates areas of flexibility and opportunity.[5]

Both films portray Eastern European countries as the new frontier also in visual terms. The customs between Italy and Yugoslavia that *Il toro* chooses to show is the one for cattle. Here, Loris and Franco mix with Italian and Eastern European truck drivers, and cattle is seen either staying for the night or being moved around. The presence of these animals sets the atmosphere for the rest of the film, which is strongly reminiscent of the western, and is conveyed not only by typical themes such as the journey itself and virile friendship, but by specific episodes that are straightforwardly taken from the Hollywood genre, for instance the ford of the river, dancing as a romantic moment, the passage of the herd, and the barehanded fight. Similarly, *Lamerica* is visually shot as a western and in fact adopts the cinemascope, which was chosen by Amelio 'in order to highlight that mine is a foreign gaze, not an Albanian one … From this also derives the choice of a certain "epic" pace' (quoted in Volpi 1995: 153; see also O'Healy 2004: 246). It must be noted that the cinemascope not only was the typical format of early 1950s Hollywood, but was also a trademark of the Spaghetti western.

In the classical western, the frontier is represented as lack of civilisation and law, as well as lack of domesticity. It is an overwhelmingly virile space, in which masculinity is coupled with mobility, exploration, self-determination, conquest and violence. As well as being alluring and promising, the frontier is also perilous and can be deadly. We have already stated how the frontier has been subsumed and transformed into the concept of the road to be found in the Hollywood road movie. In fact, although they are so different, the two couples of male Italian characters in *Il toro* and *Lamerica* resemble each other in that they drive through Eastern Europe almost as characters from a western, and look at it as a tempting but also menacing frontier.[5] As they across the border, they perceive themselves as having exited the space of civilisation and law and as faced by a different, less developed world, if not by wilderness. Their perception is of course distorted, as Franco and Loris find out when the new British owners of the Duna Farm refuse to buy their stolen goods and treat them with contempt, as thieves. Similarly, and even more traumatically, Gino realises that his perception of Albania was false

Fig. 12 Carlo Mazzacurati's *Il toro* (*The Bull*, Italy, 1994) © Cecchi Gori Communications

when the police officer who interrogates him tells him, barely hiding his despise, that even if the Albanian economy is dead, 'in a civilised country the dead are not left to the dogs in the streets'.

The impact of Italians with the Eastern countries is therefore not unproblematic, and in some cases is even tragic. In *Lamerica*, Gino arrives to Albania feeling superior and untouchable because, as he keeps yelling whenever faced with a problem, he is Italian; he feels that his Western identity protects him and grants him rights far superior to those of the Albanians. His journey, however, transforms into a true descent to hell, during which he is robbed of his belongings, spends time in prison, experiences fear and hunger, and finally leaves the country as an illegal emigrant. Amelio called Gino's transformation his 'albanisation' – at the end of the film, stripped of all the signs of his belonging to Western society, he looks exactly like the Albanians immigrating to Italy, also because, after the process of divestment, his Mediterranean and southern identity resurfaces. Although less dramatically, also Loris and Franco in *Il toro* have a mixed impact with the Eastern countries they traverse – moments of beauty and of a surprising sense of belonging and déjà vu alternate with times in which the characters are at a loss and experience fear and humiliation.

Overall, Eastern Europe in these films is ambivalently characterised as a virgin land to conquer and as a place of entrapment for Italian characters. This dichotomy can also be expressed in another way: on the one hand Eastern Europe is characterised by these two films as the frontier, thus as the promise of a better future; on the other, it is visually constructed as the (recent) past of Western countries, and of Italy in particular. At the core of *Lamerica*, for instance, is the idea that Albania in the early 1990s strongly resembles Italy in the 1950s. It is useful here to translate a comment by Amelio regarding a hotel in Durazzo where the troupe was hosted:

> From the terrace, on Sundays, I used to see families going to the beach and roasting a lamb, listening to songs of thirty years ago, Adriano Celentano and his immortal *24mila baci*… Like the summers on the beaches of Calabria when I was a boy. (1994: 19)

This marked similarity between 1990s Albania and 1950s Italy (Amelio was born in 1945), an image which also has a pop soundtrack, recalls a sequence of *Il toro* set in a small Hungarian farm where Loris and Franco listen to a 1950s Italian song and dance with the young hostess. Two ideas can be traced behind this discourse of resemblance: that Eastern Europe has become almost like a dump for the recycling of old Italian and, by extension, Western cultural products and myths;[7] and that Italy chose to forget and remove its recent 'Eastern European-like' past, made of postwar destruction, poverty, physical labour, farming culture and mass emigration, in order to sport a different image, that of an industrialised, modern country proudly belonging to the First World. Furthermore, as *Lamerica* suggests, Italy chose to forget its past as a colonialist country, and therefore its ties with and responsibilities towards the countries that once formed its empire. Italians have rapidly erased their national culture and historical memory, as well as their regional identities, in order to adopt a proud First World and global identity, which is epitomised by the protagonist of *Lamerica*, Gino – well-dressed, full of gadgets and status symbols, he shows a self-assurance which vacillates once he is stripped of his passport, car, clothes and dark glasses. Across the border Italians find a mirror image of Italy's past, which some of them recognise (like Loris), while others – the majority – prefer to ignore and continue to look down on Eastern Europeans and their plea.

Language is rightly indicated by these films as being an important component of a person's makeup, and as a key to the reclamation of lost identities and to the shaping of new ones. In *Lamerica*, the fact that most Albanians can speak Italian is experienced by the protagonist Gino as a usurpation of 'Italian identity'; he feels both surprised and threatened by the fact that Albanians can speak his language and thus 'become him'. During the film we learn that Spiro, the Albanian sleeping partner, is in truth an Italian named Michele Talarico, a Sicilian like Gino. Michele left Italy in the 1930s, at a time when the process of creation of an Italian national identity was in its early period and regional identities were amply prevalent. Michele cannot speak Italian, but he can communicate with Gino in Sicilian dialect and 'speak to' his deep roots of poverty and deprivation, but also of honest manual work and good sense, which Gino preferred to erase. *Il toro* also points to the premodern past of rural life, values and work as the common denominator of both Eastern and Western European countries. Whereas *Lamerica* seems to exclude a positive way out of our world's increasing rootlessness and loss of memory, *Il toro* with feeble hope suggests that we start again from the land and from past expertise and knowledge if we want to create zones of opposition to the current global tendencies. In general, though, and in agreement with the post-grand narratives perspective typical of postmodern thought, these films mistrust generalised solutions and large-scale counter-tendencies, and rather place faith in the ability of the single human being to rebel and make a difference in his or her journey.

Elvjs e Merilijn and *Vesna va veloce*: the Adriatic Sea, a fluid border

Contrary to the Italians in *Lamerica* and *Il toro*, the Eastern European characters in *Elvjs e Merilijn* and *Vesna va veloce* perceive the frontier between East and West as a fluid border, beyond which is the promised land of the First World.

In *Elvjs e Merilijn*, an Italian manager organises in Bucharest a competition of imitators of famous stars, which is won by Bulgarian Nicolaj, a mechanic married with two daughters, and Romanian Ileana, employed in a waste disposal site, who imitate Elvis Presley and Marilyn Monroe, respectively. Talking to one another in a basic Italian learnt from television, they prepare to exhibit in discos and night clubs in Emilia Romagna, but at the departure from Bucharest their passports are requisitioned. A Roma friend helps them to cross the border, but their trip through the territories of the former Yugoslavia turns into a chain of dangerous and violent experiences. Finally landed in Italy, their show is a fiasco; their managers first try to turn them into porn stars and then almost kill them. Nicolaj and Ileana remain penniless, disillusioned, but together and free – even if their future is very uncertain.

In *Vesna va veloce* a 21-year-old girl from a small Czech village arrives with other compatriots in Italy by bus for a shopping tour in Trieste, just over the border, but does not return home with them. Without money, hoping to settle in wealthy Italy, Vesna travels south towards Rimini, hitchhiking on the highway. At a filling station she witnesses the tragic death of a compatriot. When in Rimini, it soon

Fig. 13 Carlo Mazzacurati's *Vesna Va Veloce* (*Vesna Goes Fast*, Italy, 1999) © Cecchi Gori
Communications

becomes clear to her that her only hope of achieving her dream is to become a
prostitute; with her first earnings, Vesna begins to buy clothes and other consumer
goods. Vesna befriends one of her clients, Antonio, a contract builder who hosts
her and cures her after she is stabbed by a member of the organised crime gang
who would like to become her pimp. A love story begins, but Antonio and Vesna
are too different: Antonio has rejected consumerism and leads a frugal life, whereas Vesna has grander aspirations. She decides to move to alluring Milan, but Vesna
and Antonio have a car accident. She is found without documents by the police,
and is escorted to Florence from where she will be repatriated. During the trip on
the highway Vesna tries to escape but dies in the car crash she has provoked.

Both films concentrate on a specific Italian area, the so-called Third Italy, a
region that is today rapidly acquiring importance. Sociologist Arnaldo Bagnasco
(1977) called Third Italy a region that comprises the Centre (excluding Rome and
its region, Lazio) and the North East, or *Nordest* (in its turn made up of Veneto,
Friuli and Trentino Alto Adige). After a long economic recession, Third Italy and
the Veneto in particular moved into a period of startling economic dynamism,
with its small entrepreneurs among the most successful in all Europe (Ginsborg
2001: 66–7). Formerly a centre of emigration, particularly towards Germany and
the Americas, today a very wealthy region, but presenting strong social polarisa-

tion, the *Nordest* has become the recipient of much immigration. The Eastern European characters in *Vesna va veloce* and *Elvjs e Merilijn* try to settle in two cities of Third Italy, Rimini and Riccione respectively.[8] As we will see below, the choice of these two cites, traditional tourist and entertainment centres, is symbolic of the way in which the immigrants perceive Italy.

Similarly to the Italians in *Lamerica* and *Il toro*, Vesna, Nicolaj and Ileana also travel in search of new opportunities. Nevertheless, whereas Italian characters mainly go east behaving as neo-colonialists, who intend to make use of a situation in turmoil and then return home, hoping to safeguard their identity in the process (although they are not always successful), Eastern Europeans travel to Italy in order to follow the dream of relocating, of changing identity, and of joining forever the wealthy First World. Vesna does not have problems crossing the border: she travels by bus with a day visa, but then stays in the country illegally, as she does not have a work permit. Moreover, during the narrative her passport is stolen, thus she resides without documents. Nicolaj and Ileana, instead, all set to leave from Bucharest by plane with an invitation and a job contract, had their passports requisitioned by an arrogant representative of the local border authorities with a bureaucratic pretext (a communist and thus by now irregular stamp on Ileana's document). A trip that was supposed to be perfectly legal thus transforms into the odyssey of two illegal migrants. They travel by car with Eva, a Roma woman who knows where to cross the frontier avoiding checkpoints, through Romania, Bulgaria and the former Yugoslavia; but the trip is long and perilous, and Nicolaj and Ileana are repeatedly humiliated and in danger of dying. When they finally make it to the coast, they cross the Adriatic Sea on a fishing boat; the process of securing this passage is not shown, and the trip is represented as easy and short: also in their case, therefore, perforating the border is not a problem – what is difficult is the trip towards the border, and then life in Italy.

Nicolaj and Ileana, precisely like Vesna, believe that wealth and 'la dolce vita' will be within easy reach once they have entered the country, with or without legal documents. This illusion is created primarily by their having been exposed to a false image of the country as constructed and conveyed by television. The role of the national channels in the formation of the future emigrants' idea of Italy was that of a vehicle of 'anticipatory socialisation'.[9] Both in *Lamerica* and *Elvjs e Merilijn* Eastern Europeans often watch Italian popular programmes like soaps or light entertainment shows. The most meaningful instance can be found in *Lamerica*, when a group of starved Albanians in a neglected bar intently watch a programme called *OK, il prezzo è giusto*, the Italian version of an American show, which runs on a Berlusconi channel and in which the contestants must guess the price of consumer goods. The contrast between the poverty of the spectators and this game, which is based on a situation of diffused wealth and the logic of consumer society, illustrates simultaneously how the West has come to be seen as a dreamland of opportunities by Easterners, and how television is an instrument of cultural imperialism for the West.

The impact with the country is unforgiving: Vesna quickly learns that she must become a prostitute if she wants to achieve some prosperity;[10] Nicolaj and Ileana's dreams of success are shattered and at the end of the film their future is very uncertain. As for *Lamerica*, the film closes on the boat full of Albanians still sailing for Italy, thus apparently in a phase of hope – but we know that when they reached the Italian coastline, these refugees were detained in a sports stadium by the police, and were eventually repatriated. All the more, Italians generally do not help to make the Eastern European characters' lives easier. Painted as dodgy businessmen when away, when at home they treat Eastern Europeans as prey to be exploited; this is the case with Vesna, who mainly meets people who want to take advantage of her, and also with Nicolaj and Ileana, whose Italian manager and his friends try to introduce them to the world of porn shows. With few exceptions, Italians are portrayed as feeling superior to the immigrants and authorised to humiliate and exploit them, particularly on the sex market. Some Italian characters dissociate themselves from their countrymen's widespread neo-colonial attitude, namely Loris and Franco, the two protagonists of *Il toro*, and Antonio, the contract builder who befriends Vesna. Interestingly, these are all men who live, more or less willingly, at the margins of Italian neo-capitalist society. Loris tried to avoid conforming to current practices and remained tied to an old rural lifestyle; he set up a cooperative and attempted to be a farmer, but his love for the earth and for honest working practices did not pay off. His friend Franco worked for nine years in a farm, only to be fired at the first signs of crisis, without even been paid his redundancy money. Antonio in *Vesna va veloce* lives by his own choice at the margins of consumer society, refusing to buy useless goods, devoid of a real home, and moving to wherever he finds work.

For their part, Eastern European characters are eager to shake off their pre-Berlin Wall identities. Rather than aspiring to becoming Italian, they elect as their model fantasy images of the wealth and success they associate with the First World. The clearest examples of this phenomenon are Nicolaj and Ileana, who choose to embody two symbolic commodities of Western society, Elvis Presley and Marilyn Monroe. What Nicolaj and Ileana fail to see is that their models are two ambiguous myths, the victims of the star-making machine of the entertainment industry. Furthermore, lacking the necessary sophisticated familiarity with the rules of the 'society of the spectacle', Nicolaj and Ileana can only become mediocre copies of their Western models, like the little Albanian girl who in *Lamerica* dances to

Michael Jackson's music and hopes to appear on Italian television, or like Vesna, who in Trieste looks at a lavish shop window with a poster of Audrey Hepburn elegantly dressed and covered in jewellery. Manni's *Elvjs e Merilijn* pitilessly indicates how these imitations are perceived by sophisticated Western spectators. The sequence of their show in Riccione asserts once again that Eastern Europe is the dump for the old Western world's goods, including popular culture products, which are spread as a vehicle for Western imperialism. The same sequence also portrays the East as being naïve and vulnerable to the society of the spectacle, as much as the West used to be in the past, thus reinforcing the idea of the East as a mirror of the recent past of Western society.

As much as Eastern Europe appeared to Italian characters as a dichotomy – both frontier and forgotten past – Italy in *Vesna va veloce* and *Elvjs e Merilijn* has contradictory characteristics in the eyes of Eastern Europeans. Vesna, Nicolaj and Ileana expect Italy to be a sort of Disneyland – and in fact the cities in which they try to settle are Rimini and Riccione, eminent symbols of the national popular entertainment industry. When Vesna arrives there from Trieste, Rimini is presented as an Italian Las Vegas, a neon strip of shops, restaurants, bars and discos open for business round the clock, shot in slow motion to emphasise the lure of crowded streets full of strollers and consumers. Soon, though, it becomes clear that the images of pleasure, material comfort and widespread amusement, so typical of the representation of the Riviera in Italian cinema, are only a promise that will not be kept; the Rimini that emerges is that of isolated roads walked by prostitutes, fragments of the deserted city in the early hours of the morning, ugly and hot hotel rooms, beaches whose names (Talisman, Florid) stand in ironic contrast to their state of abandonment. Initially, Riccione is similarly epitomised by the crowded, fashionable disco owned by Nicolaj and Ileana's manager and his friends, as well as by a hotel room embellished by the character's love dream (which merges with their dream of success). Even in this early image, though, the presence of an underside manifests itself through the allusive, soft-porn decorations of the disco, and becomes patent after the fiasco of the Elvis and Marilyn show. Ileana retreats to the disco's restroom, which is invaded by the waste of the night: empty glasses and pieces of toilet paper; in order to escape a lesbian who followed her into the restroom, she ends up in a backyard full of litter and empty cans. This double face of Italy – the bright lights of the Adriatic Las Vegas coupled with the waste of consumer society, intertwined with the idea of a 'dirty' sexuality – shows to the characters that their only path to success in this city is through the porn shows and the sex market.

Although the *belpaese* seems truly at hand, almost already integrated in the make-up of the post-communist immigrants, who can speak the language and have been exposed to Italian popular culture, or even to Italian colonialism, Italy is extraordinarily distant and inaccessible to them. This idea of simultaneous proximity and distance is best rendered by the characters' journeys and by the question of the crossing of the border. In *Elvjs e Merilijn*, as in *Lamerica*, it is the sea that offers the pathway to Italy. As seen from the Eastern coast, the Adriatic Sea is pictured in our films as a thin membrane, an open door, a forgiving site that allows the reshaping of identities. As seen from the Italian coast, whereas it does suggest the idea of arrival and departure, of mix of cultures, of fluidity, the sea is, in Carlo Mazzacurati's words, 'a Mediterranean which is no longer warm. In its affluence, it has become a little unhappy' (quoted in Fornara 1996: 10). No Eastern European character, while standing on an Adriatic beach, ever looks back in the direction of the opposite shore, either with nostalgia or with indifference. Home in fact no longer exists on the other side; the past is quickly being erased in this post-Iron Curtain phase of change. In this, our films remind us, once again, of postwar Italy – in the 1950s the emigrants who were leaving their villages and homes for the industrialised cities of Northern Italy thought that one day they would return home with more money and respectability. Home, though, was already disappearing as they were leaving it, as Ciro, the young brother in Visconti's *Rocco and His Brothers*, had already guessed, thanks to the a-historical insight of which he was endowed by the director.[11] Something similar, but with increased speed, also happens to the Eastern European characters in our films. Having been displaced from a bygone centre, no desire to 'become Italian', and no true possibility of settling in contemporary Italy, they have become members of the post-communist diaspora.

chapter seven

WHEN WOMEN HIT THE ROAD: IMAGES OF FEMALE MOBILITY IN POSTMODERN EUROPE

One attribute consistently attached by critics to the road movie is that of its being a masculine genre. For Timothy Corrigan, the road movie is 'traditionally focused, almost exclusively, on men and the absence of women' (1991: 143). David Laderman elucidates:

> Most road movies … retain a traditional sexist hierarchy that privileges the white heterosexual male, in terms of narrative and visual point of view. As in typical Hollywood films, the road movie tends to define the active impulse (here, to drive) as male, relegating women characters to passive passengers and/or erotic distractions. (2002: 20)

Ron Eyerman and Orvar Löfgren describe how the car 'structures the relationships between the travellers, exploring the social psychology of front and back seat, of taking the wheel or staying behind', and that women generally 'must content themselves with rather predictable supporting roles, the motherly or cynical waitress at the roadside diner, the damsel in distress or the seductive hitchhiker' (Eyerman & Löfgren 1995: 65). This happens, according to Marsha Kinder (1974), even in road movies displaying well-developed female characters, as is the case of *Bonnie and Clyde*, *Badlands*, *The Sugarland Express* (Steven Spielberg, 1974) and *Thieves like Us* (Robert Atlman, 1974) – for Kinder, the power of the female characters in these films is, in fact, always ambiguous. As Laderman suggests, such a sexist situation has recently been challenged and partly modified by feminist and gay road movies of the 1990s. The watershed was, famously, Ridley Scott's *Thelma & Louise*, with its two heroines behind the wheel and in charge of their route and destiny. Yet the two women pay dearly for their act of rebellion: chased by their partners and the police, they end up becoming criminals and conclude their flight with a suicidal jump into the void. Critics alternatively took *Thelma & Louise* as the ultimate feminist film, or saw in its finale a classical example of 'punishment' of the heroine who dared too much, with the consequent reestablishment of the patriarchal order.

Although the patriarchal imprint is a recognised characteristic of most if not all Hollywood genres, critics consider it to be particularly strong in the case of road movies, perhaps because of the presence of the technological element (embodied by the car or motorbike), which is classically associated with masculinity. According to Eyerman and Löfgren, for instance, 'the automobile – and of course the Harley Davidson – serves both as an extension of male potency and an intoxicant' (1995: 65). And then there is the question of the derivation of the road movie from the western, an inherently masculine Hollywood genre. For Shari Roberts, the two genres are linked precisely by their vision of masculinity: 'As portrayed in the western and alluded to in the road movie, frontier symbolism is propelled by masculinity and a particular conception of American national identity that revolves around individualism and aggression' (1997: 45). For Steve Cohan and Ina Rae Hark, 'the road movie promotes a male escapist fantasy linking masculinity to technology and defining the road as a space that is at once resistant to while ultimately contained by the responsibility of domesticity: home life, marriage, employment' (1997: 3). Hitting the road is therefore seen as an escape from sedentariness and from familial duties, which are traditionally associated with woman. This is, obviously, not an exclusively cinematic question but, more amply, a cultural one. Geographical as well as social mobility have always been limited for women:

> The first explorers often refused to take women on board because they were believed to bring bad luck and to distract the men from their task. Bourgeois culture evolved the home as the temple of femininity. Domestic life was radically segregated from the public sphere. Although women obviously inhabited public space, they did so under the protection of a chaperon. Women who attempted to roam the metropolis freely struggled with deep male prejudices regarding sexuality and space. (Rojek and Urry 1997: 16)

As a consequence, the woman 'on the road' has often been seen as a woman 'who walks the streets', as a prostitute, as confirmed by etymology:

> Like *diaspora*, *nomad* is of Greek origin. It comes from *nomas*, a word for feeding or pasturing … *Nomas* used with a feminine article could also mean 'prostitute', suggesting an enduring pejorative link between mobility and femininity (compare the English *tramp*) and pointing to the long masculine gendering of travel. (Peters 1999: 26)

Similarly to American road movies, in European films before the late 1980s and the 1990s rarely did women travel alone. It is our aim in this chapter to investigate how women travellers are represented in recent European films, in comparison with previous portrayals. We will address Western and Eastern European films separately, because Western women traditionally enjoyed more personal freedom and access to mobility than women in Eastern Europe did. This historical difference obviously impinged on cinematic portrayals of female mobility.

Nowhere to run: women in Eastern European road films

Travel films that were produced in the Eastern Bloc, and especially in Poland, during communist times typically concentrated on the adventures of a single man or a group of men. If a woman appeared on the road at all, she tended to play only a passive role: she was the one who allowed herself to be kidnapped, as in *Kto wierzy w bociany?* (*Who Believes in Storks?*, 1971), by Helena Amiradżibi and Jerzy Stefan Stawiński, or who failed to escape while her male friend succeeded, as in *300 mil do nieba* (*300 Miles to Heaven*, 1989) by Maciej Dejczer, based on the true story of two teenage boys who fled to Denmark hidden in a lorry. Czechoslovak cinema in this respect was more versatile than Polish cinema. One of its most memorable female travellers is Andula in *Lásky jedné plavovlésky* (*A Blonde in Love*, 1965) by Miloš Forman, perhaps the best known example of Czech New Wave cinema, in which the protagonist left her boring village to pursue a man who appeared to be in love with her. Other noteworthy characters are the two teenage Marias in Věra Chytilová's *Sedmikrásky* (*Daisies*, 1966), whose travelling had several dimensions: they roamed through their hometown, fooling and duping a number of men (thus reversing the scenario of the majority of American road movies, where men encounter, seduce and then abandon women); they moved from the city to the country, appearing on an idyllic meadow, then returned to the city; and they travelled in history, observing such events as the explosion of a nuclear bomb. At the same time as emphasising the mobility and freedom of her heroines, Chytilová drew attention to the lack of direction and purpose of their actions. It felt as if their carefree movements covered up the hopelessness and despair attached to the position of women in a socialist country, which, as the director poignantly demonstrates, is deeply patriarchal. On the whole, in common with Polish women in travel films, Czechoslovak women were rarely in charge of vehicles and they had little control of their destiny. Men drove cars, offered lifts to hitchhikers, or passed them by.

Although road films featuring women as main characters were a rarity in Eastern European cinema during communist times, we can identify a number of films made in the Soviet Bloc, especially in the 1950s, presenting a different generic formula, which addressed the mobility of hundreds of thousands of women living there: their largely enforced migration. This migration had two principal directions: from the province to large towns in search of work and a more prosperous life, which was predominantly the case of young, uneducated women; the second, opposite direction of movement was toward provincial, underdeveloped towns and rural areas, largely in the Eastern part of Poland, in order to meet the shortage of highly-skilled workers, such as doctors and teachers. The theme of migration was present in many Polish socialist realistic films with female characters. Wanda Bugajówna in Maria Kaniewska's *Niedaleko Warszawy* (*Not Far from Warsaw*, 1954), Krystyna Poradzka in Jan Rybkowski's *Autobus odjeżdża 6.20* (*The Bus Leaves at 6.20*, 1954), Hanka Ruczajówna in Leonard Buczkowski's *Przygoda na Mariensztacie* (*An Adventure at Marienstadt*, 1954) and Irena Majewska in Jan Fethke's *Irena, do domu!* (*Irena, Go Home!*, 1955) all move from the provinces to large towns, such as Warsaw or the conurbations of industrial Silesia. These films combined the motif of migration with the issue of emancipation and upward mobility on the social ladder through work, where the notion of 'work' referred to employment traditionally regarded as a male domain. The protagonists work as a technical supervisor in a steelworks, a welder, a bricklayer, even a taxi driver, and it was suggested that they could not find such jobs in their hometowns and villages, where they either were confined to the domestic sphere or had more traditionally feminine occupations, such as a hairdresser's assistant, which did not allow them to fulfil their ambitions and intellectual potential. To comply with the socialist realistic ideology, these films celebrated the migration of their female protagonists, showing that in the new place they found both higher social status and romance, while ignoring any negative effects of their movement, such as cultural maladjustment in their new 'home', or the gap caused by their departure in their families and wider communities. The films of later periods, including *A Blonde in Love* by Forman, as well as the Polish *Bez miłości* (*Without Love*, 1980) by Barbara Sass, and the Russian *Moskva slezam ne verit* (*Moscow Does Not Believe in Tears*, 1979), by Vladimir Menshov, were much more critical of female migration, showing how it often led to boredom, cultural void and, in the case of Marianna in Sass's film, unplanned pregnancy.

After the collapse of Communism travel cinema in Eastern Europe grew in volume and variety; this type of film proved to be an excellent vehicle to explore the various upheavals experienced by Eastern Europeans due to socio-political change. The films using the motif of travel as a metaphor of the wider changes which took place in Eastern Europe around the year 1990 include the following: Marek Piwowski's *Uprowadzenie Agaty* (*Kidnapping of Agata*, 1993); Michał Rosa's *Farba* (*Paint*, 1998); *Jízda* (*The Ride*, 1994) and *Kolja* (1996) both directed by Jan

Svěrák; David Ondricek's *Samotári* (*Loners*, 2000); Alice Nellis' *Vylet* (*The Journey*, aka *Some Secrets*, 2002); and Zdenek Tyc's *Smradi* (*Brats*, 2002). There was also an upsurge in travel films concentrating on the experience of young women migrating from impoverished areas of Eastern Europe to its more prosperous regions or to Western Europe, a motif that, as seen in the chapter dedicated to the post-communist diaspora, is also a recurring theme of Western road films made in the 1990s. However, in Eastern European cinema we not only find young women, but also both older women and girls on the road. For example, in Nellis' *The Journey* the protagonist Milada, in order to fulfil her husband's final wish of having his ashes buried in Slovakia, loads up two cars with her mother, two grown-up daughters, a son-in-law and a grandchild for a trip across the Czech Republic. In Dorota Kędzierzawska's *Wrony* (*The Crows*, 1994) two girls, one about nine years old and the other about three, roam their native city of Toruń in search of adventure and new identities.

In this section, we want to investigate the situation and experience of young Eastern European women on the road, when they travel in their own country. We have chosen three films: one from the Czech Republic, Svěrák's *The Ride*, and two from Poland: Rosa's *Paint* and *Torowisko* (*Track-way*, 1999) by Urszula Urbaniak.

Anna: looking for autonomy

Anna in *The Ride* only enters the narrative after over twenty minutes of the film. The introductory section is preoccupied with two men in their twenties, Radek and Franta, who leave Prague in a second-hand car, a convertible assembled from the remnants of several Western vehicles which had been destroyed in accidents. Their aim is to find joy and adventure, especially of a sexual nature. In an early conversation they mention the advantages of foreign prostitutes, who are cheaper than local girls and, because of the language barrier, cannot complain if something goes wrong. They go as far as joking about burying them in a forest after 'having had fun' with them. Soon after their exchange, Anna appears in the frame. They find her, like a prostitute, by the side of the road, with no possessions, but, unlike a prostitute, she does not stand and wave to the passing cars; instead she sits and examines her shoes, as if unconcerned whether anybody will notice her presence. It is not even clear whether she is waiting for a car to stop. Moreover, she is Czech and not foreign, and with her waif-like figure, delicate features, a simple, loose dress and no make-up she hardly fits the stereotype of a prostitute. Hence, the parameters of her filmic existence are established: she is not an independent traveller, but an object in somebody else's travel; she is not and does not look like a prostitute, but is given such or a similar role by the men who offer her a lift. What follows can be interpreted as her efforts to assert her autonomy as a traveller in unfavourable circumstances.

There is nothing uncommon in Anna's position as an object of somebody else's pursuit, who gains access to the road thanks to sexual services paid to men, as opposed to being a traveller or tourist in one's own right, which is the privilege of male travellers. Travel and tourism, as Chris Rojek and John Urry maintain, 'can be thought of as a search for difference. From a male perspective, women are the embodiment of difference … they are, as it were, "imagined territories". The activity of leaving home to travel involves for men sexual adventure, with "finding a woman" … The loosening of everyday ties and responsibilities opens the male self for sexually-coded assignations' (1997: 17). Eeva Jokinen and Soile Veijola (1997) add that prostitutes are regarded as the epitome of the female traveller, and in fact are described as 'women of the streets'. The association of women on the road with prostitution became particularly strong in Eastern Europe after the collapse of Communism, due to the influx of prostitutes from the Balkans and the ex-Soviet Union to more prosperous post-communist countries, such as East Germany, the Czech Republic and Poland (as well as to Western countries). These women became a common feature of the busy roads, easily recognisable thanks to their crude make-up and shiny and exposing clothes. One consequence of their arrival was the virtual disappearance of 'ordinary' women, who in the past stood on the edge of the road looking for a lift, for which they paid the drivers in cash. There was nothing ambiguous, indecent or disrespectful in their status. Nowadays, women are too afraid of being mistaken for a prostitute and raped to risk this kind of transport.

We learn that Anna ran away from her rich boyfriend, Honzik, who is also the owner of a Western car, but much newer and more expensive than Radek and Franta's convertible. The reasons for her escape are not spelled out, but she suggests that she became exasperated with his possessiveness and constant presence in her life. She claims, for example, that he beat a man who showed interest in her, and did not allow her to wear any clothes other than those he gave her. His desire to be in total control of her life makes him reminiscent of a pimp, especially of the Eastern European variety, who treat prostitutes as their own property. This association is confirmed by his persistent attempts to track Anna down. He appears in the same towns and villages which the three travellers visit, and once even tries to stop their car, risking a serious accident.

Anna is both repelled by Honzik and attracted to him. His wealth flatters her, allowing her to 'travel light', without any luggage or money, which for Anna is more a question of choice than a result of her modest resources. We feel that, being used to affluence, she does not mind that Radek and Franta have little money; on the contrary, it is a pleasant change for her, opening new possibilities of adventure, such as stealing and running away. She admits that, thanks to Honzik, she was able to pursue her dream of being mobile; whenever they quarrelled or were bored they boarded the car and hit the road. Such restlessness makes her similar to heroines of some contemporary road films, especially Agnès Varda's *Vagabond*. There are also similarities with the women in the Czech New Wave films, especially those of Věra Chytilová, including the two Marias in her *Daisies*, who would rather die than settle down. However, these women were not as dependent on men in their desire to be mobile. Not only does Anna stay in contact with Honzik by telephone all the time when she is with Radek and Franta, but in the end she leaves the two friends and returns to him.

Although the owners of the convertible openly admit that on the road they look for 'simple' sex in which they will be the masters of the situation, their behaviour towards Anna suggests the opposite. Not only do they fail to take sexual advantage of her, but they give in to her wishes and go to great lengths to impress her. They get Anna her favourite food, alcohol, and share their supply of marijuana with her, and despite their modest financial resources they book into a cheap hotel to secure a comfortable night for her. In the end, anxious that she might abandon them, they even offer her a lift to wherever she wishes to go.

How did Anna manage to reach this position of power? Firstly, despite admitting that she does not know how to drive and has no money, she does not content herself with taking a back seat either in the literal or metaphorical sense. Inside the car Franta, the only one who can drive, is usually behind the wheel, Anna next to him and Radek in the back seat. Hence, the female is in a more privileged position than one of the men. We see her standing on the front seat and revelling in the wind blowing through her clothes when the car is moving, even shouting out of joy, as if the car has allowed her to express her freedom. On another occasion she sleeps on the back seat while the friends in the front seat hardly talk to each other in order not to disturb her, as if they were her chauffeurs. The young woman also behaves as if the car was a toy for her, a kind of lapdog. Nowhere is this shown better than in a scene (reminiscent of Jean-Luc Godard's *Bande à part* (*Band of Outsiders*, 1964) where, encouraged by Anna, they all run after their car while freewheeling. Eventually, Anna asks the friends to allow her to drive, and later challenges them to remove the car key while they are driving, risking a serious accident. They agree, but nothing dangerous happens, only the car stops in the middle of a field and later Anna brings a tractor to recover it back to the road. Her whole behaviour conveys the idea that she is in control of the car, able to communicate with it intimately and use it in any way she fancies, while for Radek and Franta it is only a means of transport. Anna also has a much more adventurous attitude to travel: all the unexpected events which take place on the road happen thanks to her. She initiates excursions to small, sleepy villages where they steal food and money. They also break into somebody's summer house, largely to please their female companion, who requires comfortable sleeping conditions. She also brings a kitten into a hotel room where they spend the night. Unlike earlier Eastern European travel films, which foregrounded the extremities of the journeys, the starting point and the destination, Svěrák in his film is more concerned with the journey itself – most of the film narrative is set in the car and he adopts various cinematic means such as changing point of view and tracking shots to emphasise mobility. Still, in this very mobile film Anna is the most mobile element. When Radek and Franta are resting, she is restless: investigating the neighbourhood, chasing butterflies or running purposelessly, searching for help when their car is broken, dancing to some old music. Her restlessness adds to her male companions' perception of her as an enigma who must be deciphered, and increases their interest in her.

The second reason why Anna has reached a position of authority over Radek and Franta is that she facilitates their 'travelling in time' and becoming tourists, in the positive sense of exploring, even conquering new places and cultures. For example, on her request she and Radek visit an old monastery, transformed into a museum, where the monks lived hundreds of years ago. Moreover, she acts as a link with the communist period (and its cinematic representation in the New Wave) via her affinity with objects and customs from earlier times. One example is her utter joy on finding some records of Czech singers popular before the collapse of Communism in the house into which they broke; another is her joining in the fire-fighter's feast in a provincial town, which bears similarities with Miloš Forman's *Hoří, ma pánenko* (*The Firemen's Ball*, 1967). Radek and Franta accompany in her these nostalgic pursuits, but never initiate them, as if lacking the imagination to engage with the world in new ways. Each place they visit Anna enriches with some personal touch, as when she mentions the specific smell exuded by monasteries resulting from the solitary lifestyle of the monks. All this suggests that as far as travel in time is concerned, Anna is a much more sophisticated tourist than Radek and Franta, who are mesmerised by her ideas and unpredictability. Her leading role as a tourist is conveyed also visually – whenever the camera adopts a subjective point of view, it is usually Anna's. Only after she directs her gaze at a particular object, Radek and Franta notice it.

The third and principal reason why Anna has so much power over her male companions is the way in which she manipulates her sexuality. She projects herself in contrasting ways, as somebody who is alternatively easy or difficult to seduce, a whore, a mysterious beauty and a tomboy. The impression of an 'easy girl' is first given by her choice of underwear. When Radek and Franta first invite her on their car, she does not wear any knickers and draws their attention to this fact by leaving their car immediately after boarding it, returning to the other side of the road and collecting her knickers from there. Then, she provocatively holds her knickers in her hand and only after some time puts them on in a bar toilet. When the friends notice that Anna's clothes are more complete than at the beginning, they comment that the task of seducing her has become harder. Indeed, in this 'outfit' she becomes more detached and mysterious. She is even reluctant to tell her name to Radek, who fell in love with her, and keeps secret the precise circumstances of her departure from Honzik. Likewise, she tells them little about her family and travel plans, but simultaneously demands that they disclose who they are, where they want to go and whether they have any money. She refuses to have sex with Radek saying that she is not excited. Instead of accepting the role of a passive object of the male erotic gaze, she inspects Radek with the attitude of one who picks her sexual partners according to their physical attractiveness. Particularly memorable is the episode when, after a swim in the lake, she gazes at Radek's genitals for some time and eventually tells him that it must be very humiliating for a man to swim naked, because in cold water his penis shrinks. Anna's gaze in this scene is not reciprocated: the friends do not see her naked, as she swims some distance from them. As suggested above, it is an accepted critical opinion that most road movies retain a traditional sexist hierarchy which privileges the heterosexual male not only in terms of narrative, but also of visual point of view (see Laderman 2002: 20). Hence, this scene clearly goes against the sexist tradition of the road movie. Anna's erotic strategy is to behave in a sexually provocative manner (for example, she lies in the grass with Radek, allowing him to touch her legs), but refuses sex when the man is most excited, in order to maintain her position of power and even to humiliate him.

After some chocolate ice-cream kept in a carton placed on her knees melts, leaving her white dress dirty and provoking her horrified reaction,[1] Anna replaces her semi-transparent, albeit simple dress with a T-shirt and jeans borrowed from Radek. When wearing jeans, Anna behaves as if she was one of the boys, for instance when they all roll while sitting inside tyres or run freely in the field. As time progresses, Anna comes across as being not more, but less sexually accessible to Radek and Franta, thus reversing the 'romantic' road scenario. Alternatively, her change of clothes can be interpreted as a sign of her gradual liberation from her possessive and abusive boyfriend and growing attachment to and empathy with Radek and Franta. When Anna's dress dries, she wears it again, and Radek tries to seduce her once more. This last attempt, which starts like a sadomasochistic game, in which the woman ties the man up, leads to Radek's violence towards the girl and to a fight between them which precipitates her departure. Without any warning

Anna leaves the friends and returns to her old boyfriend. Radek and Franta's last encounter with her is at the scene of a car accident, whose dead victims are Anna and Honzik. Although Honzik was behind the steering wheel, it is clear that Anna caused the crash, performing the same trick with the car key which she had attempted earlier with the old convertible. The accident can be interpreted as Anna's assertion of her power and autonomy as a female traveller. She did not allow men to decide if and where to go with her and when to stop, but shaped her own as well as their itinerary. At the same time, this finale shows that extreme measures must be taken by a travelling woman to prove that she is in control of her destiny. Svěrák's heroine, not unlike the main character in Varda's *Vagabond*, paid the ultimate price for this 'achievement'.

Farba: how not to be fixed and find a home

Michal Rosa, the director of *Paint*, is renowned for depicting the lives of young people in post-communist Poland, although not in a way sympathetic to their plight, but rather critically. This is also true of *Paint*, which was regarded as a film that subtly but persuasively conveyed a right-wing condemnation of the lifestyles of the bulk of Polish young people.

The title character, Farba, is in her late teens and neither works nor goes to school. Instead, she travels from one town to another by train, usually without a valid ticket, which is partly the result of her financial situation, and partly a sign of her rebellion against authority. She is accompanied on her journey by a boy of her own age nicknamed Cyp. The ultimate purpose of Farba's journey is to visit her grandmother, whom she has not seen for many years, but she is not in any hurry to reach her destination. Travel for travel's sake appears to be a reason at least as important to her as finding her relative. The third motivation behind her travel is that it allows her to earn money in a way which would be almost impossible to accomplish if she stayed in her hometown. Farba is expecting a baby and in each new town she visits a number of gynaecologists, to whom she suggests that she does not want to keep her child. In response, many of them propose to arrange an illegal abortion (under the strong influence of the Catholic Church, abortion has been strictly forbidden in Poland since 1993), albeit at a high price. After their proposal Farba reveals that she has taped their conversation and, together with Cyp, blackmails the doctors. Most of the gynaecologists agree to pay, rather than risk their reputation or even a sentence. Farba and Cyp use the money to buy food, sleep in a cheap hotel (if they do not manage to run away without paying their bill), and acquire soft drugs. We could describe Farba's journey, paraphrasing the famous expression 'abortion tourism', as 'pregnancy tourism', or 'fake abortion tourism'.

Fig. 14 Michal Rosa's *Farba* (*Paint*, 1998) © Adam Bajerski

Although Farba and Cyp need each other to continue with their unusual business, gradually their friendship disintegrates. Cyp feels uncomfortable with Farba's provocatively coarse manners and has some qualms about the way they use her approaching motherhood. Farba, on the other hand, cannot stand Cyp's apparent naïvety and prudishness (he tries to cover her with a towel when she bathes naked in a fountain). The relationship reaches a crisis when the couple are joined by a young woman named Szachara of Gypsy, Georgian or perhaps Armenian origin. She is an ex-prostitute who was brutalised and ran away from her pimp. Farba shows Szachara some sympathy and help, but she does not want her to stay with them indefinitely, particularly as she is aware of Cyp's interest in the pretty girl. Eventually the group splits up: Cyp and Szachara stay together while Farba sets off on her own to find her grandmother, who is in hospital dying of cancer. The relationship between Cyp and Szachara also ends, when she comes across some compatriots and refuses to leave them at Cyp's request. In the end all three travellers go their separate ways, much to Farba and Cyp's grief, when they both realise that they would have preferred to stay together.

As with many characters in road movies, it is much easier to establish what Farba rejects and wants to escape from than what she accepts and seeks. She dislikes her own family, the Catholic Church, the sexual hypocrisy of her peers, the poverty and backwardness which she sees everywhere, and society in general, which she finds constraining. Most of all, however, she rejects stability, which is symbolised by her constant changing of hair colour; hence her nickname Farba, meaning paint or dye. In her rejection of permanence she is similar to Anna in Svěrák's film and in neither film is it clearly established why the heroine refuses stability. Yet consciously or subconsciously, Farba yearns for what she openly rejects: home, family, love, even having a child. The ultimate sign of her acceptance of her imminent motherhood, and perhaps even of her Catholic outlook on family life, is her decision not to use the illegal service offered her by the doctors. The further Farba goes, both literally and metaphorically, the more she shows how much she needs a stable home and someone to support her. This distinguishes her from her Czech counterpart, who with the passage of time became more and more reckless and unwilling to settle down. Farba is deeply upset by the death of her grandmother, partly because she craves a safe and warm place for her child, and partly because she needs some reconciliation with her family and her past. She even starts to idealise her childhood, reminiscing over the good old days when her grandmother used to read her fairytales. The last scene shows her completely broken and terrified, when she realises that Cyp is not on the train on which she hoped to find him. Paradoxically, the end of her journey is more tragic than that of Anna, as the latter shows that even in death she is in control of her life, while Farba reveals herself as most vulnerable when being most self-reliant.

Farba's decision to blackmail the gynaecologists was discussed in the Polish press mainly in the context of her apparent immorality, cynicism and appetite for a life in which sex and money are easy to obtain (see Sobolewski 1997: 6; Maniewski 1998: 74). The director himself described his heroine contemptuously as belonging to the 'popcorn generation' whose lifestyle unreflexively imitates the fictitious world of glossy Western magazines which flooded Poland in the 1990s (Chyb 1998: 56). At the same time, Rosa shows that such imitation is doomed to failure in the sense that Poles, at least those belonging to the social strata represented in his film, are unable to emulate Western ways successfully. Every imitation of the West included in the film is a very poor one, often making the imitators look ridiculous, for example the shabby hotel full of prostitutes and pimps from Eastern Europe, poignantly named 'Ric'.[2] Farba's homelessness or near-homelessness (she probably could stay with her mother, but at the price of living in an overcrowded environment and enduring humiliation at the hands of her family) is also a testimony to Poland's poverty; as with many other pregnant Polish teenagers, she cannot even dream about getting a council house or welfare support (there is much truth in the claim that the Polish state nowadays cares more for unborn children than for those who are already here). Young Polish women appear to pay more than once for the changes brought about by the shift from Communism to post-Communism. First-ly, they seem particularly susceptible to the temptations of consumerism and the easy life offered to them by colourful magazines and gigantic adverts decorating the cities, while having less material resources than most members of society to fulfil their consumerist desires. It must be added that travel constitutes an impor-tant element of the 'Western life' which attracted Poles after 1989. Going abroad for tourism or sport, especially skiing and surfing, became almost as important an indicator of belonging to a budding Polish middle class as having a new Western car or a spacious house.[3] Similarly, extensive coverage of tourist attractions and ad-verts of travel agents became a normal feature of most glossy magazines. Secondly, they are the victims of conservative and patriarchal attitudes which dominated of-ficial political and cultural discourses in Poland in the 1990s, and of which the new restrictive abortion law is the most poignant indicator. Consequently, *Paint* shows that many of them risk being lost on the darker streets of democracy, where crime, drugs and prostitution dominate the impoverished landscape. Still, the situation of Polish young women is better than that of the emigrants from other ex-communist countries, as the fates of Farba and Szachara indicate. The first chooses where to go and for most of her journey decides the itinerary of her companions. Moreover, at least Farba considers and starts an independent journey, however challenging and unsuccessful this journey turns out to be. Szachara, by contrast, is resigned to the role of an 'attachment' to other travellers. Not knowing the language and grateful to get a chance to stay with somebody who does not abuse her physically and gives her some food, she has no say in their route and contents herself with following obediently first her Polish 'masters', then a man who promises her (most likely lying) a better life in Germany. First wearing uncomfortable high heels and then walking barefoot and clad in a narrow-fitting dress (the model outfit of a cheap prostitute), she does not even have the strength to keep up with Farba and Cyp, who wear simple clothes and rucksacks appropriate to travelling, and often lags behind them like a tired dog.[4] While Farba's attitude is defiant and rebellious, Szachara's is modest and demure.

In common with Svěrák's film, *Paint* differs from earlier Eastern European road films as a result of being more preoccupied with travel itself – trains and railway stations feature prominently in the narrative. Moreover, Rosa extensively uses cinematic means which suggest mobility, such as tracking shots, handheld camera and fast editing. Critic Tadeusz Sobolewski writes that the camera behaves as if looking for a frame in which to lock the characters, who always manage to escape (1997: 7). This is particularly true of Farba – she comes across as somebody difficult to catch physically and whose true opinions and dreams are impossible to track down. In our opinion, Rosa's vision of travelling, at least when the traveller

is a female representative of the young generation, is very pessimistic – the road is
not a means of self-discovery, but only leads to being more and more confused and
uncertain about one's 'inner route'.

Marysia and Krystyna: trapped on the track-way

A dislike of their life circumstances and environment and a desire to find another, more interesting and happier place to live also characterises Marysia and
Krystyna, the main characters in *Track-way*. They are of a similar age to Farba and
live in a small, provincial town – Aniołowo. Although they are friends, they have
very different personalities and attitudes to life. Marysia, who is the focus of the
viewer's identification, once wanted to work in a local library. After this was closed
down, she found employment in the railway station, combining the jobs of signal
box manager and freight train controller. She is serious and modest, as signified
by her plain hairstyle and long skirts, as well as diligent – she helps her widowed
mother financially and agrees to share her bedroom with her older brother, who is
now unemployed. Marysia also takes care of Andrzej, a feeble-minded young local
man, who is her constant companion. She does not like her small town, finding it
completely boring, or her home, where she is reproached by her mother for not yet
having her own family and home. The situation worsens when her mother begins a
romance with a local plumber and the atmosphere between her and her son dete-
riorates. Marysia often openly expresses her desire to leave Aniołowo. She conveys
her dream to travel through the postcards from around Poland and other parts of
the world which decorate the signal box, and even by her chosen occupation. At
the same time, she is reasonable enough not to object too much to her situation,
when she has no clear strategy to change it.

   Krystyna, by contrast, does not have a permanent job. She keeps leaving Aniołowo to pursue erotic adventures and a better life. However, on each occasion she
returns home promptly, as her plans regularly fail. She gets involved with a local
railway worker and moves in with him, but later discovers that he is married with
children and does not want to leave his family. He even beats her up after Krystyna
wrote a letter to his wife, informing her of their relationship. Krystyna also tries
her luck in a big city, where she seeks employment in an escort agency, but returns
again to Aniołowo claiming that 'her work was fun', but in order to be successful
in the job, one has to speak foreign languages. Although she tries to put on a brave
face, it is clear to Marysia and the audience that Krystyna is deeply disappointed.
Confirming the connection between women's travels and paid sex, her adventures
end tragically: she is raped by one of the railwaymen and soon discovers that she
is pregnant. At first she decides to arrange an illegal abortion and for this purpose

Fig. 15 Urszula Urbaniak's *Torowisko* (*Track-way*, Poland, 1999) © Radosław Pełczyński and Studio 'Indeks'

borrows money from Marysia. Later, however, she changes her mind and marries another railwayman, the only one who agrees to marry her in her pregnant state.

Although in *Track-way* the women reveal a great desire to leave their roots, only men make the most of their opportunities to travel. Travelling is an essential part of the railway workers' and, naturally, of the train drivers' occupation. All these men are promiscuous and hedonistic; they do not mind where and with whom they make love (the engine cab is the usual place for their erotic pursuits) or what might result from their erotic pleasures, as long as they get sex for free. Moreover, almost all the men in the film have cars, while Marysia and Krystyna cannot afford one. To be an independent traveller or tourist rather than an object in somebody else's travel is a luxury that Marysia and Krystyna do not even consider. In their peregrinations they have to rely on a very poor public transport system,[5] the kindness of their male acquaintances, or hitchhiking. Moreover, unlike Anna, who enjoyed the choice of men willing to serve her as chauffeurs, they find it difficult to come across anybody willing to give them a lift. Sometimes they wait for hours without success and in the end must return home. Even Andrzej, Marysia's weak-minded companion, is more mobile than her, as he usually rides a bike. On the road the girls are always 'second-class citizens', shouted at and abused by other road users. This attitude is the consequence of the fact that, after the collapse of Communism, many drivers assumed that women standing at the side of the road are hookers, or at least deserve to be treated as such. Urbaniak also suggests that the position of young, unmarried female travellers is worse than that of travelling married women. This is revealed in the episode in which a man driving a foreign car offers Marysia and Krystyna a lift. However, as he travels with his wife sitting next to him, the girls have to content themselves with back seats and must endure the derogatory comments made by the driver's wife.

Mise-en-scène and camerawork emphasise the heroines' static and claustrophobic life, hence the contrast between their dream of travel and reality. Often we see Marysia and Krystyna in the signal box, from where they observe passing trains, workers on the track and cars crossing. Marysia's brother describes her workplace as a 'glass coffin'. The camera also draws attention to the barrier between the signal box and the trains; in order to approach the trains, Marysia and Krystyna must cross it. For Krystyna this hardly constitutes a problem, but for Marysia it is a major obstacle, as she is not allowed to leave her signal box when the barrier is down. Even when Marysia and Krystyna do travel, the actual journey is rarely shown; we only see them waiting for a car on the almost deserted local road, or for a train at the station, or getting off the train. Marysia and Krystyna's frustration at their confinement and powerlessness is best revealed when they scream under the railway bridge while the train crosses: their shouts and the train's speed make the bridge tremble.

The female characters' failure to travel successfully partly results, as with Farba in Rosa's film, from their lack of solidarity and cooperation. Between them there is rivalry and envy, which are rooted in their romantic beliefs. At work Marysia reads romances and falls for Zbyszek, a handsome engine driver who charms her with his smooth talk about her beautiful eyes and legs. The fact that Krystyna is also interested in Zbyszek drives a wedge between the girlfriends, as well as stopping Marysia from seeking Zbyszek's favours. Marysia takes her revenge when Krystyna is raped; although she witnesses the incident and is deeply disturbed by it, she does not intervene, leaving her friend at the mercy of the rapist. Neither does she tell Krystyna that she knows about the rape, when she asks Marysia for money. She also refuses to admit that she witnessed the rape when questioned by Krystyna's fiancé, Zenek, and other rail workers. On this occasion, however, it is not clear if she hides her knowledge to compound Krystyna's downfall, or in order not to spoil her girlfriend's prospect of marriage. On the whole, for Marysia and Krystyna their relationships with men are much more important than their friendship.

Paradoxically, although Krystyna is the one who shows a greater appetite for fun and freedom, and seems to know more about the world than her shy girlfriend, in the end she finds herself more restricted, both geographically and socially (she must stay in Aniołowo, married to the rather unattractive Zenek) than Marysia, who was more reconciled to her confinement (see Szpulak 1999: 7). Moreover, Krystyna's travel experiences fail to teach her any lessons about men or how to prosper, but helps Marysia to mature and give up her romantic illusions. They also precipitate her decision to leave Aniołowo. Marysia leaves her hometown with a substantial sum of money (in addition to her savings, she takes part of her brother's earnings from drug dealing) and few expectations on men, suggesting that on her journey she will be more successful than her girlfriend.

In common with Michal Rosa, the director of *Track-way* shows that in Poland there is one moral code for men and another for women. Men are allowed to be reckless and promiscuous, cheat on women and even rape them, and are never punished for their actions. By contrast, reckless and promiscuous women pay a very heavy price for their mistakes: they become pregnant, have unplanned children, marry men whom they loathe and are for ever confined to domesticity. Otherwise, they risk being rejected by their local community or even going to jail.

Although the setting of *Track-way* is limited to a handful of locations, Urbaniak skilfully maps the social and moral landscape of provincial Poland. On the one hand, she includes images of girls in their immaculate, white communion dresses, shows Marysia's confession in church and a railway man asking rhetorically 'What will the world do without a Polish Pope?', thus implying the importance of Roman Catholicism in the lives of Poles, at least in towns such as Aniołowo. The power of the Catholic Church is also conveyed by reference to the issue of illegal abortion: the protection of the 'unborn child' being the focus of the most persistent and successful 'moral crusade' of the Polish Catholic Church. On the other hand, Urbaniak draws attention to the immoral and corrupt side of Aniołowo. Although the town is very small and does not even have a library, it boasts a large sex shop whose proprietor is regarded as the richest man in the neighbourhood. The sex shop is also the place where drug dealers ply their trade. Ironically, it is located next to a funeral parlour and nobody seems to question the proximity of these two businesses. It could be suggested that the power of the Church as the principal source of a moral code, the extremely illiberal abortion law and the emphasis of Catholicism on women's chastity is very conducive to sexual hypocrisy and the proliferation of such institutions as sex shops and brothels. Apart from the doubtful pleasures of sex shops and drugs, Aniołowo does not enjoy any benefits from Poland's transition from Communism to a market economy. On the contrary, it is suggested that the change only worsened the situation of the inhabitants of Aniołowo and similar places, bringing them unemployment, insecurity and an inferiority complex towards city dwellers. Although both men and women fell victims of the new circumstances, in common with Rosa's film, women are depicted as suffering more than men. In spite of the many benefits that post-Communism promised them, their 'road' to obtain them is as long as before the fall of Communism, if not longer.

Young Western women touring: roadways to horror

Similarly to both Hollywood and to Eastern European cinema, until recently in Western European films women generally did not travel alone, and were also represented more often as passengers than as drivers. Nonetheless, perhaps reflecting the easier access to mobility available to Western women, there are instances of heroines on the road who are at least co-travellers, endowed with a dignity similar to their male companions. Classical examples are Rossellini's *Voyage to Italy*, Bergman's *Wild Strawberries* and Antonioni's *L'avventura*. In *Voyage to Italy*, Ingrid Bergman's character does not drive, but enjoys some freedom of movement as a tourist in Naples – although mainly as a result of her being in conflict with her husband, whose touristic and sentimental freedom is indeed much more significant. In Bergman's film there are two travelling women: the character played by Ingrid Thulin, the protagonist's daughter-in-law, and the Bibi Andersson character, a young student travelling in the company of two male friends. Thulin and Andersson play very strong and complex women, who, while being on the road for different reasons (respectively to return home to her husband and for tourism), are in control of the route and, often, of their male companions. Thulin even drives the car and once ejects from it a rowdy couple of hitchhikers, thus setting the rules of the trip. In *L'avventura*, Monica Vitti's character is always transported (by the boat of her rich friends, by the car of Anna's fiancée, by the train), but it is her will to find Anna, her disappeared friend, that pushes the film forward, although in an indeterminate and ultimately aimless way. Her presence as a continental, glamorous female traveller in 1950s Sicily turns heads and highlights the passage from a closed society which confined women to the house to a more modern and open-minded society in which women could travel rather freely, although still in the company of men. All these examples, though, are of well-to-do women, thus suggesting that female mobility in Western Europe was, for a long time, mainly a question of class. In fact, in the same 1950s, when a woman of a different social class is represented on the road, her role returns to be ancillary to that of the male traveller, as is the case of Gelsomina, the poor waif assistant of the strongman Zampanò in Federico Fellini's *La strada*, who pays for her mobility with her life.

The portrait of a different type of woman traveller, neither affluent nor destitute, is finally offered in the 1970s by a rare example of a European female road movie: Chantal Akerman's *Les Rendez-vous d'Anna*. Anna, a young Belgian film director who travels by train through Germany to promote her new film, is widely regarded by her family, friends and people whom she meets as very lucky, because she has a creative occupation which allows her to travel extensively. On the other hand, it is subtly suggested to her more than once that her status is unusual for a woman and that, by not having firm roots, she will probably never get married and have children and, consequently, achieve happiness. Akerman clearly advocates her protagonist's right to freedom and movement, and also shows that women who do marry and have children are not necessarily happy; on the other hand, she does suggest that Anna's unhappiness is connected to her extreme mobility and lack of permanence in her life. Travelling for Anna means to go from one hotel room to the next, living in artificial non-places that look much the same, and lacking the time to form deeper relationships. She is also obviously a metaphor for the condition of displacement lived by the intellectual in modern times; her trip is both in space and time, as en route she has the opportunity of looking at the past of Europe as well as of her family.

In 1985 another novel figure of female traveller arrives on the scene of Western European cinema, only to leave a deep mark: Monà, the character played by young Sandrine Bonnaire in Varda's *Vagabond*. Not a rich woman, nor an intellectual, Monà is a secretary who chooses the freedom of the road and of solitude. The frozen landscapes of provincial France that she traverses towards her death have nothing idyllic about them; her filthy appearance and coarse personality remove all romanticism from the idea of freedom associated with hippy counterculture by films such as *Easy Rider*. Monà was a model for many female travellers of subsequent films, including several of those explored in this chapter.

The 1990s saw a great increase of Western European films with or about travelling women. Many of these characters come from Eastern European countries in search of love and bread.[6] Still very few are the middle-aged Western women who travel on their own, examples being the unsettled protagonists of a number of Italian films: Silvio Soldini's *Le acrobate* (*The Acrobats*, 1997) and *Pane e tulipani* (*Bread and Tulips*, 2000), whose protagonists leave their domestic security in search of a more fulfilling life; or the main characters in *Benzina* (*Gasoline*, 2001) by Monica Stambrini, two lesbians who leave the petrol station where they work in order to avoid being accused of murdering the mother of one of them. The majority of films encompasses young characters, many of whom have deranged personalities or are outlaws of sort, as in Bertrand Blier's *Merci la vie* (*Thank You, Life*, 1991) and Katja von Garnier's *Bandits* (1997). A large proportion of these films engage with the model of the Hollywood road movie genre. The chaotic, surreal *Merci la vie*, for instance, overtly mocks stylistic stereotypes of the genre, such as the synthesisers that the two girls always hear when they hit the road, as well as its thematic *topoi* – for instance the idea of 'highway solidarity'. The unimpressive *Bandits* is a naïve MTV-style retelling of *Thelma & Louise*, in which a group of female convicts, the victims of the system and of male violence, break away from prison but are killed by the police at one step from securing their freedom. Ridley Scott's hit is also the main frame of reference for the more accomplished full-length feature debut of Stambrini. Not only are the two protagonists represented as having only each other (apart from a dog who dies in the course of the narrative) in a world full of hostile, misogynistic and primitive men, but their suicidal and spectacular death, shot in slow motion, reminds us strongly of the demise of Thelma and Louise.

More interestingly, Michael Winterbottom's *Butterfly Kiss* (1995), Atom Egoyan's *Felicia's Journey* (1999) and Lynne Ramsay's *Morvern Callar* (2002), three films mostly set in Britain and Ireland, put young women on the road, revealing obscure, unpresentable sides of the experience of female travel, and bordering on the horror genre. The road movie has often crossed paths with the horror. As fairytales such as *Little Red Riding Hood* suggest, the road is supremely dangerous for women. Many American road movies are violent, and hitchhiking is often the catalyst of all atrocities; as a critic put it, 'in road movies, picking up hitchhikers is almost always a bad idea … and being a hitchhiker is even worse' (Morton 1999: 120). Examples are classics such as *Detour* (Edgar G. Ulmer, 1947) and cult films like *The Hitcher* (Robert Harmon, 1986). The latter is also an example of the formula of the pursuit which, adopted by many American 'highway horrors' (including Steven Spielberg's *Duel*, 1971), somehow takes the idea of 'road rage' to its extremes. Often the killer on the road is a pure psychopath, who takes lives without apparent reason. In horror road movies, women and men are equally likely to be the victims of violence and the slayers. Interestingly, it is more often the hitchhiker, be it male or female, who turns out to be vicious, rather than the opposite, as exemplified by films such as *The Hitcher*, *The Hitch-Hiker* (Ida Lupino, 1953), *Roadgames* (Richard Franklin, 1981) and *Kalifornia* (Dominic Sena, 1993). In these films, the director's concern was the threat posed by lonely, deranged travellers to the private, protective space of the car rather than the much more concrete danger run by people, and particularly women, who travel on their own and hitch a lift.

In the three films that we analyse below, women are apparently 'weak' travellers, in the sense of lacking a car and, consequently, power and autonomy. Yet not all of them are victims. Only Egoyan's Felicia is a classic figure of woman-on-the-road: the young, naïve female hitchhiker who steps into the wrong car. Winterbottom's Eunice and Miriam are psychotic murderers, and Ramsay's Morvern is a holidaymaker playing with tourist identities.

Eunice and Miriam: the monstrous-feminine goes astray

Many were the heterosexual couples of outlaws who senselessly spread death in road movies, from *Bonnie and Clyde* to *Badlands*, from *Kalifornia* to *Natural Born Killers* (Oliver Stone, 1994). Although in films of the 1990s lesbians are frequently portrayed as killers (for instance in Barbet Schroeder's *Single White Female*, 1992; Paul Verhoeven's *Basic Instinct*, 1992; and Peter Jackson's *Heavenly Creatures*, 1994), the British *Butterfly Kiss* is a rare example of a road movie with a lesbian couple of murderers. Eunice is a young woman who roams the motorways of Northern England looking for Judith, her lover, whom – she says – was supposed to meet her at a filling station. Nervous and aggressive, she kills a petrol station cashier who is guilty of not being Judith and of not helping her find the tape of a love song that she is desperately seeking. At another station she comes across Miriam, a lonely and mousy cashier who treats her sympathetically. Eunice kisses her, and Miriam takes her home to her bedridden mother. After making love, Eunice disappears, but Miriam finds her again on the motorway and sticks to her even after realising that she is a murderer. Eunice hitchhikes, lures her victims into sex and kills them, and then appropriates their vehicles. The two girls drive aimlessly around in the victims' cars, looking for Judith and for chance encounters with death. In images of a police interview with Miriam, which intersperse the narrative, we learn of the girl's feelings for Eunice: Miriam believes that Eunice must have had her good reasons, and suggests that we should accept people for what they are. Eunice, who is always testing her partner's faithfulness, believes that Miriam will soon turn bad – one night she kills a travelling salesman guilty of sodomising Eunice. Heartened by this proof of her devotion, Eunice finally reveals her plan and asks Miriam to kill her. In the morning, the girl drowns Eunice in the sea.

Butterfly Kiss is not a straightforward horror movie, because it does not overindulge in splatter and horrific details, however it presents clear elements of the genre – and in fact it was given an '18' certificate in the UK. Eunice is a true psychotic; she exudes danger, and wears tattoos and heavy chains dangling from her pierced nipples. Some of the killings are shown in full, and are violent and bloody. The corpses are also sometimes lingered on by the camera. Although the girls' travelling is aimless, *Butterfly Kiss* is also a true road movie – it opens on the road and on the road it develops and ends. Large sections of the film are devoted to framing the landscape as seen from the car windows, or even to showing the road unfolding ahead of the travelling car. Although a true sense of freedom and exhilaration is rarely attached to the girls' experience of travelling,[7] the hip all-female soundtrack adds to the classic feeling of 'hitting the road' conveyed by so many films belonging to this genre. It is most useful to look at *Butterfly Kiss* as a horror road film.

Eunice and Miriam are not simply two women on the road, or even two lesbians on the road – they are true monsters. Critical literature on horror traditionally describes woman as the victim of ruthlessly violent males, but Barbara Creed's (1993) contribution used psychoanalysis to shed light on the figure of the female slasher. Referring to Julia Kristeva's (1982) theory of abjection, Creed was able to look in a productive manner at the ways in which horror is linked to the feminine.

Kristeva describes abjection as the mechanism of separating the human from the non-human, the fully constituted subject from the partially formed subject. Abjection is a violent, obscure revolt of the being against an unthinkable, intolerable threat that seems to come from either the outside or the inside. This threat, which is both repulsive and attractive, does not come from a definable object, but it is still a 'something', which opposes and threatens the self. Sources of abjection are the improper and the unclean (for instance bodily functions, the corpse); yet, as Kristeva explains, 'It is … not lack of cleanliness or health that causes abjection but what disturbs identity, system, order. What does not respect borders, positions, rules. The in-between, the ambiguous, the composite' (1982: 4). Abjection is in fact about borders, that which crosses or threatens to cross the border – and Creed rightly suggests that the horror movie is also about borders, those between human and inhuman, natural and supernatural, good and evil, normal and abnormal (for instance in sexual desires and gender roles). Kristeva also links abjection to religion, and indicates that the 'various means of *purifying* the abject – the various catharses – make up the history of religions' (1982: 17). Abjection also has much to do with woman and particularly with mother, whose body is a site of conflicting desires for the child who tries to break away from her and become a separate subject, but who also simultaneously fears and desires to sink irretrievably into the mother.

Eunice in *Butterfly Kiss* is a monstrous-feminine and, as such, a figure of abjection. Creed discusses various facets of the monstrous-feminine in conjunction with Kristeva's theories – all being aspects of the maternal and reproductive functions. She also discusses the monstrous-feminine in relation to Freud's theories of castration. According to Creed, the slasher film 'deals specifically with castration anxieties, particularly with the male fear of castration' (1993: 125). Some of these films show a female slasher who is psychotic (rather than a woman looking for revenge, usually after having been raped), and 'her victims are mutilated/murdered because they engage in sexual activities' (1993: 126). Creed suggests that in these films the woman refuses to conform to her 'proper' role, thus becoming psychotic. These women, who are usually represented as both castrated and castrating, are invariably beautiful and intelligent and their allure is used by the film to terrify the male spectator about their castrating powers.

Eunice has elements of the woman as castrator. She lures her male victims by exciting them sexually and kills them during intercourse. It is significant that we never see her killing her female victims, with whom she does not have sex: a service station assistant and a waitress at a roadside café. We only see their dead bodies some time after the killings, which are thus less vivid and meaningful to us. Two out of three killings of men are instead fully shown, and all three are associated with sexual intercourse. In this sense, Eunice is part of the subgenre explored by Creed: she is a psychotic lesbian who has rejected her 'proper' feminine role. Her body is represented both as castrated (the wounds left by the chains on her chest) and as castrating. Eunice is not an intelligent and beautiful woman as the slashers analysed by Creed, and we suggest that her erotic power on men is consequently described as even more abominable. She has made of her body a site of abjection, through corporeal aberration (the tattoos, the piercing, the chains), sexual immorality and perversion (her lust, bisexuality and masochism) and filth (her dirty clothes). More than anything, she is linked to the idea of religious sacrifice, both in the sense that she performs human sacrifices and that, at the end of the film, she offers herself as a sacrificial victim to God. Her demeanour during the whole film is that of an abominable priestess; she quotes from the Bible, she looks for Judith (the biblical Judith severed Oloferne's head after seducing him), she cries that God has forgotten her. In the sequence of sadomasochistic sex with the salesman, she recalls the episode of St Thomas putting his hand in Christ's wound, and she licks his blood. Before she is drowned by Miriam, she recounts the biblical story of Elias's sacrifice.

We suggest that, in the light of Kristeva's analysis, Eunice is abominable because she has not preformed the shift from sacrifice to taboo as imposed by the Bible. Both sacrifice, including human sacrifice, and taboos (dietary, sexual and moral taboos) partake of the logic that sets up the symbolic order. By performing a separation from what is impure and threatening, they subordinate maternal power (mother, women and reproduction being both historically and subjectively the site of such threat) to the symbolic order 'as pure logical order regulating social performance, as divine Law attended to in the Temple' (Kristeva 1982: 91). Nevertheless, for Kristeva there is a fundamental distinction between sacrifice, in which 'the killed object, from which I am separated through sacrifice, while it links me to God it also sets itself up, in the very act of being destroyed, as desirable, fascinating, and sacred', and taboo, thanks to which 'the abjected object from which I am separated through abomination … tears me away from the indifferentiated and brings me into subjection to a system' (1982: 110–11). Rather than a religion of abomination, Eunice is the priestess of a religion of the sacred, a sacrificial religion which has not yet tempered the fascination of murder.

The question that remains to be explored is why Miriam allows herself to become captivated by Eunice. During the narrative, the two girls begin to call one another 'Eu' and 'Mi'. The psychoanalytical suggestion is clear: Eunice is the 'you', the 'other' of Miriam. Miriam somehow is the 'I', the subject explored by the film. The police videotape that intersperses the narrative gives us many opportunities to gain insight into Miriam's mind; through it, we assist her mutation from an exceedingly introvert and immature young woman into a psychotic individual. Whereas Eunice is the same from the beginning to the end of the film, Miriam mutates and somehow 'becomes herself'. We know nothing of Eunice's life and background: she is first seen walking along a motorway, and her claims about her love story with 'Judith' are dubious (in fact, we are more than once offered a glimpse of her photograph of Judith – the reproduction of a sculpture representing the biblical Judith holding Oloferne's head). Instead, we know and see Miriam's background; she lives in a flat with her paralytic mother, who, in the few scenes that concern her, is sketched as a paranoid woman who sees evil everywhere, and as a monstrous mother who has kept her daughter tied to her and removed from the world. At a closer analysis, it becomes clear that it was Miriam who never let go of her mother. When she takes Eunice home with her, she states: 'She is not my mother as such. She is my grandmother. She forgets and I don't like to cross her'. This statement is very odd, given that it follows a video-sequence in which Miriam admits: 'Not a lot to say about me. I lived with my mother until I met Eunice'. Is the old lady Miriam's mother or her grandmother? Even for Eunice things seem strange: 'That does not feel right', she exclaims after Miriam told her about her 'grandmother'. Later in the film, Miriam refers to her as her mother again: 'Mother, Auntie Katie, a girl at swimming, and Eunice, are the people who kissed me.'

If the old lady truly is Miriam's grandmother, this shows how Miriam never let go of her own mother and even replaced her with an immobile and persecuting mother-like figure, who calls her 'Mi'. If the old lady, instead, is her true mother, this might show how Miriam is aware of the strangeness of their close relationship, and justifies it by maintaining that she is an absent-minded granny who must not be upset. Either way, it is easy to see how Miriam is attracted to Eunice: rather than forcing her to separate from 'mother', Eunice actually offers her an opportunity to sink even further and irretrievably into the abject female, maternal body, into the site of the tempting threat of indistinction. Eunice is abject because she reminds Miriam of an 'object' that she has always already lost – she takes Miriam's ego 'back to its source on the abominable limits from which, in order to be, the ego has broken away' (Kristeva 1982: 15). Interestingly, whereas Eunice is constructed as filthy, improper, excessive and perverse, Miriam is her opposite – clean, tidy, modest and appropriate. Eunice is what Miriam separated from, but never renounced.

Eunice and Miriam's mother could not be more diverse as maternal figures: the old lady is completely static, and admits: 'I never go anywhere – mind you, if you never go out, you will do no evil, will you?' Eunice, who is instead exceptionally mobile and restless, replies: 'Evil is in your heart, if you don't go out you never get away from it.' Both women are thus trying to stay away from evil, one by sitting at home, the other by compulsively moving around. It is therefore highly significant that Miriam and Eunice's relationship starts, develops and ends on the road. As Kristeva writes:

> The one by whom the abject exists is thus a *deject* who places (himself), *separates* (himself), situates (himself) and therefore *strays* … Instead of sounding himself as to his 'being', he does so concerning his place: '*Where* am I?' instead of '*Who* am I? … A deviser of territories, languages, works, the *deject* never stops demarcating his universe whose fluid confines – for they are constituted of a non-object, the abject – constantly question his solidity and impel him to start afresh. A tireless builder, the deject is in short a *stray*. He is on a journey, during the night, the end of which keeps receding. He has a sense of the danger, of the loss that the pseudo-object attracting him represents for him, but he cannot help taking the risk at the very moment he sets himself apart. And the more he strays, the more he is saved. (1982: 8)

Eunice does not travel towards a specific place – she wanders off, she drifts, she strays. Once she exclaims: 'I always get lost and I always end up in the woods – always in the woods, over and over again.' Whereas Miriam thinks that it would be possible for them to go somewhere (although only to a mythical location, an imaginary Spain she knows very little about), Eunice wants to continue to stray. Miriam's journey does have an objective – sticking to Eunice, and conquering her love; Eunice's journey, instead, is easily described as that of Kristeva's *deject*. Eunice situates herself in relation to the abject, she always tries to steer clear of it while continually coming upon it. When she first appears in the film, walking along the motorway, she introduces herself by locating herself, when she compulsively repeats: 'Look who it is. It's me. *Here* I am.' Eunice is a deject as long as she keeps straying and, as long as she strays, in line with Kristeva, she is saved. It is when she stops travelling that her end comes – when she allows Miriam to seduce her, to transform into Judith and to perform her sacrifice.

During the whole film Eunice 'never stops demarcating her universe', one which is characterised by 'fluid confines'. Northern England's motorways and adjacent landscapes are indeed constructed as a border, as a liminal, fluid territory. Its constituents – the endless tarmac, the identical filling stations, the grimy roadside cafes, the ordinary motels and the Americanised theme park – are too unexceptional to coalesce into a solid, recognisable world that could be explored with a map, a possibility that Miriam even suggests at some stage, but that is immediately discarded by Eunice. It is impossible for the spectator ever to geographically locate the girls during their trip. The film constructs their journey as a compulsive, mad back and forth motion, as a repetitive to and fro movement that does not progress spatially, and that never crosses physical boundaries (the river which the girls do not negotiate, the sea they do not traverse). This lack of direction and progression is epitomised by the scene in which Miriam and Eunice meet at a service station a father who is hitchhiking with his young daughter, and offer them a lift. Eunice suggests that it is no problem for them to take them to their destination, since they are going there too. The man is puzzled, and comments: 'But it is in the opposite direction', at which Eunice simply turns the car around. The road in this film is not used to go from one place to another, but as a liminal space in which to tirelessly search the boundaries between proper and improper, between subject and object, between deject and abject. Such a reading of the road as the quintessence of liminality, of a universe with fluid confines, or even of a non-place, and of travelling as a dangerous journey whose end keeps receding, is obviously not unique to *Butterfly Kiss*, but is a trademark of the highway horror.

Butterfly Kiss, by adopting many characteristics of the horror road movie, and by constructing its protagonists as castrator and castrated monstrous-feminines going astray, reaffirms the traditional pejorative link between femininity and mobility. Perhaps the most interesting aspect of this film is that it associates this monstrous female mobility to a specific landscape, that of Northern England's motorways. Eunice appears so suddenly at the beginning of the film that she looks like an embodiment of that specific motorway; and Miriam is carefully constructed, through clothing, accent and manners, as a local girl. As one critic has noted, 'This is a film that takes delight in the small details of modern English life. Miriam reads *The Puzzler*, wears anoraks and home-knitted cardies. Her home life in a council block … testifies to a social isolation that seems peculiar to this country' (Francke 1995: 42). Then again, the British locale is little more than a variation of well-known characterisations of femininity.

Felicia: things take a (wrong) turn

The eighth full-length feature of Armenian-Canadian director Atom Egoyan, and his first to be filmed in Europe, *Felicia's Journey* is a US-Canadian co-production based on Irish writer William Trevor's novel of the same title, although the original story underwent significant changes to become a film. As several critics have felt, despite the changes Egoyan respected the novel's atmosphere, and yet he made a film that is very much his own, reflecting some of his most frequent concerns – the family and the relationship between parent and child; the influence of past traumas; the role of the media; the reflection on images and on the cinema as a means of expression.

The story is told with many flashbacks, as is customary in Egoyan, and also through several dream sequences; some flashbacks, as often happens in his films, are made up of video footage. Felicia is a young Irish girl from a small village who, despite her father's stern opposition, dated Johnny, a young boy from a family that historically collaborated with the British. Johnny left for England, officially to work in a factory in Birmingham, in reality to join the British army. When she realises that she is pregnant, Felicia travels to Birmingham to trace him, but does not have his address. A kind-hearted catering manager, Hilditch (Bob Hoskins), gives her directions and the address of a bed and breakfast. Hilditch lives in an old house, a sort of shrine dedicated to his mother Gala (played by Egoyan's wife and regular actress Arsinée Khanjian), the star of a 1950s cooking programme in which she often humiliated her chubby son. But Hilditch is not just an eccentric who loves cooking and watching videos of his mother's programme: he is a true monster, who gives lifts to distressed girls, videos them with a hidden camera and then kills them. When he meets her again, Hilditch offers Felicia to drive her to a more distant factory, where they might find Johnny. He makes up a story about his wife being very sick in hospital, in order to win her trust. He then pretends that his wife has died, and steals Felicia's money, so that the girl is forced to move in with him. Finally Hilditch convinces Felicia to abort. He then prepares to kill her and bury her in his garden, but has a sudden crisis of conscience, instigated by the visit of two nutty evangelical missionaries. He allows Felicia to escape and hangs himself. Some time later, Felicia is working as a gardener in a city park.

Reviewers concentrated on the figure of Hilditch's overassertive and flamboyant mother but, although Gala is undoubtedly the direct cause of Hilditch's psychosis, we suggest that – as always in Egoyan – it is paternal figures that dominate the film. To begin with, Hilditch's father, whose absence had catastrophic consequences on his childhood. In psychoanalytical terms, a strong paternal figure would have been essential in redressing the balance of a devouring mother, who could only express her affection for Hilditch by stuffing him with food, keeping him in a pre-symbolic, oral phase. It is unsurprising that the abject also surfaces in this film, in Hilditch's duplicitous reaction of disgust and fascination for the obliterating relationship with an archaic, devouring mother such as Gala. Abjection emerges violently in young Hilditch's act of vomiting the piece of raw liver forcibly introduced by Gala into his mouth, and later in his life of other foods linked to the memory of this trauma. Other paternal figures have important roles in the narrative: Felicia's rigid and unforgiving father, but also – and perhaps less obviously – Hilditch himself. Hilditch functions as a paternal figure for many characters: for his employees, with whom he is a severe but rewarding father, who elicits respect and devotion; for the girls of his videotapes, to whom he offers the understanding and support of a paternal figure; and, most importantly, for Felicia. Hilditch replaces her true father, who has let her down, and in fact at one point exclaims: 'Sorry for being fatherly. I cannot help but being fatherly!' In his made-up story about his dying wife, Hilditch suggests that they could not have children, a 'terrible disappointment', thus portraying himself as a trustworthy and willing father-figure. Hilditch continuously expresses concern for Felicia, gives her sensible advice and protects her. Above all, he continually directs her, he shows her the way. This leading, though, is in truth a misleading – as Hilditch himself admits with an ironic remark: 'I wouldn't like to think that I misled you.'

Felicia's journey is all a matter of misleading, in the literal sense of being 'shown the wrong way'. Felicia is represented in Egoyan's film almost as a child – the choice of actress, her clothes and make-up and her general demeanour hint at a liminal identity, in-between childhood and womanhood. When he confesses to her his previous crimes, Hilditch suggests that Felicia is different from all the other girls he killed, whom we saw in his creepy videotapes: 'You are a special angel, heaven is in your eyes', he explains. Hilditch's murderous folly is hardly characterised in sexual terms – the only image that suggests his sexual desire is that of Felicia's legs in his first videotape of her. What distinguishes Felicia from all the other girls is thus not her sex appeal, but her childlike, immature manners and looks, her huge faith in goodness – as in the song that opens the film: 'What a wonderful world we would live in if we had the faith of a child's heart.' Felicia is thus in a liminal phase, in-between dependence on paternal figures (it must be noted that Felicia's mother died many years before) and self-determination. Her journey is also the fruit of her liminal state – partly triggered by her emerging will to autonomy and self-reliance, partly instigated by her dependence on men. Felicia is initially misled by her father, in the sense that she is 'led out of home' by him – instead of helping and supporting her when she most needs him, he imposes her to abandon her family and her fatherland. His misleading factually initiates Felicia's journey. She is then misled by her boyfriend, who promised her to send his address, but never did, thus making it very difficult for her to reach him; furthermore, his claims to have gone to work in a factory put her on the wrong track. Finally, Hilditch continually misleads Felicia; he purposefully keeps her on the road by sending her or driving her to several 'wrong' destinations (a factory; a bed and breakfast; a pub; another, more distant factory; a hospital; a clinic where she is made to abort) all of which lead her away from her true destination – Johnny. 'She asked me for directions' he pleads to the evangelical missionaries at the end of the film, but Hilditch is precisely guilty of having given Felicia wrong directions, over and over again. 'Things take a turn', he justifies himself, but it is a wrong turn that things constantly take for Felicia.

Whereas Johnny, Felicia's young lover, straightforwardly wanted to get rid of the girl, the two father figures in her life meant to achieve exactly the opposite: keep her close to them, lock her in their house, and make her immobile. Her real father does not want Felicia to grow up and be a woman – as he says to her, 'a child must listen'. When Felicia objects that she is no longer a child, he steps away from her. Once it has become clear that she is now a woman, who claims her freedom of choice, her 'mobility', he shuts the door on her. Hilditch's strategy of misleading, instead, first aims at attracting Felicia into his home, and then at keeping her there for ever, even if this means killing her and burying her in the garden. Both men thus try to keep Felicia in her childhood state. The problem is that Felicia is no longer a child, even though she might still look like one. Her determination is huge, and ultimately prevails, although aided by chance – it is Hilditch who at the end of the film unlocks the door and lets her escape.

Felicia's trip is thus metaphorical, a typical coming-of-age tale, with gender-specific overtones. She is not only on a journey from childhood to adulthood, but also on a traditional feminine quest – she is looking for the man who impregnated her, seeking his love and support. In this two-faced pursuit, she is invariably looked upon by people, and particularly by all the men involved, as a child, despite her body being mature enough to carry a baby, and despite her will to embrace her responsibilities and become an adult. On the road, she is shown by Egoyan as an inexperienced traveller, who naïvely goes to Britain without personal documents, who traverses moments of despair and fear, who searches for the help and guidance of a paternal figure and of a spiritual leader, although in both cases stumbling upon the wrong ones. Yet, as children often are in fairytales, she is shown as a tremendously strong and stubborn young woman, with a huge faith in goodness and will to reach her goal. Also the other women in the film, Hilditch's several victims, are painted as distressed travellers, running away from negative experiences with men – Egoyan's film, in fact, seems to suggest that women are forced to leave home and travel as a consequence of male violence, but on the road only run the risk of encountering more of the same. Whereas all the other victims are portrayed as mature and experienced, Felicia seems to prevail precisely because she still has 'the faith of a child's heart'. Her success is even more remarkable because she is a fragile and passive traveller who, like the other victims, ends up as a passenger in Hilditch's car. Like the others, she was won by his fatherly, passé manners and accepted a lift, in the cosiness and protection of the passenger's seat. This position, in truth, proved to be uncomfortable and dangerous, as signified by the images produced by Hilditch's hidden video camera: the women are squeezed on one side of the frame, their image fragmented and flattened by the magnetic support.

As one critic has noticed, 'the film is not, despite appearances, a fairytale warning to innocents not to stray abroad, for Hilditch's problem is that he has never left home. Home, or surrogates thereof, prove to be hostile: Felicia finds succour in an evangelical hospice, but the ark turns out to be a madhouse' (Romney 1999: 35). Felicia and Hilditch's homes are portrayed as static and stagnant environments. Both are frozen in time – a distant, almost mythical past has seized these places, adding to the metaphorical, fairytale quality of the film. The past of Felicia's home is that of the Irish troubles and the civil war, which turned neighbours into enemies, and of a rigid Catholicism that sees sin everywhere. Hilditch's home is frozen in the past of 'the aspic of 1950s English suburbia' (Romney 1999: 34), but also of an archaic relationship of fusion with a devouring maternal figure. Leaving home is a necessity – but it is also a very difficult if not impossible task, given the weight of the past (personal, historical and mythical). Hilditch does not succeed. Felicia, instead, does: paradoxically thanks to Hilditch, who manages to make her stray long enough for her to decide never to return home. This, of course, happens at a cost. For Jonathan Romney, 'the cost might be lesser in the film: Trevor's Felicia ends up a nameless, homeless wanderer. Here, she not only achieves freedom but also becomes the symbolic redeemer of Hilditch and his victims, finally intoning a voice-over memorial blessing' (1999: 35).

In Egoyan's film, Felicia does not end up a nameless wanderer, but her situation at the end of the narrative is far from being stable and safe. Firstly, she is definitely homeless, as she cannot return to Ireland and her native village. Secondly, she is shown planting bulbs in a municipal park, a job that, beyond the affirmative metaphor of the good seed that she hides in the ground (but it could also be the 'evil seed' to which her father referred when he disowned her), has nothing stable about it. Working in a park is a characteristically impermanent job, often done by foreign or underprivileged young people. Felicia, though, is shown as a mature and independent young woman, a change connoted by her new clothing style, jeans and jacket having replaced her schoolgirl skirt and cardigan. More importantly, for the first time in the film she seems to be in control of her space – we see her giving directions to a passer-by, with the demeanour of one who knows her way around. Her traumatic experiences, as in a typical coming-of-age tale, made her grow up, although maintaining her pure, gentle style (the teddy bear she returns to a girl to whom she smiles sweetly). Nevertheless, the park is constructed by the camerawork (the closing, spiralling pan around the trees) and by the soundtrack (the mysterious tune, the litany of the names of Hilditch's victims uttered by Felicia's voice-over) as a dangerous, enveloping place, perhaps referring to the woods of *Little Red Riding Hood*, the fairytale that Egoyan mentioned in relation to his film. When the spiralling camera returns to the place in which we expect to see Felicia, in fact, the girl is no longer there.

As well as being a metaphorical journey from childhood to womanhood, from the paternal home to independence (although a precarious one), *Felicia's Journey* shows a true voyage across the sea, from Ireland, a country depicted as rural, archaic and immobile, to a more modern, industrial, but equally unappealing England. Egoyan's England is 'middle England', in many senses of the word: geographical, as the director depicts the region of the Midlands, which is widely associated with a monotonous landscape; economic, as the inhabitants of this part of the country are regarded as neither particularly rich nor poor; and cultural, having few touristic attractions and being imprisoned in an industrial, pre-Fordist era, marked by large factories, industrial estates and urban decay. Due to the aforementioned perception, the Midlands are rarely shown on screen, in contrast to London and the North, which are even directly associated with particular periods of British cinematic history. Egoyan accepts such an image of the Midlands and even reinforces it, by demonstrating that its supposed mediocrity conceals monstrosity. However, he also suggests that, in order to discover such monstrosity, one has to take, like Felicia, a 'wrong turn'.

Morvern: off the beaten track

Often hypnotic, stylistically austere, *Morvern Callar* is the second feature by Lynne Ramsay (*Ratcatcher* was her 1999 debut), based on Alan Warner's acclaimed novel of the same title. Morvern Callar (Samantha Morton) is a young woman who works in a supermarket in a small Scottish coastal town. The film begins when she finds her partner on the floor of their kitchen, with his wrists slashed – he committed suicide, and left her a goodbye message on his computer, without explanations but with the instructions for sending to a publisher a novel that he wrote. Morvern goes to the train station to phone the police, but then changes her mind. It is Christmas, and she goes out with her best friend, Lanna. The two girls drink and take drugs, and go to a party with some boys they met in a pub. The party is wild, and Morvern and Lanna have sex with one of the boys. In the morning, they walk back home and stop to see Lanna's grandmother. Morvern decides to submit the novel for publication (but first she puts her name on the typescript), and to saw and bury her boyfriend's corpse. Although Lanna confesses of having slept with her boyfriend, Morvern – who has received a letter of acceptance of the manuscript – uses the money he left for his funeral to buy for herself and for Lanna a ticket to Spain. Soon after they arrive, Morvern forces Lanna to leave the tourist resort and travel inland, without destination. Lanna dislikes the place they get to, and after a night on the road, in the middle of nowhere, Morvern leaves Lanna and continues her journey alone. She receives a visit from the publishers, who offer her £100,000 for her book. Eventually she returns home, finds the check in the post, packs a bag full of records, offers Lanna the chance to go with her, and leaves again, alone.

Morvern Callar, as so many road movies, is as much about home as it is about being away from it. Morvern is an orphan (she once points at a spot on the other side of the lake and tells Lanna: 'There is where my foster mum is buried'); she is not from the coastal town where she lives (as is revealed by her accent, and as she confesses to an unknown person with whom she speaks over the phone, at the train station). We are never told where she comes from, in fact we are told very little about Morvern's past; we only know that she has been living in this town for a long time. 'Home' is thus both here and elsewhere, or perhaps in neither place. The dingy flat that she shared with her boyfriend until his death is painfully simple and bare: stripped walls, basic furniture, a Christmas tree with cheap lights that keep flashing intermittently, making the house look even more bare and eerie with their electric on-and-off sound and reddish glow. Although Morvern must have experienced it as a meaningful locus of her relationship with Johnny, it hardly makes for a warm, welcoming home; rather, it is a signifier of her entrapment in poverty, as much as the town in which she lives is a signifier of her entrapment in provinciality. Although we never have the certainty that she dislikes her flat, there is a scene that tells us of Morvern's yearning for a true home – when she goes to visit Lanna's grandmother, makes some soup for her, sits in the cosy warmth of her sitting room and contentedly looks at granny eating in her armchair. Significantly, in the middle of this sequence, Lanna's granny enigmatically lifts her hand and wordlessly points out of the window, at the outside world. Is it a suggestion to Morvern to leave, and go look for what she seeks elsewhere?

We are not told how and why Morvern takes the decision to buy tickets to Spain for herself and for Lanna; granny's gesture and Morvern looking at a foreign postcard on a friend's fridge are the only two feeble indicators of the girl's developing desire to leave. Director Lynne Ramsay is nevertheless able to convey with subtlety the reasons of Morvern's departure. In an interview, she suggested that 'she saw buried in [the novel] a modern girl's "black fairytale"' (quoted in Williams 2002: 10). This 'black' quality of *Morvern Callar* resides in what we could define as the protagonist's ability to perceive the horror of the everyday. While not being an exceptional character in other ways, Morvern is endowed by a unique dark side,

Fig. 16 Lynne Ramsay's *Morvern Callar* (UK, 2002) © Robyn Slovo

which is conveyed visually in many ways. She often wears scarlet clothes and caps, which recall blood rather than passion. This impression is reinforced by the eerie red Christmas lights rhythmically flashing in her flat; by the red of the varnish that more than once she applies on her fingernails; and by the red of Johnny's blood on his wrists, which she caresses, on her naked body as she severs his limbs in the bathtub, and on the linoleum floor which she later cleans. In a mysterious scene set in a graveyard in Spain, Morvern moves a red flower from one tomb to another. The camera frames her in close-up on the left-hand side of the screen, next to a tomb, then pans away showing a series of tombs, and when it stops Morvern reappears on the right-hand side – the scene constructs Morvern as a supernatural apparition. Often the girl spots worms or crawling insects which, also thanks to the sinister soundtrack, recall the idea of physical decay – like the worm on the carrot in the supermarket, or the insects in the water after she buried Johnny's remains, or the cockroach on the floor of her room in Spain, following which she ends up in the bedroom of a boy who is crying because he has learnt of his mother's death.

We do not know whether Morvern was always able to see the horror of the everyday, or if her heightened sensitivity was induced by the atrocious experience of finding her loved one with his wrists slashed, on the kitchen floor – a room in which normal, daily activity happens, one of the hubs of a home. By leaving his corpse laying there, Morvern cohabits for days with physical decomposition – as we are reminded when she sprays the house to get rid of the stench of rotting flesh. Nevertheless, we are not given the impression that by travelling Morvern wants to escape horror and decay – rather, she travels because she is close to them. It was her boyfriend who, through his Christmas presents for Morvern, already imagined her as a traveller: a padded leather jacket, a walkman, and a lighter – the basic equipment of a modern young tripper. Furthermore, when she confesses to Lanna that 'something horrible has happened', she tells her that Johnny left her, and is not going to come back, because he went 'to another country'. Going to another country for Morvern is consistent with being close to Johnny, as well as to death.

Many reviewers asserted that Morvern's trip is a question of change of identity. We claim instead that in her journey, consistently with a postmodern traveller, Morvern does not change identity but plays with it – more precisely, she plays with tourism and tourist identities. Travelling is a state that favours this activity; when travelling, one is a stranger to the people he or she meets, and can easily pretend to be somebody else – something much more difficult to achieve in a small town where one is known by everybody. It has been suggested that, by erasing her boyfriend's name from his novel, Morvern becomes an author, or even that she becomes Johnny (see Williams 2002). This is not quite true – Morvern only plays at being an author or, more specifically, she plays at being an author on vacation in Spain. In the chapter dedicated to the cinema of Eric Rohmer, we discussed tourism and tourist identities within the framework of scholarly writing on this topic. By referring to the same body of work, we now want to investigate the tourist identities with which Morvern plays or that she comes to embody in her journey.[8]

Initially, Lanna and Morvern's trip could be seen as an example of what has been described as the 'McDonaldisation' of tourism. George Ritzer and Allan Liska (1997) use this term to define tour vacations that are highly predictable, efficient, calculable and controlled. Despite the appearances, the girls' stay in the Spanish coastal resort only looks like an attempt at losing control (through drugs, alcohol and casual sex). The young people who, like Lanna and Morvern, bought this package holiday to Spain are not seeking extraordinary experiences, as in a form of exotic sextourism, but a more intense and concentrated repetition of their ordinary life and activities. The raving parties, clubbing and drugs of the Spanish resort are not different from the ones we saw in the Scottish section of the film. Also, there is hardly the danger of meeting a Spaniard in this package holiday – everybody is British, apart from the hotel staff, who speak English anyway. The sexual encounters and new friendships are not with locals, but with other British tourists. If it were not for the sun, the hotel and its environs (made up of a swimming pool and a disco) would not look particularly Spanish either. 'The McDonaldisation thesis leads to the view that people increasingly travel to other locales in order to experience much of what they experience in their day-to-day lives' (Ritzer and Liska 1997: 99). The first incarnation of Morvern as a tourist is, therefore, that of the McDonaldised package-holiday tripper or, better, of the version of this type of tourism targeting teenagers and young people.

Except for a few moments of happiness (for instance, when Lanna and Morvern play at being two German tourists with a couple of British lads who try to chat them up), Morvern is not contented with this identity. She sits on the small balcony of her room and looks at the depressing view of toilet rolls being thrown from tens of balconies exactly like hers. In the morning, at the swimming pool, at the opposite of Lanna, Morvern does not join in the eroticised and humiliating game led by the hotel's entertainment organiser, an exchange of swimming costumes between male and female holiday-makers.

Morvern soon, and suddenly, decides to leave. She forces her friend on a taxi, which – filled with gadgets and driven by an unusual singing driver – assists their almost magical transit from the coast to the inland, from the McDonaldised resort to a true village and desert, from a highly predictable package holiday to an erratic, adventurous trek. This movement somehow recalls another film about a travelling woman, Bertolucci's *The Sheltering Sky*, in which Kit (Debra Winger), after the death of her husband, joins a caravan of nomads and with them traverses the Algerian Sahara desert, departing more and more from civilisation. Bertolucci represents her experience as both liberating and constraining, pleasant and traumatic. It is liberating, because it allows Kit to change her identity, or at least be treated as somebody different from her old self. It is constraining, because her new identity – that of a woman in a harem – forces her to adjust to a culture which she hardly understands. It is pleasant, because it offers Kit intensive experiences, especially of the erotic kind, but also traumatic – because it allows her little authority and dignity, not mentioning bringing physical discomfort. Ramsay, by contrast, illuminates only the positive sides of 'venturing into wilderness' for her heroine, but at the price of representing wilderness as less dangerous than Bertolucci's Sahara.

Caught in the middle of a traditional fiesta, Morvern and Lanna must leave their taxi, and find themselves completely alone, with only one suitcase, 'in the middle of nowhere', as Lanna complains. Inland Almeria, with its almost lunar landscape of hot desert, sandstone and dried up riverbeds, has been a popular setting for filming Spaghetti westerns (*Lawrence of Arabia* was also shot here). It makes a huge contrast with the cold and wet Scottish sequences. Lanna is hugely uncomfortable and does not understand why they are not clubbing at the resort, and must instead spend a night out, surrounded by frightening noises. 'This is so depressing', Lanna comments; Morvern, instead, exclaims: 'This is amazing!' The image of tourist that Morvern here embodies is that of the adventurous trekker, who purposefully loses her way (she is shown on the top of a hill, choosing the direction in which to go in a casual way) and is rewarded by the discovery of a perfectly preserved village in which a real and not a touristy religious procession and fiesta are taking place. Morvern, therefore, (once again, bearing similarities with Kit in *The Sheltering Sky*) first experiences the heritage of the region and then the adventure of spending one night in the desert, having lost her way. She is set in contrast to Lanna, who experiences the fiesta as a version of rave club-bing and who is frightened and annoyed of being lost in the middle of nowhere, unable to see beauty and excitement around her. Morvern's ecstatic enjoyment of this phase of her vacation is in agreement with the idea that being a 'traveller' is better and more authentic than being a 'tourist' (what she was in the first phase of her vacation). On the other hand, this belief is easily critiqued by the point of view that sees the traveller as yet another form of tourist. This opinion seems to find confirmation in the fact that the villagers are clearly displeased by the girls' intrusion in their celebrations, and by the 'cinematic' quality of the desert in which the girls spend the night – Morvern seems to be visiting not the real desert but an abandoned film set.

In the early morning, Morvern decides to leave Lanna and continue on her own, embarking on a new phase of her journey, and becoming yet another type of traveller, one which is closer to her personal inclinations. Although much of the discourse on tourism is centred on the gaze, on sightseeing, and on photograph-ing (see Urry 1990; Crawshaw & Urry 1999), the analysis of other senses should be used here to describe Morvern's third travel identity. Her experience of places and landscapes, both at home and abroad, is multi-sensory. She inhabits space in a sensual way and makes it her own, particularly through touch and hearing. When in Scotland, she goes everywhere with her walkman, listening to the music that Johnny recorded for her as a Christmas present. The music shapes and trans-forms her experience of place. This is seen particularly well in a sequence set in the supermarket where she works: Morvern walks down the aisles while listening to her music; the images in slow motion and the low camera angle create a hypnotic, heightened experience of a space which should otherwise appear as customary and uninteresting. Another example is the last sequence of the film (which, how-ever, is not necessarily the last in chronological order), with Morvern standing in the middle of a chaotic disco, but listening to her own music, the Mamas and Papas' 'Dedicated to the One I Love'. Morvern's sensual experience of landscape and of space includes scenes set both in Scotland and in Spain. When she buries her partner, for instance, she climbs a hill, and looks for the 'right' spot by spinning

around – her body twirls in space, both enjoining it and making it her own. Afterwards, she takes pleasure in touching some budding branches, and in immersing
her hand in the cold water of a stream. When in Spain, during the last phase of
her vacation, we see her sitting under a tree, sensually touching the sandy earth.
Morvern's reaching out and her desire to experience things by touching them is
exemplified also by several sequences, in which she stretches her hand after var-
nishing her nails, and looks at it against different backgrounds.

Although Morvern's sensorial experience of space is achieved both in rural
Scotland and in rural Spain, the last phase of her Spanish vacation stands out as
extremely satisfactory for her. It is by abandoning the routes of mass tourism and
by going off the beaten track that Morvern seems to achieve happiness. And when
she does, the film stops showing her moving around. Her last bit of holiday has
nothing to do with traditional sightseeing, or even with the adventurous trek in
the desert; in fact, her vacation becomes a sedentary affair. We never see her travelling; we see her sitting in a café, listening to a group of Spaniards singing a popular
song; wearing a new flowery dress, which is more in tune with her environment;
sitting under a tree, enjoining the heat and the contact with nature; and sitting on
her bed in her room, looking out at the sea. This immobility is ever more striking
if compared to Morvern's previous restlessness. For most of the film, she was seen
vigorously walking around – in her town, with its wet and dark streets; heading
home after the Christmas party; going up the hill to bury Johnny; trekking in the
Almeria desert. Even when she was sitting in a car, she often put her head out of
the window, enjoying the wind in her hair.

The tourist identity that Morvern develops in this last phase of her vacation is
that of the non-tourist, almost of a resident, or of a guest of the community. Her
attitude here suggests that the best way of travelling is not travelling: 'The irony
of tourism is that for many tourists they achieve the highest levels of satisfaction
when they feel that they have ceased to be a "tourist"' (Ryan 1991: 35). Yet the identity of the non-tourist, although apparently being highly satisfactory for Morvern,
does not seem to be final and stably adopted by her – it is only one more form of
playing. This is proved by the fact that, even in this phase, Morvern takes also up
other tourist identities – with a Spanish family who gives her a lift she plays at
being 'Jackie' (the name on a necklace that she found and wears throughout the
film), a 'rucksack-type' young British traveller; and with the two London publishers who come to discuss her contract she plays the cultural tourist, the intellectual
on vacation. Furthermore, also the phase of the non-tourist ends, when Morvern
returns home.

Morvern's travelling, her 'on the road' game of identity playing, is possible only
thanks to a man and to his intellectual and monetary power. It is by taking the

money that Johnny left for his funeral that Morvern can become a tourist; and it is by cashing the publisher's check for his novel that she can go back on the road. The film does not engage with what kind of traveller she will become, with £100,000 in her pocket and a suitcase filled with vinyl LPs. Somehow, *Morvern Callar*'s journey is the rehearsal of another, probably longer journey, which we will not see. Lanna does not understand her friend's desire to leave again. She is a local, and she does not see the point of going elsewhere. As she says to Morvern before her friend leaves again, everybody she knows and cares for lives in this town: 'There is nothing wrong with here; it is just the same crap as everywhere else.' For Morvern, instead, what counts is that, with money in her pockets, 'you can go anywhere you like', and – we would add – be anybody you like, play some more identity games. At least until the money lasts.

It is worth adding that, in Alan Warner's novel, the eponymous heroine in the course of her travel becomes pregnant, carrying in her belly 'the child of the raves', as the author puts it. Although Warner does not say it explicitly, this event seems to be a crucial factor in Morvern's decision to return to Scotland for good, or at least with no intention to travel back to Spain in the near future. Ramsay's unfaithfulness to the novel in this respect, in our opinion, reflects her unwillingness to constrain her heroine by domesticity or any other factor. It could be argued that, in order to make Morvern a winner on the track, Ramsay constructed her as childless, single and rich. It seems to us that men do not need to fulfil all these conditions to become (successful) travellers. Accordingly, it can be said that women have a long way to go before they can even start travelling.

Conclusion: female mobility in postmodern Europe

Female mobility is a phenomenon on the increase both in Eastern and Western Europe, as is reflected by the growing number of European films that portray women on the road, who travel for various purposes, including emigration, adventure, tourism, escape and relocation. Numbers, both in terms of real movements and of films made, seem to indicate that travelling in Europe for women has become easier, and is now an experience open to females belonging to middle as well as to lower social classes, rather than being restricted to upper-class women or intellectuals as before. However, our analysis has evidenced that, at least according to recent films, going on the road and travelling is still very difficult for women of all ages and classes, both in Eastern and in Western Europe. Leaving home is usually hard for them, for economic, social and psychological reasons; it requires a special effort and carries the risk that, upon their return, their position will be worse than at the outset. This can be seen in *Track-way*, whose protagonists keep returning home because they cannot afford to move or at least spend some time in a new location. Moreover, they lack ideas regarding what to do outside their home village, aside from looking for romance, something that will bind them back to domesticity, precisely what they tried to escape by hitting the road. We observe a similar set of difficulties in *Felicia's Journey*, in which Felicia with great anguish flees her inflexible father, only to meet a man who becomes for her an even worse 'father'.

Finances are always an issue; in order to travel, women must rely on money and on vehicles invariably belonging to men, as happens to Anna in *The Ride*, to the protagonists of *Felicia's Journey* and *Track-way*, and to Morvern Callar; women are often passengers in men's cars, thus adopting a passive and subaltern positioning. The danger of being a hitchhiker for a woman is shown in *The Ride* (in which Anna for being on the road is exchanged for a prostitute) and in *Felicia's Journey* (where several hitchhikers become the victims of Hilditch's manic violence). It is true that some of these women manage to prevail and overturn their condition of dependence, but this is usually at a high cost – Anna establishes her independence only in death; Felicia escapes Hilditch but at the price of the loss of her unborn child and of her home. Farba goes her own way, leaving her boyfriend behind, but then becomes lonely and despairs and tries to return to him. Morvern, despite an appearance of great independence, owes her mobility to her dead boyfriend. Even Eunice and Miriam in *Butterfly Kiss* are ultimately defeated: one dies, the other faces murder charges.

Despite the many similarities in the message that these films convey about female mobility, there is a clear difference between the Eastern and Western European films that we have analysed: the first group of films looks at female mobility from a rather realistic perspective; in the second group, instead, references to genre (the horror movie, and more specifically the highway horror), to recurrent themes of travel narrative (the coming-of-age tale) and even to fairytales (particularly *Little Red Riding Hood*, with its perilous forest) abound. Thus, generalising somehow, Eastern European directors see the growing female mobility against a background of real social and economic issues; conversely, Western European directors, although not completely disregarding such issues, prefer to inscribe their stories within more mythical and rhetorical boundaries and place them on an a-historical plane, in which the timeless pejorative link between femininity and mobility is reinstated.

chapter eight
TRAVELLING TO THE MARGINS OF EUROPE

'The problem for Europe is to learn how to marginalise itself.'
                                                    – Ien Ang

Critics and filmmakers alike from the 1980s have drawn attention to the crisis experienced by national cinemas in European countries. Dimitris Eleftheriotis writes:

> This crisis is evident on many levels, from the critical-theoretical to the economic. Indeed the very term 'national cinema' is riddled with conceptual contradictions, and its theoretical, pedagogic and practical usefulness has been repeatedly challenged in recent years. But perhaps more relevant is the realisation that shrinking domestic markets have become in most cases inadequate for the financial survival of national films. As a result more and more filmmakers have to rely on state or European funding (and in many cases both) for their productions. This in turn brings into play the contradictions in national and European policy ... and raises dilemmas of criteria and priorities: for example, is funding offered to films asserting difference or those relying on an assumed shared repertory of 'European' themes and values ... Co-production is emerging as an important strategy for the survival of European cinema ... The recent significant shift towards co-production represents ... a qualitative leap as the norm will almost certainly become (if it is not already) transnational rather than national production. (2000: 93)

Repeatedly in this book we have argued that road cinema provides an excellent opportunity to explore the following issues: the variety and differences of European national and regional cultures; the common 'European identity', of which migration and travelling are often regarded as an important component (see Hall 1992b: 46–7); and the areas of potential conflict and domains of cooperation. It also offers the opportunity to re-examine and re-negotiate the relationship between the centre of Europe and its margins, which seems to us a crucial prerequisite for any meaningful discussion concerning a new, united Europe. In practical/institutional terms, road films are also a natural opportunity for co-production.

In this chapter we examine how Europe's core and peripheries are represented in three recent films – three European co-productions with a significant financial input from German investors. Two of them are by German directors, Wim Wenders' *Lisbon Story* (1994) and Peter Lichtefeld's *Zugvögel … einmal nach Inari* (*Trains and Roses*, 1998), and focus on a German man travelling from his native country to the geographical margins of Europe, Lisbon and Northern Finland respectively. The third is Atom Egoyan's *Calendar* (1993), about a journey to Armenia. Although both director and protagonist are not German, and not even European, but Canadian, this film is relevant to the problems investigated in this chapter, namely a traveller's perception of the meaning of 'margins' or 'periphery' of Europe (as well as its 'centre', because these concepts operate dialectically). Another reason to group these films together is their strong metacinematic aspect; travel to the margins of Europe is used by their directors, especially by Wenders and Egoyan, as an opportunity to discuss the importance of media representations in constructing travel experiences and identities. This feature seems to us to be a characteristic trait of European versions of road cinema, therefore worth exploring.

Before discussing the films, it is worth referring to the meaning of margins in the discourse on travel and tourism. This part of our analysis is particularly indebted to the essay by A. V. Seaton (2000), 'The worst of journeys, the best of journeys: Travel and the concept of the periphery in European culture'.

Margins as geographical and socio-cultural concept

A. V. Seaton, echoing the views of such eminent cultural historians as Edward Said (1979), Mary Louise Pratt (1992) and Stuart Hall (1997), observes that the connotations and denotations of the concept of 'periphery' or 'margins' depend on the power relations existing between people living in different countries, regions, or even different parts of the same country and city:

> The geographical and social conception of periphery is an inherently dyadic, relativistic one, predicated upon explicit or implicit, binary contrasts between two constructed spheres of contrasted spatial and social difference. Moreover, these spheres of spatial difference have normally been constructed and defined by agents deriving their perspectives, self-definition, and not infrequently, their power and authority from membership of the constructed core sphere, rather than membership of the constructed, peripheral one. (2000: 322–3)

Seaton identifies four main 'discursive strata' on the periphery, 'each of which accumulated, through time, upon the previous one, but never to an extent that did not allow residual sedimentations from earlier periods to project and intermingle with later accretions' (2000: 323): the periphery as the discursive site of fabulation, salutary myth and sacred truth; the periphery as the discursive site of observational physical and social science, and prescriptive social engineering; the periphery as the discursive site for the spiritual raptures, archaic identifications, physical retreats and challenges of romanticism; the periphery as the discursive site of the imperial mission of adventure (2000: 324).

For our purposes the third discourse is of particular importance, as in the chosen films peripheries are represented or constructed largely according to the premises of this discourse. The elements of Romanticism which according to Seaton had the greatest impact on the way the margins were represented and projected in travel discourses are: a greater emphasis on feeling and emotional response in life and art; a greater awareness and, in some instances, near-worship of nature as a form of spiritual communion; the cult of the child as a paradisial innocent whose perceptions were superior to those of worldly adults; and an interest in mystery and abnormality (2000: 329). Seaton regards the romantic discourse as the most benign of the four. It is the only perspective in which the periphery is perceived as more noble and admirable (at least in some respects) than the centre. Yet the attraction to the inexplicable and the sublime, which is typical of Romanticism, often undergirds colonialising desire (see for instance Bernstein 1997: 9).[1] Not surprisingly, as Seaton observes, the romantic attitudes to peripheries were immersed in contradictions. For example, the inhabitants of Arabia, regarded as a paradigm of periphery in romantic discourses, 'on the one hand, were seen as carriers of archaic values of stoic nobility, loyalty and bravery; on the other, they were deemed to be treacherous and barbaric' (2000: 333).

Seaton argues that it is possible to divide the attributes of cores and peripheries into three different domains, which can be compared on an axis of binary contrasts: physical, politico-economic and psycho-cultural. We cannot present all the features of the periphery that the author discusses, but it is worth listing some of them: in physical terms, the periphery is regarded as distant, having an extreme climate, and being sparsely populated; from a politico-economic perspective, it is conceived as backward, rural and poor; and from a psycho-cultural viewpoint, it is seen as romantic, dangerous, natural and spiritual.

Lisbon Story: being European

'American? No, European' (Philip Winter, *Lisbon Story*)

Lisbon Story, a Germany-Portugal co-production, was directed by Wim Wenders, a leading figure in European road cinema, if not the most famous European director who consistently engaged with this genre. Consequently, it is inappropriate to consider this film independently of Wenders' other films, especially those set on the road. Wenders himself encourages us to treat *Lisbon Story* in conjunction with his earlier films, by including in it many of his 'trademarks', such as the protagonist's encounters with children, water as an important element of the *mise-en-scène*, and such extra-diegetic means as casting his favourite actor, Rüdiger Vogler, and calling him Philip Winter, the same name of Vogler's character in *Alice in the Cities*. One of the two main characters in *Kings of the Road* was also called Winter, although his first name was Bruno.

The link with *Alice in the Cities*, which featured a German photo-journalist returning to Europe after failing to write an article about the United States, is particularly important. While in *Alice in the Cities* Wenders offers a critical representation of America as 'an offensively noisy world that bristles with the vulgar sights and sounds of pop and commercial culture' (Sandford 1980: 107), his film is also about the 'negative uniformity' of Europe, especially about European cities as lacking a distinguishing (national or regional) character and looking all the same (see Sorlin 1994). Thus, the protagonist of *Alice in the Cities* moves from one unappealing location to another. The opinion that Germany (and, by extension, Europe) lacks a distinctive identity and needs to find or rediscover one, is a persistent motif of Wenders' films. The main reasons for this lack, as seen by Wenders, is the erasure or concealment of the old national culture, due to its association or even equation with Nazism, and the famous 'colonisation of the German subconscious' by American culture. It could be argued that largely for this reason Wenders' films often borrow a form of literary genre that is regarded as characteristically German: the *Bildungsroman*, a model of which is Goethe's *Wilhelm Meister's Apprenticeship* (1795), the novel that inspired Wenders' *Falsche Bewegung* (*The Wrong Movement*, 1974). Wenders' young characters in his films of the 1970s, often played by Vogler, look for a personal identity, for a story which they can tell about themselves, in the same way their country looks for a new identity.

If we assume that Philip Winter of *Lisbon Story* is the same Winter of *Alice in the Cities* and *Kings of the Road* but twenty years older, we can ask whether his quest for a new identity was fulfilled. The same question can be asked in reference to Germany and Europe. Did they change enough to claim that they now have a new story to tell? We believe that Wenders gives positive answers to these questions. His new German man is a happy citizen of Europe; his new Germany is a country voluntarily subscribing to and immersed in a new, united Europe, rather than an American colony.

Lisbon Story's Philip Winter is a sound engineer working in films, who travels from Frankfurt to Portugal's capital. On his way to Lisbon he muses on how Europe becomes more and more like one country – in contrast to the old Europe which was divided by wars. This country, he says, is his true homeland; to emphasise his Europeanness he repeats the word 'homeland' in several European languages. Later on, asked by a barber in Lisbon if he is American, he answers 'European', further reassuring us of the strength of his European identity. The part of Europe Philip crosses, including Germany and France, at the time of his journey was, indeed, peaceful. However, other regions, such as the Balkans and, it could be argued, Northern Ireland and Turkey, were still divided by wars. One can assume that these troublesome areas of Europe do not constitute 'Winter's Europe'. This is confirmed by the choice of languages that he uses to express his European patriotism: Turkish, Irish or Serbo-Croatian are not amongst them.

On his way to Portugal Philip observes that borders still remain, but no longer matter. Jokingly, he addresses the absent or indifferent border guards, asking: 'Don't you want to see my passport or check what I am smuggling in the boot of my car?' His announcement of the 'United States of Europe' is supported by images of cars swiftly passing border controls or the borders between countries, such as that between Spain and Portugal, without any controls at all, and only marked by a sign with the country's name. Borders, as David Sibley observes, are typically erected to defend oneself against outsiders, as well as to confirm and energise the differences between 'us' and 'them'. They can provide security and comfort, as well as lead to an experience of constraint and rejection – depending on who constructs the borders and why (see Sibley 1995: 32–48). The informality of national borders in the part of Europe depicted by Wenders suggests that there is no need for states and nations to defend themselves against the threat of the other, or to pronounce their difference from the surrounding nations.

The landscape that Winter passes changes significantly, becoming more rocky and dramatic, but the townscape and 'motorway-scape', with the same road signs, petrol stations and types of cars, remain the same. Hence, the space traversed by Winter comes across as a more balanced melange of uniformity and difference than that offered in *Alice in the Cities*. Winter uses the long journey to Portugal to learn Portuguese, not so much out of necessity but for interest and respect for the country he visits, and maybe for his own European identity, understood as resistance against American culture, of which the English language is a privileged element. In fact, since he goes to Lisbon to meet a friend, an American director named Friedrich Monroe who asked him for help in finishing his film, Winter could assume that he will not need Portugese to communicate when performing his job. However, the problems Wenders' character encounters on his journey with his broken-down car, as well as the disappearance of Friedrich before he even arrives in Lisbon, demonstrate the usefulness of his knowledge of his host country and its language.

The remaining part of the film is filled with Philip's exploration of Lisbon and recording the sound for a film about this city which Friedrich Monroe started to shoot there to commemorate the hundredth anniversary of cinema, a project he eventually abandoned. This film is strongly inspired by silent cinema, especially by Soviet Formalism. As films made before the invention of sound, it does not include any recognisable spoken words, but possesses a soundtrack, consisting of music and city noises. Gradually, Philip becomes fascinated with Lisbon and Friedrich's project, trying to capture the sounds of Lisbon on his recorder to be used in the film. He also becomes charmed by Teresa, a singer in the *fado* group Madredeus, whose songs were to be used by Friedrich on the soundtrack of his film. A model Mediterranean beauty, with long, black, simply done hair, black eyes, clad in a dark, long dress, and singing songs inspired by Portugese folklore, Teresa can be regarded as a symbol of Lisbon (and perhaps Portugal), and Philip's enchantment with her is symbolic of his love of this city and country.

Lisbon is placed on the geographical edge of Europe – it stands at the westernmost point of the European mainland. It is also represented by Wenders as politically and economically marginal, conforming to the view that geographic marginality is typically a mark of being a social periphery (see Seaton 2000; Shields 1991: 3). This marginality relies on Lisbon resisting values such as speed, pursuit of money and efficiency which, albeit associated primarily with America, are increasingly widespread and dominant in large European cities. From Wenders' perspective, Lisbon hardly changed since the nineteenth century. The principal means of transport are old-fashioned tramways; we even see a wandering knife-grinder on an ancient bike and women hand-washing clothes in special basins in front of their small cottages. The lifestyle is very relaxed and communal, with neighbours knowing each other well and people stopping the tram drivers in order to ask for directions. The clothes hang outside windows or on ropes over the narrow streets, more like in a village than a large city. Along with the almost nonexistent traffic, the communal lifestyle makes the inhabitants feel very safe. Unlike in contemporary metropolises, anonymous and dangerous as a result of crime and drug abuse, children are not afraid to play in the streets or approach strangers. The village character of Lisbon is also revealed by Friedrich and Philip, who leave unlocked their flat and editing studio, where they keep valuable equipment, without any fear of burglary. Furthermore, Lisbon is depicted as a city which remembers, respects and makes use of its history. The importance of history lies in the memories of the past, which old inhabitants recollect in conversations with Winter, in the songs written and performed by Madredeus, and in the prominence and functionality of the old buildings, such as the ancient aqueducts and the large areas of excellently preserved old cottages. It is worth mentioning that most of the film was shot in Lisbon's Old City, Alfama; the new estates with their high-rise flats are shown only at the end of the film and it is suggested that they are not typical of Lisbon. Philip, who finds Friedrich there, amongst ugly blocks of flats, advises his friend to leave the neighbourhood immediately.

When these features of Lisbon are recorded by Friedrich for his film, using the same hand-cranked camera which Buster Keaton, Dziga Vertov (whose *Man with a Movie Camera* was also largely a film about the 'poetry' of tramways) and other masters of early cinema used, in sepia colour, the city looks even more as if frozen in time. The very fact that Friedrich Monroe (and Wim Wenders) chose Lisbon to make a film about the old world and to commemorate cinema's jubilee suggests that they found Lisbon a quintessentially nineteenth-century town, more so than Paris or Berlin (not mentioning any American city). This suggestion is confirmed in one of the interviews Wenders gave in connection with *Lisbon Story*: 'For me [Lisbon] was the essence of everything I loved in Europe: France, England and Germany re-united in one country, but with a jump of thirty years backwards in time' (quoted in Colusso 1998: 76). It is worth mentioning here Jean Baudrillard's observation on his return from America that Paris (and by extension Europe, understood as the Old World) gave him the impression of living in the nineteenth century (see Baudrillard 1988: 73). It could be argued that, for Friedrich and Wenders, by being more nineteenth century than Paris, Lisbon is also more European than Europe's geographical centre, in spite of being situated at the geographical periphery of the Old Continent. Wenders even talks in an interview of Lisbon as a metaphor for Europe: 'I represented a metaphorical city, a metaphorical Lisbon, because I took Lisbon as a metaphor for Europe' (quoted in Colusso 1998: 79).

We can single-out three types of European marginality/centrality in *Lisbon Story*: geographical, political/economic and cultural. Whereas it is depicted as marginal according to the first and second meanings, in terms of the third meaning Lisbon is represented as central. According to Wenders, it is precisely due to its geographical and political marginality that Lisbon remained true to itself and, consequently, to its nineteenth-century, European character. Such an exaltation of the European geographical and political margins implies a criticism of the old European centre (wherever this centre is placed). Although the idea of the old centre's inferiority is not overtly discussed, it is conveyed by suggesting that in the twentieth century central Europe took a wrong turn, both politically and cultur-ally, first by engaging in wars and secondly by imitating America.[2] The perception that a place on the margin is a locus of noble values, which the centre abandoned or forgot, brings Wenders close to the romantic discourse on the periphery. The only difference is that the Romantics tended to extol the margins as a site of nature, while Wenders glorifies its culture. However, one can argue that Lisbon's culture is more 'natural' than the culture of the centre, as it is less manufactured and more human.

The discovery of Lisbon's nineteenth-century character and the making of a 'neo-silent' film about the city is meant to awaken nostalgia for the cultural (if not political and social) past and for the old cinema. In Friedrich's opinion, which Winter shares, and which can be identified with Wenders' own stance, old movies have an innocence and purity which contemporary cinema lacks. Friedrich complains that today images have lost their natural connection with the world; instead, they are used to sell products. After weeks of shooting with a crank camera, he abandons the idea of the silent film and embarks on a new project, which consists of shooting without really operating a camera: he hangs it on his back, allowing it to record images at random. Neither does he review afterwards the footage he produced in this way. He claims that such non-reflexive shooting is the only way to make a film which will reflect reality truthfully, not as a director or anybody else conceives it. Winter is not so radical in his attitude to filming, but deeply dislikes video; he calls the children whom he befriends in Lisbon 'vidioten' (video-idiots) because they use their video cameras constantly. Although this problem is not discussed overtly in *Lisbon Story*, one can assume that what makes Winter (and Wenders) so hostile towards video is its instantaneity, which contributes to the decline of the media that show a greater respect for narrative and for human history, such as film (see Virilio 1994).

Germany is never mentioned by Winter. It feels as if he traded his German identity or, more exactly, his German identity as reshaped by American culture, for a European one. Still, he comes across as more American than German. For example, on various occasions he pronounces his surname as if it was an English name and prefers to read some parallel texts of Portugese poetry in English rather than in German. Even the fact that the people whom he encounters assume that he is an American, and his friendship with an American film director testify to his being to a certain extent a product of the American cultural colonisation of post-war Germany. Obviously, cultural influences cannot be washed away overnight by the sheer power of will of one individual; having a European identity does not preclude the possession of other identities, at least in a residual form.

Bridges, roads and various means of transport, such as trains, cars and ships, feature prominently in Wenders' film. They testify to the fact that Lisbon is an important place of cultural encounter and exchange. There are also frequent images of water surrounding Lisbon and of aqueducts, and the characters themselves talk of the importance of water for Lisbon. One of Madredeus' songs is dedicated to the river Tagus. As Dimitris Eleftheriotis observes,

> water is a material and visual manifestation of fluidity and … fluidity involves first and foremost a renegotiation of identity. This entails a restructuring of the relationship between similarity and difference that supports any identity. In a geographical sense water seems to reproduce this dynamic relationship between similarity and difference, union and separation: seas and rivers are not only physical frontiers and markers of national borders, but also routes of communication linking and connecting ports, peoples and cultures. (2000: 99–100)

In Wenders' film, water might refer to Winter's own position as a man who 're-negotiates' his identity in Lisbon, but it might also stand for Lisbon/Portugal being open to various cultural influences and 'flooding' other peoples and countries with its own culture. Looking at the Tagus and the Atlantic Ocean surrounding Lisbon it is difficult not to think about the city's colonial past. Lisbon was both an object of foreign invasion and an invader: captured by the Moors in the eighth century, in the twelfth century it was conquered for Christendom by Alfonso Henriques, assisted by a Christian crusade of Normans, Flemish and English. With the opening of the sea route to India and the discovery of Brazil, Portugal became very rich and powerful, both in Europe and globally. It was also from Lisbon that the Invincible Armada sailed in 1588 (see Bradford 1973: 24–54). Interestingly, the issue of colonialism and post-colonialism, and of Lisbon's multiculturalism, is almost completely erased from Wenders' film. There is no reference to Lisbon's Moorish past and the only allusion to Lisbon's connection with the old colonies (which might be completely accidental and insignificant) appears when Philip asks Teresa about her artistic tour of Brazil. Moreover, apart from Friedrich and Winter, no strangers or immigrants feature in *Lisbon Story*. One suspects that the memory of the 'ultra-European' Lisbonians heading for South America to kill and exploit the natives, as well as of any tensions between Christians and Muslims living in Lisbon, will not suit the film's message about a civilised, peaceful and presumably Christian Europe. The oversight or, perhaps, the denial of Portugal's and by extension of Europe's colonialist past, coupled with the nostalgia for a ultra-European, nineteenth-century past, adds to Wenders' idealised vision of new Europe and narrows the parameters in which the discussion of Europe and its margins is conducted. Such omissions are regrettable, as the issues are crucial for any meaningful discussion of European margins and European identity.

Wenders shows that first Friedrich and then Philip fell under the spell of Lisbon and of Teresa. The best testimony to Philip's love of the city is the fact that it is thanks to him that the film will be finished, after Friedrich decided to abandon his project. However, we argue that in spite of Winter's enchantment with Lisbon, his learning Portuguese, and his longer-than-planned stay in this city, he remains a tourist, who keeps a safe distance from the place he visits. Firstly, his very interest in historic Lisbon, at the expense of the contemporary city, betrays a typical touristic attitude. Philip is reluctant to watch what his young friends shot with their video cameras and which reflects their everyday life. This unwillingness partly results from the previously mentioned distaste Winter has for the medium they use, but also from a lack of interest in the reality they try to record. Secondly, his enchantment with Teresa does not lead to any true love or romance, or desire to live together, which was even lamented by some critics (see Gansera 1995: 37). He admires her as a beautiful object, in the same way a tourist admires a palace or a church, without planning to take it home, at very most only in the form of an image on a postcard. The same can be said about Monroe. His way of filming Lisbon, using a camera placed on his back, suggests as much his desire to get a true image of the city, as his unwillingness to explore it, to have any personal contact with it. His distance from Lisbon and enclosure within his private obsessions is also signified by the place he occupies: a small, strange car on the outskirts of Lisbon. Furthermore, it is remarkable that Friedrich uses as his guide to Lisbon a boy who is mute, as if he was afraid that an articulate Lisbonite could destroy his preconception of the city. The whole film can be regarded as a kind of tourist guide to Lisbon and praise of touristic pleasures. Hence, although nominally Winter and Wenders reached the margins of Europe, metaphorically they did not travel very far.

Winter's unwillingness to commit himself seriously to his love for Teresa and for Lisbon is typical of Wenders' characters and the director's own *Weltanschauung*, which was accurately summed up by Robert Phillip Kolker and Peter Beicken: 'He makes homelessness a virtue, an aesthetic' (1993: 161). This unwillingness can also be interpreted as a testimony to Winter's prioritising his Europeanness over any national or regional identity. This is because identity can only be constructed through demarcating oneself in relation to some other. As Paul Gilroy observes, 'nobody ever speaks of human identity' (1997: 301). We will suggest that there are two principal 'others' in relation to Winter's pan-European identity: one is American culture, the other European national cultures. Consequently, to remain a true European, he cannot allow himself to identify too strongly or exclusively with any particular national culture within Europe. Strong nationalism goes hand in hand with lack of enthusiasm and sometimes even with open hostility, as in the case of Britain, towards such quintessentially pan-European institutions as the European Parliament in Brussels or the common European currency. Also, patriotic feelings towards Europe are still a rarity amongst ordinary European citizens, which prob-

Fig. 17 Wim Wenders' *Lisbon Story* (Germany/Portugal, 1994) © Road Movies Filmproduktion

ably explains why Europeanness is rarely represented or projected in 'high' art. Consequently, to use Godard's phrase, today's Europe is styleless (MacCabe 1992: 100). *Lisbon Story*'s attempt to change this fact was not entirely successful.

Trains and Roses: becoming Finnish

'Not even a fool would flee to Finland' (The border guard, *Trains and Roses*)

Trains and Roses, a German-Finnish co-production, deals with many of the issues discussed by Wenders in *Lisbon Story*, but in a more discreet way or, as one could say, in the shadow of the narrative. The film tells the story of a lorry driver from Dortmund, Hannes Weber, whose hobby is to memorise train timetables. His ambition is to win a world timetable competition, which takes place in Inari, in Lapland. In order to attend the event, he asks his new boss if he can take a week of unused holiday. His boss, who was brought into the haulage company to rationalise its operations, meaning making many employees redundant, fires him, regarding his wish to go on holiday as a sign of insufficient commitment to work. Weber, who did not have any time off for several years, finds his boss's attitude unacceptable; he punches him and leaves for Finland. Several hours later the boss is found dead in his office and Hannes becomes the prime suspect in the murder investigation. The police and border controls in several countries are informed about the crime and try to intercept Hannes on his way to Inari. This international and costly operation, however, proves unsuccessful. In the end Stefan, the detective responsible for the case, flies to Finland to arrest Hannes only minutes before the competition starts but, on his plea, allows him to take part in the event. Hannes loses by a very small margin, but is allowed to walk free, as during the competition the detective discovers that the true killer of Weber's boss was his secretary.

The narrative of Hannes' journey from Dortmund to Inari, as with Phillip Winter's journey from Frankfurt to Lisbon, allows the director to examine the relationship between national and European identities and cultures. Hannes is portrayed as a very un-German German. Instead of listening to German music, he is a fan of Italian singer Adriano Celentano; he does not like football, the favourite pastime in his native Dortmund; and even avoids drinking beer when in his hometown. Neither does Hannes' flat reveal any sign that its owner is German. It is furnished in a most basic way and looks more like a railway station information office than a home, with maps of railway connections, train timetables and a large railway clock on the wall. Even his job as a truck driver, spending a substantial part of his life travelling, presumably also abroad, suggests a lack of strong national and regional identity. Dortmund is depicted by Lichtefeld as a nondescript, monotonous and ugly townscape. We usually see the less attractive sides of the buildings: the backs of supermarkets and of a stadium, a truck depot and identical-looking blocks of flats. The camera never shows an overview of the city, only revealing small parts of streets and locales, giving the impression of Dortmund as being fragmented and a locus of alienation. It could be argued that such a place is hardly conducive to patriotic feelings. When Hannes writes a postcard to his friend, entitled 'Greetings from the beautiful Dortmund', it looks like a bad joke.

Hannes' obsession with timetables, particularly his efforts to find the fastest routes between European cities, can be interpreted as a sign that being a citizen of Europe matters more for him than being German. On the way to Inari he confesses his ambition to become a railway expert, working for the European Union to develop the fastest European railway transport possible, which will be unified and standardised, and thus replace the currently fragmented national railways. Although he does not say it, his project will bring Europeans closer together, at the same time as making their lives more efficient. Lichtefeld also shows that Europe is already well connected and cooperating in many areas, such as trade (legal and illegal), policing and border control. For example, it takes only minutes for Stefan, who investigates the murder of Hannes' boss, to inform the border controls and police in Sweden and Finland that the main suspect is trying to cross their frontiers. On the other hand, people manage to cross borders illegally and criminals succeed in escaping the international police, confirming the widespread opinion (particularly strong in Great Britain) that European bureaucracy is excessive and inefficient. Lichtefeld also shows, perhaps unintentionally, that there are some shortcomings in living in a unified and standardised Europe, such as having similar food served on the trains and on ferries in Germany, Sweden and Finland.

The railway in *Trains and Roses* can be interpreted as the epitome of Continental Europe, understood as a place where states still own and control large sections of the industry and where people are encouraged to use public transport to avoid road congestion, reduce pollution and travel more safely and comfortably. In this respect, a train may be contrasted with the private car, symbolising America as an individualistic country, dominated by corporations and unconcerned about the natural environment. It also encapsulates the distinctiveness of European road cinema, as in American films characters almost always travel by car or motorcycle. Trains in Lichtefeld's film work almost perfectly: there are no delays, carriages are clean and well equipped, conductors are polite, tickets are reasonably priced and there are no vandals on board. Not every European country can boast such an ideal railway system. An example is the British one, ineffective both in reality and in the way it has recently been depicted by the media, especially in Ken Loach's *The Navigators* (UK, 2001).[3]

Hannes feels much more at home on a train or ferry than in his company office or in his Dortmund flat. At work he is awkward and shy, unable to express himself adequately or stand up for himself. He is oblivious to what people tell him and think of him, and does not notice the attention of a young woman who works in a supermarket. On a train, however, even in a foreign country, he is nobody's fool. He knows the precise prices of different seats and sleeping compartments, he knows how to defend his territory when somebody tries to take his place and, of course, he knows the fastest train connections. Moreover, although Hannes is regarded by his fellow employees as a loner, during the journey he reveals well-developed social skills, befriending a string of different people, including a conductor involved in money counterfeiting and a Finnish woman, Sirpa, who lives in Helsinki, but dreams about cultivating roses in a Finnish village. In the end he falls in love with her, and it is suggested that he will remain in Finland with her.

Nationality plays little part in the contacts Hannes makes on his way to Inari, as neither he nor his fellow travellers mind whom they talk to. For example, the Finnish couple whom Hannes meets on the last train enjoy the fact that they are all professional drivers; doing the same job is for them more important than coming from the same country. Moreover, the man says that it does not matter where one lives or what nationality one has; what is really important is 'having a good woman at one's side'. Speaking different languages is hardly a problem in transnational connections, as everyone in *Trains and Roses* knows at least two: their mother tongue and English. The majority of Finns also speak fluent German and Swedish. They learn foreign languages not simply out of necessity, but due to curiosity, to find out about foreign cultures, as revealed in the episode in which a Finnish train driver switches on the radio tuned into a German station, to demonstrate how she learnt almost perfect German.

The film also draws attention to the fact that there are more important differences than those between nations, such as divisions between city and country, between people who put profit first and those who cherish love, friendship and life in tune with nature more than economic success. The last one is largely a gender division; in Lichtefeld's narrative Sirpa abandons her Finnish boyfriend because he does not want to move to the country, where she inherited a rose nursery. We never see or hear her boyfriend; he is so busy with his work that he hardly visits their flat, only leaving messages for Sirpa on his computer or on their answering machine. Neither does he look after her favourite roses; upon her return from Germany, she finds them all withered. By contrast, it is suggested that Hannes, being a 'new man', will be happy to live with Sirpa close to nature, as he greatly enjoys walking in the forest with her and exploring Lake Inari in Lapland. The best indication of him embracing her values is his behaviour at the competition. Asked about the best route from Munich to Inari, Hannes does not answer by giving the details of the fastest route, but the longer one, which Sirpa described to him the day before as her favourite. This is a route in which the traveller reaches his destination in the morning, relaxed and satisfied with his journey. As a result, Hannes loses the competition beaten by one Ms Higgins (probably an American), who answered by providing the fastest route, but wins the heart of Sirpa, demonstrating his good memory of her travel tips and his faithfulness to her values. The film's author fully endorses the more rural, one could say marginal, lifestyle which Sirpa hopes to enjoy once she moves to the rose farm, and which Hannes discovers on his way to Inari, and condemns as inhuman the city culture, based solely on financial success. By doing so, Lichtefeld promotes the idea of a Europe that does not want to go the American way, given that the values which Sirpa opposes are representative of the USA even more than of any European country.

The scenery significantly changes during the film, with Germany looking extremely industrialised, urbanised and grey, almost devoid of nature, while Finland is depicted as sparsely populated, only lightly touched by civilisation and, contrary to the northern stereotype, rather colourful, with green, yellow and brown leaves on many different types of trees. The Finnish landscape is shot with long takes, and a bird's-eye view is often used, to allow the spectator to contemplate the magnificent landscape. The towns, however, look very similar along the whole route between Dortmund and Inari, with almost identical railway stations, blocks of flats and large corporation buildings standing in prominent positions in Hamburg, Stockholm and Helsinki. Thus, the main difference between Germany and Finland is that large towns are a rarity in Finland, while Germany is heavily urbanised.

On many occasions Finland is described as being located on the margins of Europe; the characters simply say that 'Finland is the end of Europe' and its peripheral status appears to be an important component of the country's identity. Not only the Finns recognise their distance from the European centre, but the region which is peripheral within Finland, northern Lapland, is considered as playing a crucial role in defining its character. Attention is drawn to such extreme phenomena as Lake Inari, the most northerly lake in the world, the austere climate and the long periods of complete winter darkness which, as Sirpa puts it, 'lie heavy on the soul', making people sleepy, slow and inactive. The Finns are portrayed by Lichtefeld as very friendly, relaxed, but also self-deprecating and slightly sad. Testimony to their dead-pan sense of humour is a scene which takes place on the border between Sweden and Finland. The Finnish border guards receive a photograph of Hannes by fax, but do not identify him amongst the passengers leaving a ferry and comment that not even a fool would decide to flee to Finland. They quickly lock up their checkpoint, without ensuring that all the passengers have crossed the border, allowing Hannes, who overslept and missed the ferry's arrival, to enter Finland undisturbed. This episode bears strong similarities with the films of Aki Kaurismäki, who also plays down Finland's economic and cultural importance. Another reference to Kaurismäki's cinema is the appearance of his favourite actress, Kati Outinen, as a taciturn Finnish woman married to a truck driver, whom Hannes meets on a Finnish train. The reference to Kaurismäki's work can be interpreted as proof that, as Timothy Corrigan observes, contemporary road cinema deals more often with images, with 'simulacra', than with reality (1991: 152). It might also suggest the desire on the part of the director of *Trains and Roses* to depict Finnish people and their culture from the perspective of the insider, rather than that of the ignorant tourist.

The construction of Finnish national identity around the Lapland discourse is reminiscent of the construction of Canadian national identity around the myths of the Arctic and Sub-Arctic (see Shields 1991: 162–206). In spite of the fact that only a small proportion of Finns and Canadians actually live in the North, in both cases the northern periphery plays a crucial role in establishing what being a 'true' Finn or Canadian means:

> The myth of the 'True North Strong and Free' has been appropriated as one symbol of specific Canadian nationalistic discourse which, although not com-

pletely hegemonic, attempts to reconcile regional viewpoints. This myth resides within an oppositional spatialisation whereby Southerners construe the North as a counter-balance to the civilised world of the Southern cities, yet the core of their own, personal, Canadian identity … The 'True North Strong and Free' is a perverse case of building a cultural identity from both sides of the equation civilised/uncivilised or culture/nature: of defining a dichotomy and then reappropriating elements which are often rejected because the dualism becomes associated, metaphorically, with other black and white categories such as good/bad … Such a dualism provides a foundation for Canadian nationalists because it provides the possibility of setting a 'Canadian nature' (The 'True North') off against 'American mass culture' entirely originating, or so we are asked to believe, south of the border. (Shields 1991: 163)

Similarly, the 'Finnish national character' equated with 'Lapland character' in Lichtefeld's film (as in the films by Aki Kaurismäki) is set off against metropolitan Finnish culture, epitomised by the lifestyle of Sirpa's boyfriend and condemned as fake and inhuman.

Although Finland is at the end of Europe and apparently content with its peripheral position, the organisation of the first world rail timetable competition in Inari suggests that the country tries and succeeds, albeit on a small scale, to be at the centre of Europe, or even of the entire world. It also proves to be more innovative than many of the more central countries. The actual competition also makes the viewer realise that Europe extends much further than the borders of Western Europe or the European Union, as places such as Constanza in Romania and towns in the ex-Soviet Union are mentioned. The competition is, however, very modest and low-key, contrasting with many other European contests and festivals, renowned for their pomp and kitsch.

Water plays an even more important role in the setting and narrative of *Trains and Roses* than in *Lisbon Story*. A substantial part of Hannes' journey involves crossing seas and rivers and travelling near water. There is also much talk about the beauty of Finnish lakes and their importance for the country's mythology. For example, the characters discuss the holy island of Ukonnkivi which emerges from Lake Inari. The more Hannes learns about the waters of Finland, by listening to Sirpa's stories and by walking around Lake Inari, the more he is enchanted by the Finnish landscape and culture and by Sirpa herself, and the more distanced he becomes from his own life back in Dortmund, and even from his ambition of winning the contest. Hannes' change of identity from German to Finnish, from metropolitan to rural, is much more profound than that of Winter in *Lisbon Story* who had no desire to learn what Madradeus sang about. It could be suggested that in *Trains and Roses* being a cosmopolitan European is not an end in itself, but only a stage on the road to becoming a person who prefers another culture to the one in which he was brought up. Conversely, one can hardly imagine a person of nationalistic views falling in love with Sirpa and Inari as easily as Hannes. At the same time, to smooth the process of Hannes' 'becoming Finnish', Lichtefeld represents Sirpa as completely at ease with German culture. Not only does she speak fluent German, but she lived in the country for some time. She even takes precisely the same route from Dortmund to Helsinki as Hannes. Moreover, in spite of Hannes being only an unemployed lorry driver, both Hannes and Sirpa are depicted as typical Westerners who live a reasonably comfortable and safe life, unlike many of the immigrants from Eastern Europe, Africa or Asia, who in their native countries suffered poverty and fear of political or religious persecution. In common with *Lisbon Story* the issue of non-Western Europeans crossing the European borders and the encounters between the citizens of the European Union and other Europeans is not even mentioned.

The attractiveness of 'marginal' Finland for Hannes, in common with the attractiveness of Lisbon to Philip Winter, but to an even greater extent, originates from their conviction that the periphery possesses a distinctive culture which the civilised, industrialised, urban centre of Europe lacks. This conviction can be treated both as conforming to the romantic discourse on the periphery and the acceptance of the view that the West is declining due to globalisation. John Tomlinson, referring to the work of Anthony Giddens and Zygmunt Bauman, writes:

> Although the process of 'globalising modernity' may have *begun* in the extension of Western institutions (capitalism, industrialism, the nation-state system), their very global ubiquity now represents a decline in the differentials between the West and the rest of the world. In a sense the West's 'success' in disseminating its institutional forms represents a loss of its once unique social/cultural 'edge'. (Tomlinson 1999: 172)

Consequently, one can expect that, as Europe becomes increasingly more Westernised and 'global', these parts of the Old Continent, which resist the forces of globalisation even at the cost of remaining backward and parochial, will become increasingly more important from a cultural perspective.

In common with Wenders, Lichtefeld advocates travelling both in the literal and metaphorical sense. All the characters who embark on a journey benefit from it immensely. This refers not only to Hannes and Sirpa, who find each other on a train, but also to Stefan, the policeman who investigates the murder of Hannes' boss. We meet him as a man who sees no world apart from his work – he is obsessive, intolerant and difficult to cooperate with. Learning about train timetables and eventually going to Finland changes him, however, into a 'softer', more considerate and sensitive person. After finding Hannes in Inari and discovering that he did not commit the murder, he decides to prolong his sojourn in Lapland. One can imagine that in future he might even succeed Hannes in the train timetable competition.

Calendar: being neither from here nor from there

'We are both from here, yet being here has made me from somewhere else'
(The Photographer in *Calendar*)

The protagonist of *Calendar*, identified in the film credits as the Photographer, finds himself in a different position to that of the main characters in *Lisbon Story* and *Trains and Roses*, as he is not a European citizen travelling to another European country, but a Canadian of Armenian origin who visits Armenia. Armenia, similarly to Portugal and Finland, is situated at the geographical periphery of Europe, at its Eastern edge, and in common with the aforementioned countries has a low density population. However, its perceived distance from the centre of Europe is even greater than that of Lisbon and Lapland, largely because of its history of many military invasions and attempts at colonisation. The last was that of communist Russia, which resulted in its incorporation to the Soviet Union as one of its republics. During Soviet rule, Armenia was doubly marginalised: both within the Soviet Union and within Europe. Before the fall of the Berlin Wall virtually all political, economic and cultural exchanges between Armenia and the outside world were mediated by Moscow. Not surprisingly, many Europeans are not even aware that this country belongs to their continent. As Jonathan Romney observed, *Calendar*, which was co-financed by the Armenian National Cinematheque, 'is itself somewhat invested in representing Armenia to the world' (2003: 97).

It could be argued that the Photographer not only travels to a marginal location, but also starts his journey from a place on the margin, as Canada has a peripheral status within the North American context. In common with Armenia, it is sparsely populated and although its citizens enjoy a high standard of living, as testified by many previous films by Egoyan (see Mazierska 2002), it is economically and culturally dominated by its rich and powerful neighbour, the USA. Largely for this reason, as argued above, 'True North Strong and Free' has been appropriated as a symbol of Canadian national identity. On his trip the Photographer is accompanied by his wife, who is also a Canadian of Armenian origin, but unlike the

Photographer, who does not know the language of his forebears, she came from a diasporan community and speaks good Armenian. She serves as her husband's translator (her filmic name is the Translator). During their stay in Armenia, they are accompanied by the Driver, an ethnic Armenian who also acts as their guide, taking them to visit sites and explaining their history and significance. The Driver, like the Photographer, speaks only one language, in this case Armenian. Accordingly, the Translator acts as a bridge between her husband and the Driver and, by extension, between Canada/the West and Armenia/the East. The Photographer, not unlike Philip Winter in *Lisbon Story*, comes to the 'margin of Europe' to perform a specific task – he was commissioned to photograph a series of churches for a calendar.

Egoyan refers to Armenia's marginal status through various means. One is his use of *mise-en-scène*. The two most persistent images in the film are that of a flock of sheep against the hills, with no one in sight except the travellers and the churches. The first image suggests that Armenia has a small population and is a rural, even backward country. Such a conclusion is corroborated by the few scenes set in an urban environment which looks like a model Eastern European 'sink estate' with ugly, dilapidated tenement blocks and poorly-clad people. It might be regarded as paradoxical to list Christianity as one of the principal reasons for Armenia being at the periphery of Europe and the Western world. However, by constructing the Photographer as a man who does not hold any religious beliefs, and indeed lacks any spirituality (he sees no point in going inside the churches which he photographs), and suggesting that he is a model inhabitant of the Western world, Egoyan succumbs to the widely held view that the West ceased being truly Christian and became secular. In many contemporary discourses on religion, Christianity, especially if practiced by praying and taking part in religious ceremonies, is regarded as more primitive than being non-religious.

However, whenever we see those aspects of Armenia that conform to its peripheral status, Egoyan makes us aware of the medium which records them: respectively photography and video. The director demonstrates that it matters to our understanding and appreciation of the landscape where the camera was situated, how a particular object was framed, or whether it was recorded by high-class or cheap equipment. In this way, Egoyan draws our attention to the fact that, as tourists and travellers, we are not free agents, observing and remembering whatever we choose to see and observe, but are governed by some pre-existing knowledge of the place we visit, which itself is largely the product of representations created and circulated by the media. At the same time, by choosing the aspects of Armenia that testify to its marginality (at the cost of excluding others) Egoyan is complicit with these stereotypical representations, which construct the country as a cultural

Fig. 18   Atom Egoyan's *Calendar* (Armenia/Canada/Germany, 1993) © Ego Film Arts

'other' of Europe and of the Western world at large, or their inferior, backward cousin.

Adding to the representation of Armenia as oriental and, therefore, un-European, the music prevalently sounds like a shepherd's lament or like prayers in a mosque. It bears strong associations with the music from Bertolucci's *The Sheltering Sky*, a film, which, not unlike *Calendar*, is built around the perceived contrasts between West and East. It is worth adding that, although this type of music is indeed popular in Armenia, the country also has composers who, at the same time as drawing on their own culture, engage in the 'central' European musical traditions, most importantly the twentieth-century composer, player and singer Soghomon Soghomonian, known as Komitas.

The narrative and the construction of the main characters further perpetuates the impression of Armenia's marginality, as conveyed by the setting and music, while adding new meanings and layers to its apparent peripheral status. Firstly, although the Photographer's main purpose is to work on the calendar, Egoyan also suggests that he visits the country to learn about his roots and become a more spiritual creature. The same is also true about the Translator. In accordance with the romantic discourse on the periphery, they expect Armenia to be a site of simple nobility, spontaneity and spirituality and, in the eyes of the Driver, the country embodies these qualities. However, in line with the contradictory character of the romantic discourse, this character can also be perceived as a simpleton and even a barbarian. Unlike the Photographer, who is bespectacled, clean shaven, has rather delicate features, wears designer clothes, and talks with great care, as if unsure of his opinions and perceptions, the Driver wears simple, crumpled clothes, has a moustache, thick features and talks very fast, as if paying no attention to his words and lacking any self-doubts and, consequently, self-reflexivity. In contrast to the visitors, who interrogate their national identity, the Driver is in tune with his country and nation. He regards himself as an Armenian and does not want to be anything or anywhere else and expects all Armenians to be like him. He even tells the couple that if they have children, they should raise them in the country of their ancestors. One can guess that this opinion prevails amongst the inhabitants of Armenia; in reality, the majority of them, even those residing in the country, operate a more open and tolerant concept of national identity than the representatives of many other European nations, resulting from the fact that so many of them live in diaspora. Virtually every Armenian family has relatives in other ex-Soviet republics, other European countries, or the United States and Canada.[4] Consequently, we argue that Egoyan constructs the Driver as more nationalistic than an 'average Armenian'.

Although the Driver is poor, in line with the romantic stereotype that 'ethnic' people are more generous than Westerners, he shows remarkable disregard for money and material goods. This is revealed in the episode in which he is offended when the Photographer shows concern that the Driver will expect them to pay extra for explaining the history of the churches, and by his desire to exceed his remit as a driver and to show the visitors the 'real Armenia' for free. In addition, in contrast to the intellectual and passive Photographer, who prefers a mediated contact with people, including his wife, whom he normally sees through the lens of his camera, rather than face to face, the Driver comes across as a virile, even macho man, who prefers to act than to meditate. In the tourist and photographic discourses, as well as feminist examination of the cinematic apparatus, using a camera is regarded as a sign of power over the objects recorded (see Mulvey 1975; Sontag 1979; Urry 1990). However, Egoyan draws attention to the fact that it can also act as an obstacle to access and possess the desired object. In particular, the Photographer, being committed to completing his photographic work on time and worried that somebody might steal his precious equipment, avoids taking part in walks with his wife and the Driver, and practically becomes immobile and powerless when the dashing native seduces his wife, which leads to the break-up of their marriage and the Translator remaining in Armenia. This, however, not only confirms the romantic stereotype that 'Oriental' men are virile, but also that they are treacherous and their apparent generosity only conceals a business-like attitude to Westerners. The use of language adds to the romantic concept of Armenia, making the Armenian characters feel mysterious and impenetrable for the Westerners: only Armenian viewers know what the Driver and the Translator are talking about, as we are not sure if the Translator translates the Driver's words truthfully or, taking advantage of her husband's lack of knowledge of the language, flirts with the Driver.

The rivalry between the Photographer and the Driver for the wife of the former can be read as a competition between Armenia and Canada and by extension, between East and West for the souls of people who are in-between cultures, undecided about their identity and values, or maybe even for those who already gravitate towards the culture which they eventually choose. Such a metaphorical interpretation is encouraged by Jonathan Romney, who writes: 'The fictional Photographer loses his wife ... to an Armenian – indeed, to Armenia itself' (2003: 101). However, Egoyan is anxious to demonstrate that this happens because from the very start the Translator feels close to Armenia. This is signalled by her excellent command of the language, which suggests that, even prior to her journey, she belonged to a vibrant Armenian diaspora, as well as her appearance and behaviour. In tune with the stereotype that women are closer to nature than men, she comes across as a 'child of nature'. Most of the time we see her running among the sheep with her long, curly hair wildly flying in the wind, wearing loose clothes, completely in tune with the untamed landscape. Similarly, it appears that she communicates with the local people not only on the level of language, but emotionally as well; they treat her as if she was one of them and she happily joins in their celebrations, rather than doing it out of politeness. Moreover, unlike the Photographer, who remains outside the churches, she goes inside, which can be read as a metaphor of her desire to belong, to participate in a culture, rather than observing it (see Mazierska 2000). Her attitude to her husband further indicates that Armenian culture or, more precisely, the Armenian culture as constructed in the romantic discourse of periphery, is closer to her than her Canadian/Western heritage. She is increasingly weary of his utterly pragmatic attitude to people, including herself. At some point she asks him if he took her to Armenia because it was practical, and he agrees. Her realisation that they stay together mainly for practical reasons puts her off her husband and increases the attraction of people who follow their hearts, rather than their brain.

By contrast, for the Photographer, whose allegiance to Armenian identity is based solely on possessing Armenian ancestors, remaining in the country of his roots for good is not a viable option. The visit only highlights the fact that he does not belong to Armenia, as conveyed in the sentence he utters to his wife: 'We are both from here, yet being here has made me from somewhere else.' Not knowing the language is an important factor in his being an outsider in Armenia; however, there are other, perhaps even more important reasons why he feels as if he comes 'from somewhere else'. For example, he looks at Armenia 'through his usual lenses', accepting and identifying only with those of its aspects which he can understand (which means rejecting or being indifferent to most of its cultural heritage), and assessing the local people by moral standards which he would apply to fellow Canadians. In particular, the Photographer likes to know the precise monetary value of objects and services, even those which are difficult to measure in money, and pay for them in accordance with their value. This attitude is visible in his worry that the Driver will expect to be paid extra for any extra services. It appears to trouble him even more than the risk that he might seduce his wife.

While in the two films previously discussed the emphasis was on the ease of overcoming long distances, crossing borders, communicating with people belonging to different countries and cultures and the fluidity of cultural identity, *Calendar* is based on a different set of premises. For the characters in this film travelling and crossing borders is difficult, communicating with people belonging to a different culture is almost impossible, cultural identities are fixed. It is worth adding that, unlike *Lisbon Story* and *Trains and Roses*, in which water featured prominently, symbolising the chance of meeting and the fluidity of identity, the main element of Egoyan's landscape is mountains – a symbol of barriers between cultures and people.

Egoyan also addresses the issue of the impact of travel and contact with different cultures on the travellers' perception of their own identity. He does this by making his main character return to Canada and ask himself and other Armenian-Canadians what it means to be a Canadian and what Canadian culture means for them. The very fact that he needs to ask this question suggests a crisis of identity on his part. The answer he receives is that being Canadian does not preclude being an Armenian, Russian, Iraqi and so on. We suggest that, contrary to the metaphor of a 'melting pot' of traditions which produce a new and richer culture, typically applied to the US, in his representation of Canadian culture and identity the author of *Calendar* opts for the metaphor of a 'common ground', a narrow set of values shared by all Canadians, irrespective of their ethnic origin. This idea is close to the previously mentioned opinion that, due to globalisation, the West has lost its distinctiveness, hence its identity. Needless to say, such a reductionist construction of national culture does not lead to a richer personal identity but, on the contrary, to an impoverished one. The Photographer experiences this particularly painfully, as after his trip to Armenia he loses any illusion of belonging to the country of his ancestors. Hence, at the end of his trip he is 'neither from here nor from there'. His only solution to this problem appears to be constructing an identity based on the culture of the media. In the end the use of photography and video defines the Photographer much more accurately than him being Canadian or Armenian.

The pessimistic assessment of travel to the margins, as offered in *Calendar*, so different to that shown in *Lisbon Story* and *Trains and Roses*, can be partly attributed to the different cultural background of Egoyan to that of Wenders and Lichtefeld, and consequently, to the different character of his films. We refer to the fact that Egoyan's films belong to diasporic cinema or even, in the opinion of Hamid Naficy, constitute a paradigm of such cinema, which he describes as 'accented cinema'. This cinema, as Naficy argues, is marked by such features as focusing on sad, lonely, alienated and internally divided characters who are continuously displaced and unsuccessfully search for home, and foregrounding the difficulty, if not impossibility, to overcome linguistic problems and problems related to communication in a wider sense (see Naficy 2001).

It is worth noting that, by representing the Translator crossing the chasm between West and East, while the Photographer remains in the West, Egoyan, not unlike Wenders and Lichtefeld, conforms to the dominant cultural practice of representing gender differences, by suggesting that men are on the side of history, culture and rationality, while women gravitate towards family, nature and instinct. The majority of feminist authors are very critical of such stereotyping, which in their opinion betrays a patriarchal and misogynist mindset, pointing out that its acceptance results in denying women the right to participate fully in society and shape their fate. Egoyan, however, does not subscribe to this conclusion in his film because, as a model Romantic, he regards culture as constraining, not as liberating. Consequently, women are for him much freer creatures than men. Unlike Wenders and Lichtefeld, who foreground the benefits of travelling by showing that contact with foreign cultures enriches one's identity, Egoyan draws attention to its dangers and risks by pointing out that by travelling we can lose our old sense of self without gaining any new one.

Conclusions

The margins of Europe in *Lisbon Story*, *Trains and Roses* and *Calendar* are represented according to romantic conceptions of periphery. Wenders, Lichtefeld and Egoyan focus on their beauty, allure and cultural richness, which in *Lisbon Story* and *Trains and Roses* surpass the attractiveness of Europe's core, Germany, and in *Calendar* of Canada. The result is the evolution of the principal characters – Winter, Hannes and the Translator – their love affairs with cultures and people of Lisbon, Lapland and Armenia respectively. At the same time, the three directors demonstrate that remaining on the margin is a viable option only for those people who are already, to put it metaphorically, 'half-way' between their old home and the new one: detached from their old country and willing to give in to the charm of the new one. By contrast, those who, like the Photographer in *Calendar*, are unable to give up their habits and make an effort to learn about the new place must return home.

It is also worth noticing that in his film Egoyan leaves out completely the question of Armenia's contribution to European culture and its post-Soviet aspiration to come closer to Western Europe, instead representing it as the West's 'other'. Similarly, Wenders and Lichtefeld operate a rather narrow concept of Europe, understood as the relatively affluent Western Europe, populated by people who have lived there for many generations: ethnic Germans, Portugese and Finns. Hence, although Germany is the most multi-ethnic country in the whole European Union (as is well documented in German cinema of the last decade), Wenders and Lichtefeld avoid the issue of 'renegotiating identity' inside the borders of Germany, between ethnic Germans and, for example, Turks, Kurds, ex-Yugoslavians, Poles or Armenians. In *Trains and Roses* there is not even the token presence of immigrants on the trains to or from Hamburg, in spite of this city having one of the highest proportions of immigrants in the whole of Germany. Literally and metaphorically, the films explore the margins of Europe from the point of view of a Westerner. These films show that Europe (and the West) is discovering its margins, but still needs to learn, as Ien Ang put it, 'how to marginalise itself, to see its present in its historical particularity and its *limitedness*, so that Europeans can start relating to cultural "others" in new, more modest and dialogic ways' (1992: 28). Time will tell if the old continent is inclined or able to gain such knowledge and skill, and how this marginalisation will affect European cinema and European culture in general.

NOTES

introduction

1   Laderman devoted the last chapter of his book to the European road movie, recognising its autonomy from the Hollywood format.
2   On the other hand, the European trip is often informed by the yearning for freedom and a new life, particularly when the journey consists of an emigration from poor regions or from repressive regimes.
3   Obviously, the car is very important also in European road films, particularly during phases of economic growth, when it becomes a powerful symbol of social progression.

chapter two

1   A seminal filmic example of tourism turned into exile can be found in *The Sheltering Sky* (1990) by Bernardo Bertolucci, based on the novel of the same title by Paul Bowles, about a rich American couple travelling in North Africa.
2   Bauman's discourse on tourism is similar to that on travelling, as presented by Buzard and Urry, suggesting that there are no meaningful, empirical differences between these two states. See Buzard 1993 and Urry 1995.
3   Adrien's hypothesis has so far little support in reality; see Seabrook 1988.
4   Yet not everybody in the film is of the same opinion as Magali: some characters enjoy the view of gigantic factory plants claiming that thanks to the industry the valley is alive.
5   Rohmer is not the only director to tackle the ambivalent character of female mobility; see Luckett 2000 for a discussion of it in reference to the Swinging London films.
6   One can notice a strong connection between Rohmer's advocating of a 'spiritually centred life' and his Jansenist version of Catholicism. For a discussion of Rohmer's religious conviction see Crisp 1988.

chapter three

1   A further discussion of *Dear Diary* can be found in chapter five.

2   Iain Sinclair observes that Paul Scofield, who provided the Narrator with his voice, 'is the whisperer, the voice in the head, the syrup keeping authorial distemper in check' (1994: 13).

3   See our discussion of these terms in chapter two.

4   This effect is to a certain extent a consequence of Keiller's use of the documentary form. As Paul Virilio observes, the temporal mode of film documentaries is that of the 'fatum', or event completed in the past (1994: 25).

5   We can talk about two types of *flânerie* in Keiller's films: as a position or condition of his characters, and as a narrative and visual device; *flânerie* in the text and of the text. We refer to stylistic features such as the lack of establishing shots and rejection of continuity editing, the adoption of Sergei Eisenstein and Chris Marker's intellectual and poetic montage, the dissociation of sound and image, the absence of visible characters with whom the viewer can identify, the episodic structure of the film and open ending. We argue that Keiller makes the viewer a *flâneur* of his films by avoiding overt judgements and encouraging him or her to find independently the meanings of his images and words, and the answers to the questions he asks. In this respect his *oeuvre* is a postmodern one, in the same way Godard's and Marker's work can be classified as postmodern.

6   The last factor, as Keith Tester argues, was already present at the time Rober Musil wrote *The Man Without Qualities*, which is one of the most important accounts of late *flânerie* (1994: 12).

7   As a postmodern *flâneur*, Robinson encounters him at the outskirts of the city, at a supermarket.

chapter four

1   *Film Lesson* (1992) is composed of eight half-hour films shot in Vienna during Herzog's time as head of the Vienna Film Festival.

2   The walk was interrupted for sickness after 2,000 kilometres (see Cronin 2002: 278–80).

3   In the middle of his 1999 manifesto, *The Minnesota Declaration: Truth and Fact in Documentary Cinema*, Herzog writes in an apparently disconnected manner: 'Tourism is sin, and travel on foot virtue' (see Cronin 2002: 301–2).

4   We will return to this topic in chapter five.

5   See for instance Davis & Jenkins 1985.

6   See for instance Horak 1983, Koning 1983, Peucker 1984, Rentschler 1986, and Koepnick 1993.

7   A more subtle and fleeting instance is the image of the poster of Akira Kurosawa's *Ran* (1985) in Martin's apartment – drawing parallels between Martin and Japanese tyrant Hidetora's tragic journey towards folly and death.

8   Think only of his statement, 'I had a higher purpose in mind', related to his will to demonstrate his love to the star by climbing Cerro Torre, and of the fact that he is convinced that the actress is still alive and runs a beauty parlour.

9   See note 3 to this chapter.

10 Ivan also brings him a book by Ernest Hemingway, whom – as the antithesis of Chatwin – is for Herzog, at least at a 'mythical' level, the representative of negative adventuring, as can be inferred from the following quote: 'I am not one of those Hemingway Kilimanjaro nostalgia people who love to track animals through the underbrush with an elephant gun while being fanned by the natives' (in Cronin 2002: 47).

11 For a detailed account of the production of *Fitzcarraldo* see Dolis & Weigand 1982.

12 Both films were commissioned by German TV; the first as part of a series called *Voyages to Hell*; the second was co-produced by BBC.

chapter five

1   See also our discussion of the desert in the cinema of Werner Herzog in chapter four.

2   This will be the subject of chapter six.

3   A further presence is that of Antonioni's films, particularly in the scenes set in Noto, as Amelio himself recognised; see Crowdus & Porton 1995.

4   It should be noted that, in the unemployment-stricken Italian South, jobs as a *carabiniere* were coveted until recent times as being secure and well-paid, as well as conveying a respectable social status.

5   The 'sedentary road' for Deleuze and Guattari has the function 'to parcel out a closed space to people, assigning each person a share and regulating the communication between shares' (1986: 50).

6   This is the form of urban nomadism that is the focus of Varda's *The Gleaners & I* (see above).

chapter six

1   It is necessary to distinguish between Weber's innovative social analysis of the migrations of the German workers in these writings, from his different and largely racist perspective on the seasonal movements of Polish migrants.

2   The thriller sequences not only point to the discourse on the exploitative nature of visual media that goes back to a film like *Peeping Tom* (Michael Powell, 1960); through the gas chamber, they are also suggestive of the Holocaust. It seems that the relevance given to these sequences in the film points to the Holocaust as the beginning of a new era, in which all human experience, including rootedness, sedentariness and citizenship, has lost its traditional significance.

3   Italy is not the only European country in which films on the 'new migration' proliferate; another example is Germany, which in the 1990s produced a series of films featuring immigrants from Turkey, Angola, Bosnia, Greece, Albania, Poland and other Eastern European countries, including *Engelchen* (*Little Angel*, Helke Misselwitz, 1996), *Plus-Minus Null* (Eoin Moore, 1998); *Nachtgestalten* (*Night Shapes*, Andreas Dresen, 1999) and *Dealer* (Thomas Arslan, 1999), all of which are set in Berlin, and *Aprilkinder* (*April*

Children, Yuksel Yavuz, 1998), *Kurz und schmerzlos* (*Short Sharp Rock*, Fatih Akin, 1998) and *Eine Handvoll Gras* (*A Handfull of Grass*, Roland Suso Richter, 2000), all of which are set in Hamburg. German critic Stefan Reinecke claims that in the 1990s a new genre has been created in German cinema: 'populares Migrantenkino' – 'the popular cinema of the migrants' (1999: 45). A distinction between the two countries must nevertheless be drawn: whereas Italian production on the post-communist diaspora is prevalently made up of road films, the German one consists of city films. This difference possibly accounts for the different status of the two countries as recipients of immigration: Italy is new to the phenomenon, and thus Italian filmmakers look at the process itself of the arrival of immigrants and refugees, which is experienced by the Italian population as an invasion; Germany instead is traditionally a country of immigration, and in fact the majority of the protagonists of the 1990s films were either born in Germany or came to the country as children. There nevertheless are exceptions to this trend – recent films such as *Auslandstournee* (*Tour Abroad*, 2000), by Ayse Polat, and *Im Juli* (*In July*, 2000) and *Gegen die Wand* (*Head On*, 2004), both by Fatih Akin, might suggest that a migrant travel cinema has started to develop in Germany.

4   For a comprehensive discussion of the role of the road in the cinema of Carlo Mazzacurati and Gianni Amelio, see Rascaroli 2004.

5   *Il toro* also shows a more dubious and hideous Italian entrepreneur, whom Loris and Franco first meet at the border, and then again later in the company of shady local partners.

6   Moreover, the means of transport that they use - a lorry for the transport of cattle and a jeep - are both symbolical of the act of traversing/exploring the frontier.

7   The idea of the dump is present in all the films here analysed, and particularly in *Elvjs and Merilijn*. Ileana works precisely in a waste disposal site in Bucharest. Refusal also appears later in the Italian sequences, after the impact of the protagonists with the bitter reality of immigration, symbolising the hidden face of the *belpaese* and of the Western system of life.

8   The Italian protagonists of *Il toro* also departed from a region of Third Italy, Veneto.

9   This concept, put forward in the 1960s by Francesco Alberoni and Guido Baglioni in relation to the internal migrations in Italy, has also been applied to the Albanian immigration (see Campani & Carchedi 1998: 16).

10 For an in-depth discussion of Vesna's transformation from traveller to streetwalker see Rascaroli 2003.

11 For a discussion of this theme in *Rocco and His Brothers* see also chapter five.

chapter seven

1   The dirty dress also serves as a premonition of her violent fate.

2   The same question of poor imitations of Western style recurs in Italian films on the new emigration explored in chapter six.

3   See the Polish Institute of Tourism website (www.intur.com.pl).

on the stage: *Aguirre*, neo–colonialism,
ique, 60, 101–30.
nigrational colonialism and the impe
& History, 24, 3-4, 67–83.
carraldo: Exotic and perverse', *Jump C*

ud', *Monthly Film Bulletin*, 432, 6–7.
lan: Il Castoro.
ology: The War Machine, trans. Brian Ma

d Schizophrenia. London: Athlone.
modernism: Decentering Privileged Cen
. Faris (eds) *Magical Realism: Theory, His*
e University Press.
loating Opera', *Film Comment*, 18, 5, 56–9
on ami', *Monthly Film Bulletin*, 654, 198–9.
rzestrzeni. *Flâneur* – szkic do portretu', in
w.anthropos.us.edu.pl/anthropos2/teksty.

e and exchange: a future for European film',

1998) 'Illegality and criminality: the differ-
ed immigrants', in Khalid Koser and Helma
don: Macmillan Press.
ncing the Road: Road Movies and Images
1, 53–79.
Christopher Lyon, *The International Dic-*
ectors/Filmmakers (London: Papermac).
ns and politics: the evolution of European
s Migration in Europe: The Legacy and the

vista a Carlo Mazzacurati', *Cineforum*, 357,

Sight and Sound, 5, 8, 42.
om Oberhausen to Hamburg. London: Co-

ma and the Postmodern. Berkeley: Univer-

Epd Film, 12, 5, 37.
Guy Debord (contro) il cinema. Milan: Il

Modernity. Cambridge: Polity Press.

4   The association with a dog is also suggested by her manner of eating – she eats quickly and secretly, as if worried that the food might be taken away from her.
5   Poland's public transport system used to be very good, but deteriorated after the country developed a market economy.
6   We have looked at some of their stories in chapter six.
7   Perhaps the only moment is the scene when they sing together: 'We are off in a motor-car … we don't know where we are…'
8   For a more complete discussion of these theories we refer the reader to chapter two.

chapter eight

1   For a discussion of the sublime and romanticism in relation to imperialism see chapter four.
2   Wenders is not the only European filmmaker who recently drew attention to Europe's past mistakes and their consequences for the issue of marginality/centrality. A similar idea is conveyed in Patrick Keiller's *London*, which was discussed in chapter three.
3   Privatised by the Major government, which, in common with the Thatcher administration, was greatly influenced by American-style economies, extremely fragmented, lacking funds, expensive, unreliable and unsafe, the British railway system is today widely regarded as one of the worst in the world.
4   The relationship between Canadians and Armenian immigrants is an important motif of Egoyan's films made prior to *Calendar*; see Mazierska 2002.

BIBLIOGRAPHY

Amelio, Gianni (1994) *Lamerica: Film e storia del film*. Turin: Einaudi.

Ang, Ien (1992) 'Hegemony-in-Trouble: Nostalgia and the Ideology of the in European Cinema', in Duncan Petrie (ed.) *Screening Europe*. London: Institute.

Armes, Roy (1970) *French Cinema since 1946*, vol. II. London: A. Zwemmer.

Bagnasco, Arnaldo (1977) *Tre Italie: La problematica territoriale dello sviluppo i logna: Il Mulino.

Baudrillard, Jean (1988) *America*. London: Verso.

Bauman, Zygmunt (1994) 'Desert spectacular', in Keith Tester (ed.) *The Flâneu* Routledge.

____ (1996) 'From pilgrim to tourist – or a short history of identity', in Stuart Ha du Gay (eds) *Questions of Cultural Identity*. London: Sage.

____ (1997) *Postmodernity and its Discontents*. Cambridge: Polity Press.

____ (2000) *Liquid Modernity*. Cambridge: Polity Press.

Benelli, Dana (1986) 'The cosmos and its discontents', in Timothy Corrigan (ed.) *of Werner Herzog: Between Mirage and History*. New York and London: Meth

Bernstein, Matthew (1997) 'Introduction', in Matthew Bernstein and Gaylyn Stud *Visions of the East: Orientalism in Film*. London: I.B. Tauris.

Bradford, Sarah (1973) *Portugal*. London: Thames and Hudson.

Braidotti, Rosi (1994) *Nomadic Subjects: Embodiment and Sexual Difference in Co rary Feminist Thought*. New York: Columbia University Press.

Brooker, Peter (1992) 'Introduction: Reconstructions', in Peter Brooker (ed.) *Mod Postmodernism*. London: Longman.

Buck-Morss, Susan (1999) *The Dialectics of Seeing: Walter Benjamin and the Arcade ect*. Cambridge, MA: MIT Press.

Burke, Edmund (1987). *A Philosophical Inquiry into the Origin of our Ideas of the S and Beautiful*. Oxford: Blackwell.

Buzard, James (1993) *The Beaten Track: European Tourism, Literature, and the W Culture, 1800–1918*. Oxford: Clarendon Press.

Campani, Giovanna and Francesco Carchedi (1998) 'Migranti, rifugiati e nomadi da cani', in Giovanna Campani, Francesco Carchedi and Giovanni Mottura (eds) *Mig*

Davidson, John E. (1993) 'As others put plays up the New German Cinema', *New German Cri*

____ (1994) 'Contacting the Other: traces of agent in Werner Herzog's *Fitzcarraldo*', *Film*

Davis, Howard and Dilwyn Jenkins (1985) 'Fit 30, 8–10.

Dawson, Jan (1970) 'Review of *Ma nuit chez M*

De Bernardinis, Flavio (1998) *Nanni Moretti*. M

Deleuze, Gilles and Félix Guattari (1986) *Nomad* sumi. New York: Semiotext(e).

____ (1988) *A Thousand Plateaus: Capitalism a*

D'haen, Theo L. (1995) 'Magic Realism and Pos tres', in Lois Parkinson Zamora and Wendy *tory, Community*. Durham and London: Du

Dolis, Geroge and Ingrid Weigand (1982) 'The

Durgnat, Raymond (1988) 'Review of *L'Ami de*

Dzionek, Michał (2003) 'W stronę antropologii *Anthropos*, 2–3. On-line. Available: http://w htm (accessed 13 September 2004).

Eleftheriotis, Dimitris (2000) 'Cultural differenc *Screen*, 41, 1, 92–101.

Engbersen, Godfried and Joanne van der Leun ential opportunity structure of undocument Lutz (eds) *The New Migration in Europe*. Lo

Eyerman, Ron and Orvar Löfgren (1995) 'Rom of Mobility', *Theory, Culture and Society*, 12

Farnsworth, Rodney (1987) 'Werner Herzog', i *tionary of Films and Filmmakers - Vol. 2: Di*

Fielding, Anthony (1993) 'Migrations, instituti migration policies', in Russel King (ed.) *Ma Future*. Chichester: John Wiley & Sons.

Fornara, Bruno (1996) 'Luoghi di confine: Inter 10.

Francke, Lizzie (1995) 'Review of *Butterfly Kiss*

Franklin, James (1983) *New German Cinema: F* lumbus Books.

Friedberg, Anne (1993) *Window Shopping: Cin* sity of California Press.

Gansera, Rainer (1995) 'Review of *Lisbon Story*

Ghezzi, Enrico and Roberto Turigliatto (2001 Castoro.

Giddens, Anthony (1990) *The Consequences of*

Gili, Jean A. (1994) 'Entretien avec Nanni Moretti: Le plaisir de reconter plus librement', *Positif*, 399, 9–14.

Gilroy, Paul (1997) 'Diaspora and the Detours of Identity', in Kathryn Woodward (ed.) *Identity and Difference*. London: Sage.

Ginsborg, Paul (2001) *Italy and Its Discontents: Family, Civil Society, State 1980–2001*. London: Allen Lane.

Gocić, Goran (2001) *The Cinema of Emir Kusturica: Notes from the Underground*. London: Wallflower Press.

Gordon, Bertram M. (2003) 'The Film, the Historian and the Tourist: A View to Future Methodology and the Role of the Male as a Travel Mentor in English-Language Films from 1890 to the Present', paper presented at the 'Tourism and Histories' conference, June 2003, University of Central Lancashire, Preston.

Habermas, Jurgen (1992) 'Modernity – an Incomplete Project', in Peter Brooker (ed.). *Modernism/Postmodernism*. London: Longman.

Haikio, Martti (1992) *A Brief History of Modern Finland*. Lahti: University of Helsinki Lahti Research and Training Centre.

Hall, Stuart (1990) 'Cultural Identity and Diaspora', in Jonathan Rutherford (ed.) *Identity: Community, Culture, Difference*. London: Lawrence and Wishart.

____ (1992a) 'European Cinema on the Verge of a Nervous Breakdown', in Duncan Petrie (ed.) *Screening Europe*. London: British Film Institute.

____ (1992b) 'The Question of Cultural Identity' in Stuart Hall, David Held and Tony McGrew (eds) *Modernity and its Futures*. Cambridge: Polity Press.

____ (ed.) (1997) *Representation: Cultural Representations and Signifying Practices*. London: Sage.

Harrison, Robert Pogue (1992) *Forests: The Shadow of Civilization*. Chicago and London: University of Chicago Press.

Herman, Edward S. and Noam Chomsky (1994) *Manufacturing Consent: The Political Economy of the Mass Media*. London: Vintage.

Herzog, Werner (1991) *Of Walking in Ice: Munich–Paris, 11/23 to 12/14, 1974*, trans. Alan Greenberg. London: Jonathan Cape.

Higson, Andrew (1986) 'Britain's Outstanding Contribution to the Film: The Documentary-Realist Tradition', in Charles Barr (ed.) *All Our Yesterdays: 90 Years of British Cinema*. London: British Film Institute.

____ (1993) 'Re-presenting the National Past: Nostalgia and Pastiche in the Heritage Film', in Lester Friedman (ed.) *British Cinema and Thatcherism*. London: UCL Press.

Horak, Jan-Christopher (1986) 'Werner Herzog or the Mysteries of Walking on Ice', in Timothy Corrigan (ed) *The Films of Werner Herzog: Between Mirage and History*. New York and London: Methuen.

Jameson, Fredric (1985) 'Postmodernism and Consumer Society', in Hal Foster (ed.) *Postmodern Culture*. London: Pluto Press.

____ (1992) *The Geopolitical Aesthetic*. Bloomington and Indianapolis: Indiana University Press.

Jokinen, Eeva and Soile Veijola (1997) 'The Disoriented Tourist: The Figuration of the Tourist in Contemporary Cultural Critique', in Chris Rojek and John Urry (eds) *Touring Cultures: Transformations of Travel and Theory*. London: Routledge.

Kant, Immanuel (1987) *The Critique of Judgment*, trans. Werner Pluhar. Indianapolis: Cambridge.

Kaplan, Caren (1996) *Questions of Travel: Postmodern Discourses of Displacement*. Durham, NC: Duke University Press.

Keiller, Patrick (1999) *Robinson in Space*. London: Reaktion Books.

Kemp, Philip (2002) 'Review of *L'emploi du temps*', *Sight and Sound*, 12, 4, 44–5.

Kilvert, Francis (1971) *Kilvert's Diary: Selection from the Diary of the Rev. Francis Kilvert, January 1870–19 August 1871, vol. 1*. London: Jonathan Cape.

Kinder, Marsha (1974) 'The Return of the Outlaw Couple', *Film Quarterly*, 27, 4, 2–10.

King, Norman (1990) 'Eye for Irony: Eric Rohmer's *Ma nuit chez Maud* (1969)', in Susan Hayward and Ginette Vincendeau (eds) *French Films: Texts and Contexts*. London: Routledge.

Koepnick, Lutz P. (1993) 'Colonial Forestry: Sylvan Politics in Werner Herzog's *Aguirre* and *Fitzcarraldo*', *New German Critique*, 60, 133–59.

Kolker, Philip Robert and Peter Beicken (1993) *The Films of Wim Wenders: Cinema as Vision and Desire*. Cambridge: Cambridge University Press.

Koning, Hans (1983) 'Review of Fitzcarraldo', *Cineaste*, 12, 4, 42–3.

Koser, Khalid and Helma Lutz (1998) 'The New Migration in Europe: Contexts, Constructions and Realities', in Khalid Koser and Helma Lutz (eds) *The New Migration in Europe*. London: Macmillan Press.

Kristeva, Julia (1982) *Powers of Horror: An Essay on Abjection*, trans. Leon S. Roudiez. New York: Columbia University Press.

Kuhn, Annette (1985) 'National cinemas and film movements', in Pam Cook (ed.) *The Cinema Book*. London: British Film Institute.

Laderman, David (2002) *Driving Visions: Exploring the Road Movie*. Austin: Texas University Press.

Laguerre, Michel S. (1998) *Diasporic Citizenship: Haitian Americans in Transnational America*. New York: St. Martin's Press.

Lash, Scott and John Urry (1994) *Economies of Signs and Space*. London: Sage.

Lewis, Robert A. and Richard H. Rowland (1976) 'Urbanization in Russia and the USSR, 1897–1970', in Michael F. Hamm (ed.) *The City in Russian History*. Lexington: University Press of Kentucky.

Lovelock, James (1979) *Gaia: A New Look at Life on Earth*. Oxford: Oxford University Press.

Luckett, Moya (2000) 'Travel and mobility: Femininity and national identity', in Justine Ashby and Andrew Higson (eds) *British Cinema, Past and Present*. London: Routledge.

Lyotard, Jean-François (1984) *The Postmodern Condition: A Report on Knowledge*, trans. Geoff Bennington and Brian Massumi. Minneapolis: University of Minnesota Press.

MacCabe, Colin (1992) 'Jean-Luc Godard in Conversation with Colin MacCabe', in Duncan Petrie (ed.) *Screening Europe*. London: British Film Institute.

Maffesoli, Michel (1997) *Du nomadisme: Vagabondages initiatiques*. Paris: Librairie Générale Française.

Maniewski, Maciej (1998) 'Zyj kolorowo', *Film*, 4, 74.

Marangi, Michele (1999) 'Nanni '90 ovvero Caro Aprile', in Giulia Carluccio and Sara Cortellazzo (eds) *Nanni Moretti*. Turin: Garage-Scriptorium.

Marcus, Millicent (1996) '*Caro diario* and the cinematic body of Nanni Moretti', *Italica*, 73, 2, 233–47.

Mazierska, Ewa (2000) 'Power, Freedom, Gender in Films by Atom Egoyan', in Elzbieta Oleksy, Elzbieta Ostrowska and Michael Stevenson (eds) *Gender in Film and the Media*. Frankfurt am Main: Peter Lang.

_____ (2002) 'Institutions and Individuals in the Films of Atom Egoyan', *Kinema*, 18, 55–74.

Mazierska, Ewa and Laura Rascaroli (2003) *From Moscow to Madrid: Postmodern Cities, European Cinema*. London: I.B. Tauris.

Mazlish, Bruce (1994) 'The flâneur: from spectator to representation', in Keith Tester (ed.) *The Flâneur*. London: Routledge.

Mezzadra, Sandro (2001) *Diritto di fuga: Migrazioni, cittadinanza, globalizzazione*. Verona: Ombre Corte.

Monaco, James (1976) *The New Wave*. Oxford: Oxford University Press.

Montanari, Armando and Antonio Cortese (1993a) 'South to North migration in a Mediterranean perspective', in Russel King (ed.) *Mass Migration in Europe: The Legacy and the Future*. Chichester: John Wiley & Sons.

_____ (1993b) 'Third World Immigrants in Italy', in Russel King (ed.) *Mass Migration in Europe: The Legacy and the Future*. Chichester: John Wiley & Sons.

Moore, Cornelius (1990) 'Africa through African Eyes', California Newsreel's Library of African Cinema Catalogue, On-line. Available: http://spot.pcc.edu/~mdembrow/africa_through_african_eye.htm (accessed: 13 September 2004).

Morawski, Stefan (1994) 'The hopeless game of *flânerie*', in Keith Tester (ed.) *The Flâneur*. London: Routledge.

Morton, Jim (1999) 'Road Kill: Horror on the Highway', in Jack Sargeant and Stephanie Watson (eds) *Lost Highways: An Illustrated History of Road Movies*. Creation Books.

Mulvey, Laura (1975) 'Visual Pleasure and Narrative Cinema', *Screen*, 16, 3, 6–18.

Naficy, Hamid (2001) *An Accented Cinema: Exilic and Diasporic Filmmaking*. Princeton: Princeton University Press.

Nicolson, Marjorie Hope (1997) *Mountain Gloom and Mountain Glory: Development of the Aesthetics of the Infinite*. Washington: University of Washington Press.

Nigro, Kristen F. (1975) 'From *Criollismo* to the Grotesque: Approaches to Jose Donoso', in Merlin H. Foster (ed.) *Tradition and Renewal: Essays on Twentieth-Century Latin American Literature and Culture*. Urbana: University of Illinois Press.

O'Healy, Áine (2004) '*Lamerica*', in Giorgio Bertellini (ed.) *The Cinema of Italy*. London: Wallflower Press.

Orr, John (1993) *Cinema and Modernity*. Cambridge: Polity Press.

Ousby, Ian (1993–95) 'Magic Realism', *Microsoft Encarta Encyclopaedia*. Microsoft Corporation.

Pearce, Philip L. and Gianna M. Moscardo (1986) 'The Concept of Authenticity in Tourist Experiences', *Australian and New Zealand Journal of Sociology*, 22, 1, 121–32.

Perniola, Mario (1998) *Transiti*. Rome: Castelvecchi.

Peters, John Durham (1999) 'Exile, nomadism, and diaspora: the stakes of mobility in the Western canon', in Hamid Naficy (ed.) *Home, Exile, Homeland. Film, Media, and the Politics of Place*. New York and London: Routledge.

Peuker, Brigitte (1984) 'Werner Herzog: In Quest of the Sublime', in Klaus Phillips (ed.) *New German Filmmakers: From Oberhausen through the 1970s*. New York: Friedrich Ungar.

Prager, Brad (2003) 'Werner Herzog's Hearts of Darkness: *Fitzcarraldo, Scream of Stone* and Beyond', *Quarterly Review of Film and Video*, 20, 1, 23–35.

Pratt, Mary Louise (1992) *Imperial Eyes: Travel Writing and Transculturation*. London: Routledge.

Pulleine, Tim (1990) 'Review of *Leningrad Cowboys Go America*', *Monthly Film Bulletin*, 57, 674, 71–2.

Rascaroli, Laura (2003) 'New voyages to Italy: Postmodern travellers and the Italian road movie', *Screen*, 44, 1, 71–91.

_____ (2004) 'Mazzacurati, Soldini & Amelio: Highways, Side Roads and Borderlines – the New Italian Road Movie', in William Hope (ed.) *Italian Cinema: New Directions*. Oxford and Bern: Peter Lang.

Reinecke, Stefan (1999) 'Review of *Aprilkinder*', *Epd Film*, 16, 2, 45.

Rentschler, Eric (1986) 'The Politics of Vision: Herzog's *Heart of Glass*' in Timothy Corrigan (ed.) *The Films of Werner Herzog: Between Mirage and History*. New York and London: Methuen.

Reynaud, Berenice (1990) 'Representing the sexual impasse: Eric Rohmer's *Le Nuits de la pleine lune* (1984)', in Susan Hayward and Ginette Vincendeau (eds) *French Films: Texts and Contexts*. London: Routledge.

Rignall, John (1989) 'Benjamin's *flâneur* and the problem of realism', in Andrew Benjamin (ed.) *The Problems of Modernity: Adorno and Benjamin*. London: Routledge.

Ritzer, George and Allan Liska (1997) 'McDisneyzation and Post-Tourism', in Chris Rojek and John Urry (eds) *Touring Cultures: Transformations of Travel and Theory*. London: Routledge.

Roberts, Les (2002) 'Welcome to Dreamland: From Place to Non-place and Back Again in Pawel Pawlikowski's *Last Resort*', *New Cinemas*, 1, 2, 78–90.

Roberts, Shari (1997) 'Western Meets Eastwood: Genre and Gender on the Road' in Steven Cohan and Ina Rae Hark (eds) *The Road Movie Book*. London: Routledge.

Robertson, Pamela (1997) 'Home and Away: Friends of Dorothy on the Road in Oz', in Steven Cohan and Ina Rae Hark (eds) *The Road Movie Book*. London: Routledge.

Rohmer, Eric (1989) *The Taste for Beauty*, trans. Carol Volk. Cambridge: Cambridge University Press.

Rojek, Chris and Urry, John (1997) 'Transformations of Travel and Theory', in Chris Rojek and John Urry (eds) *Touring Cultures: Transformations of Travel and Theory*. London: Routledge.

Romney, Jonathan (1995) 'Review of *Take Care of Your Scarf, Tatjana*', *Sight and Sound*, 5, 11, 50–1.

____ (1997) 'The Kaurismäki Effect', *Sight and Sound*, 7, 6, 10–14.

____ (1999) 'Review of *Felicia's Journey*', *Sight and Sound*, 9, 10, 34–5.

____ (2003) *Atom Egoyan*. London: British Film Institute.

Rosello, Mireille (2001) 'Agnès Varda's *Les Glaneurs et la glaneuse*: Portrait of the Artist as an Old Lady', *Studies in French Cinema*, 1, 1, 29–34.

Ryan, Chris (1991) *Recreational Tourism*. London and New York: Routledge.

Said, Edward (1979) *Orientalism*. New York: Vintage.

Sandford, John (1980) *The New German Cinema*. London: Oswald Wolff.

Sargeant, Jack and Stephanie Watson (1999) *Lost Highways: An Illustrated History of Road Movies*. London: Creation Books.

Seabrook, Jeremy (1988) *The Leisure Society*. Oxford: Basil Blackwell.

Seaton, A.V. (2000) 'The worst of journeys, the best of journeys: Travel and the concept of periphery in European culture', in Mike Robinson *et al.* (eds) *Expressions of Culture, Identity and Meaning in Tourism*. Sunderland: Centre for Travel and Tourism.

Shields, Rob (1991) *Places on the Margin*. London and New York: Routledge.

____ (1994) 'Fancy footwork: Walter Benjamin's notes on *flânerie*', in Keith Tester (ed.) *The Flâneur*. London: Routledge.

Sibley, David (1995) *Geographies of Exclusion*. London: Routledge.

Simpkins, Scott (1995) 'Sources of Magic Realism/Supplements to Realism in Contemporary Latin American Literature', in Lois Parkinson Zamora and Wendy B. Faris (eds) *Magical Realism: Theory, History, Community*. Durham and London: Duke University Press.

Sinclair, Iain (1994) 'Necropolis of Fretful Ghosts', *Sight and Sound*, 4, 6, 12–15.

Singer, Alan (1986) 'Comprehending appearances: Werner Herzog's ironic sublime', in Timothy Corrigan (ed.) *The Films of Werner Herzog: Between Mirage and History*. New York and London: Methuen.

Singleton, Fred (1998) *A Short History of Finland*. Cambridge: Cambridge University Press.

Small, Pauline (1998) 'Gianni Amelio's *The Stolen Children*: recalling the image', *Italian Studies*, 53, 150–66.

Smith, Paul Julian (1997) 'Review of *Robinson in Space*', *Sight and Sound*, 7, 1, 44.

Sobolewski, Tadeusz (1997) 'Sztuczny luz', *Kino*, 31, 9, 6–7.

Soila, Tytti, Astrid Söderbergh-Widding and Gunnar Iversen (1998) *Nordic National Cinemas*. London: Routledge.

Sontag, Susan (1979) *On Photography*. London: Penguin.

____ (1980) *Under the Sign of Saturn*. London: Writers and Readers.

Sorlin, Pierre (1994) *European Cinemas, European Societies 1939–1999*. London: Routledge.

Szpulak, Andrzej (1999) 'Nieprowincjonalna sprawa', *Kino*, 33, 10, 6–7.

Taylor, John (1994) *A Dream of England: Landscape, Photography and the Tourist's Imagination*. Manchester: Manchester University Press.

Tester, Keith (1994) 'Introduction', in Keith Tester (ed.) *The Flâneur*. London: Routledge.

Tomlinson, John (1999) 'Cultural globalisation: placing and displacing the West', in Hugh Mackay and Tim O'Sullivan (eds) *The Media Reader: Continuity and Transformation*. London: Sage.

Urry, John (1990) *The Tourist Gaze: Leisure and Travel in Contemporary Societies*. London: Sage.

____ (1995) *Consuming Places*. London: Routledge.

Van Hear, Nicholas (1998) *New Disaporas: The Mass Exodus, Dispersal and Regrouping of Migrant Communities*. London: UCL Press.

Veal, Anthony J. (1987) *Leisure and the Future*. London: Allen & Unwin.

Vincendeau, Ginette (2002) 'White Collar Blues', interview with Laurent Cantet, *Sight and Sound*, 12, 4, 30–2.

Virilio, Paul (1994) *The Vision Machine*, trans. Julie Rose. London: British Film Institute.

Volpi, Gianni (ed.) (1995) *Gianni Amelio*. Turin: Garage-Scriptorium.

Walton, John K. (2002) 'British tourism between industrialisation and globalisation: an overview' in Hartmut Berghoff, Barbara Korte, Ralf Schneider and Christopger Harvie (eds.), *The making of modern tourism: the cultural history of the British experience, 1600-2000*. London: Palgrave.

____ (2004) 'Blackpool and the varieties of Britishness', in Steve Caunce, Ewa Mazierska, Susan Sydney-Smith and John K. Walton (eds) *Relocating Britishness*. Manchester: Manchester University Press.

Watson, Stephanie (1999) 'The Western', in Jack Sargeant and Stephanie Watson (eds) *Lost Highways: An Illustrated History of Road Movies*. New York: Creation Books.

Weber, Max (1984) *Die Lage der Landarbeiter im ostelbischen Deutschland*, Max Weber Gesamtausgabe, Abteilung I, Bd. 3, 2 Halbbde., hrsg. von M. Riesebrodt. Tübingen: Mohr.

____ (1993) *Landarbeiterfrage, Nationalstaat und Volkswirtschaftspolitik. Schriften und Reden 1892-1899 Landarbeiter*, Max Weber Gesamtausgabe, Abteilung I, Bd. 4, 2 Halbbde., hrsg. von W. J. Mommsen in Zusammenarbeit mit R. Aldenhoff. Tübingen: Mohr.

White, Edmund (2002) *The Flâneur: A Stroll through the Paradoxes of Paris*. London: Bloomsbury.

Williams, Linda Ruth (2002) 'Escape Artist', *Sight and Sound*, 12, 10, 22–5.

Wilson, Emma (1999) *French Cinema Since 1950: Personal Histories*. London: Duckworth.

Woodward, Kathryn (1997) 'Diaspora and the Detours of Identity', in Kathryn Woodward (ed.) *Identity and Difference*. London: Sage.

Wrathal, John (1996) 'Review of *A Summer's Tale/Conte d'ete*', *Sight and Sound*, 6, 10, 53–4.

Zavattini, Cesare (1979) *Neorealismo ecc*. Milan: Bompiani.

INDEX

4　The association with a dog is also suggested by her manner of eating – she eats quickly and secretly, as if worried that the food might be taken away from her.

5　Poland's public transport system used to be very good, but deteriorated after the country developed a market economy.

6　We have looked at some of their stories in chapter six.

7　Perhaps the only moment is the scene when they sing together: 'We are off in a motorcar … we don't know where we are…'

8　For a more complete discussion of these theories we refer the reader to chapter two.

chapter eight

1　For a discussion of the sublime and romanticism in relation to imperialism see chapter four.

2　Wenders is not the only European filmmaker who recently drew attention to Europe's past mistakes and their consequences for the issue of marginality/centrality. A similar idea is conveyed in Patrick Keiller's *London*, which was discussed in chapter three.

3　Privatised by the Major government, which, in common with the Thatcher administration, was greatly influenced by American-style economies, extremely fragmented, lacking funds, expensive, unreliable and unsafe, the British railway system is today widely regarded as one of the worst in the world.

4　The relationship between Canadians and Armenian immigrants is an important motif of Egoyan's films made prior to *Calendar*; see Mazierska 2002.

BIBLIOGRAPHY

Amelio, Gianni (1994) *Lamerica: Film e storia del film*. Turin: Einaudi.

Ang, Ien (1992) 'Hegemony-in-Trouble: Nostalgia and the Ideology of the Impossible in European Cinema', in Duncan Petrie (ed.) *Screening Europe*. London: British Film Institute.

Armes, Roy (1970) *French Cinema since 1946*, vol. II. London: A. Zwemmer.

Bagnasco, Arnaldo (1977) *Tre Italie: La problematica territoriale dello sviluppo italiano*. Bologna: Il Mulino.

Baudrillard, Jean (1988) *America*. London: Verso.

Bauman, Zygmunt (1994) 'Desert spectacular', in Keith Tester (ed.) *The Flâneur*. London: Routledge.

____ (1996) 'From pilgrim to tourist – or a short history of identity', in Stuart Hall and Paul du Gay (eds) *Questions of Cultural Identity*. London: Sage.

____ (1997) *Postmodernity and its Discontents*. Cambridge: Polity Press.

____ (2000) *Liquid Modernity*. Cambridge: Polity Press.

Benelli, Dana (1986) 'The cosmos and its discontents', in Timothy Corrigan (ed.) *The Films of Werner Herzog: Between Mirage and History*. New York and London: Methuen.

Bernstein, Matthew (1997) 'Introduction', in Matthew Bernstein and Gaylyn Studlar (eds) *Visions of the East: Orientalism in Film*. London: I.B. Tauris.

Bradford, Sarah (1973) *Portugal*. London: Thames and Hudson.

Braidotti, Rosi (1994) *Nomadic Subjects: Embodiment and Sexual Difference in Contemporary Feminist Thought*. New York: Columbia University Press.

Brooker, Peter (1992) 'Introduction: Reconstructions', in Peter Brooker (ed.) *Modernism/Postmodernism*. London: Longman.

Buck-Morss, Susan (1999) *The Dialectics of Seeing: Walter Benjamin and the Arcades Project*. Cambridge, MA: MIT Press.

Burke, Edmund (1987). *A Philosophical Inquiry into the Origin of our Ideas of the Sublime and Beautiful*. Oxford: Blackwell.

Buzard, James (1993) *The Beaten Track: European Tourism, Literature, and the Ways to Culture, 1800–1918*. Oxford: Clarendon Press.

Campani, Giovanna and Francesco Carchedi (1998) 'Migranti, rifugiati e nomadi dai Balcani', in Giovanna Campani, Francesco Carchedi and Giovanni Mottura (eds) *Migranti, rifugiati e nomadi: Europa dell'Est in movimento*. Turin: L'Harmattan Italia.

Cattini, Alberto (2000) *Le storie e lo sguardo: Il cinema di Gianni Amelio*. Venice: Marsilio.

Chaliand, Gérard and Jean-Pierre Rageau (1995) *The Penguin Book of Diasporas*, trans. A. M. Barrett. New York: Viking.

Chambers, Iain (1990) 'An Island Life', in *Border Dialogues: Journeys in Postmodernity*. London: Routledge.

Chard, Chloe (1996) 'Crossing boundaries and exceeding limits: Destabilization, tourism, and the sublime', in Chloe Chard and Helen Langdon (eds) *Transports: Travel, Pleasure, and Imaginative Geography, 1600–1830*. New Haven and London: Yale University Press.

Chyb, Manana (1998) 'Nie – letniości', *Film*, 4, 55–6.

Cleere, Elizabeth (1980) 'Three films by Werner Herzog seen in the light of the grotesque', *Wide Angle*, 3, 4, 12–19.

Codagnone, Cristiano (1998) 'The New Migration in Russia in the 1990s', in Khalid Koser and Helma Lutz (eds) *The New Migration in Europe*. London: Macmillan Press.

Cohan, Steven and Ina Rae Hark (1997) *The Road Movie Book*. London: Routledge.

Cohen, Robin (1997) *Global Diasporas: An Introduction*. London: UCL Press.

Colusso, Paolo Federico (1998) *Wim Wenders: Paesaggi luoghi città*. Turin: Testo & Immagine.

Combs, Richard (1995) 'New British Cinema: A Prospect and Six Views', *Film Comment*, 31, 6, 52–9.

Condee, Nancy (ed.) (1995) *Soviet Hieroglyphics: Visual Culture in Late Twentieth Century Russia*. Bloomington and Indianapolis: Indiana University Press/London: British Film Institute.

Corrigan, Timothy (1991) *A Cinema Without Walls: Movies and Culture After Vietnam*. London: Routledge.

Craik, Jennifer (1997) 'The Culture of Tourism', in Chris Rojek and John Urry (eds) *Touring Cultures: Transformations of Travel and Theory*. London: Routledge.

Crawshaw, Carol and John Urry (1999) 'Tourism and the Photographic Eye', in Chris Rojek and John Urry (eds) *Touring Cultures: Transformations of Travel and Theory*. London: Routledge.

Creed, Barbara (1993) *The Monstrous-Feminine: Film, Feminism, Psychoanalysis*. London-New York: Routledge.

Crisp, C. G. (1988) *Eric Rohmer: Realist and Moralist*. Bloomington: Indiana University Press.

Cronin, Paul (ed.) (2002) *Herzog on Herzog*. London: Faber and Faber.

Crowdus, Gary and Richard Porton (1995) 'Beyond Neorealism: Preserving a cinema of social conscience. An interview with Gianni Amelio', *Cinéaste*, 21, 4, 6–13.

Darke, Chris (2001) 'Refuseniks', *Sight and Sound*, 11, 1, 30–3.

Dave, Paul (2000) 'Representations of Capitalism, History and Nation in the Work of Patrick Keiller', in Justine Ashby and Andrew Higson (eds) *British Cinema, Past and Present*. London: Routledge.

Davidson, John E. (1993) 'As others put plays upon the stage: *Aguirre*, neo-colonialism, and the New German Cinema', *New German Critique*, 60, 101–30.

_____ (1994) 'Contacting the Other: traces of migrational colonialism and the imperial agent in Werner Herzog's *Fitzcarraldo*', *Film & History*, 24, 3–4, 67–83.

Davis, Howard and Dilwyn Jenkins (1985) 'Fitzcarraldo: Exotic and perverse', *Jump Cut*, 30, 8–10.

Dawson, Jan (1970) 'Review of *Ma nuit chez Maud*', *Monthly Film Bulletin*, 432, 6–7.

De Bernardinis, Flavio (1998) *Nanni Moretti*. Milan: Il Castoro.

Deleuze, Gilles and Félix Guattari (1986) *Nomadology: The War Machine*, trans. Brian Massumi. New York: Semiotext(e).

_____ (1988) *A Thousand Plateaus: Capitalism and Schizophrenia*. London: Athlone.

D'haen, Theo L. (1995) 'Magic Realism and Postmodernism: Decentering Privileged Centres', in Lois Parkinson Zamora and Wendy B. Faris (eds) *Magical Realism: Theory, History, Community*. Durham and London: Duke University Press.

Dolis, Geroge and Ingrid Weigand (1982) 'The Floating Opera', *Film Comment*, 18, 5, 56–9.

Durgnat, Raymond (1988) 'Review of *L'Ami de mon ami*', *Monthly Film Bulletin*, 654, 198–9.

Dzionek, Michał (2003) 'W stronę antropologii przestrzeni. *Flâneur* – szkic do portretu', in *Anthropos*, 2–3. On-line. Available: http://www.anthropos.us.edu.pl/anthropos2/teksty. htm (accessed 13 September 2004).

Eleftheriotis, Dimitris (2000) 'Cultural difference and exchange: a future for European film', *Screen*, 41, 1, 92–101.

Engbersen, Godfried and Joanne van der Leun (1998) 'Illegality and criminality: the differential opportunity structure of undocumented immigrants', in Khalid Koser and Helma Lutz (eds) *The New Migration in Europe*. London: Macmillan Press.

Eyerman, Ron and Orvar Löfgren (1995) 'Romancing the Road: Road Movies and Images of Mobility', *Theory, Culture and Society*, 12, 1, 53–79.

Farnsworth, Rodney (1987) 'Werner Herzog', in Christopher Lyon, *The International Dictionary of Films and Filmmakers* - Vol. 2: *Directors/Filmmakers* (London: Papermac).

Fielding, Anthony (1993) 'Migrations, institutions and politics: the evolution of European migration policies', in Russel King (ed.) *Mass Migration in Europe: The Legacy and the Future*. Chichester: John Wiley & Sons.

Fornara, Bruno (1996) 'Luoghi di confine: Intervista a Carlo Mazzacurati', *Cineforum*, 357, 10.

Francke, Lizzie (1995) 'Review of *Butterfly Kiss*', *Sight and Sound*, 5, 8, 42.

Franklin, James (1983) *New German Cinema: From Oberhausen to Hamburg*. London: Columbus Books.

Friedberg, Anne (1993) *Window Shopping: Cinema and the Postmodern*. Berkeley: University of California Press.

Gansera, Rainer (1995) 'Review of *Lisbon Story*', *Epd Film*, 12, 5, 37.

Ghezzi, Enrico and Roberto Turigliatto (2001) *Guy Debord (contro) il cinema*. Milan: Il Castoro.

Giddens, Anthony (1990) *The Consequences of Modernity*. Cambridge: Polity Press.